TEACHING BUDDHISM IN THE WEST

T0386187

CURZON CRITICAL STUDIES IN BUDDHISM

General Editors:

Charles S. Prebish and Damien Keown

The Curzon Critical Studies in Buddhism Series is a comprehensive study of the Buddhist tradition. The series explores this complex and extensive tradition from a variety of perspectives, using a range of different methodologies.

   The Series is diverse in its focus, including historical studies, textual translations and commentaries, sociological investigations, bibliographic studies, and considerations of religious practice as an expression of Buddhism's integral religiosity. It also presents materials on modern intellectual historical studies, including the role of Buddhist thought and scholarship in a contemporary, critical context and in the light of current social issues. The series is expansive and imaginative in scope, spanning more than two and a half millennia of Buddhist history. It is receptive to all research works that inform and advance our knowledge and understanding of the Buddhist tradition. The series maintains the highest standards of scholarship and promotes the application of innovative methodologies and research methods.

THE REFLEXIVE NATURE OF AWARENESS
Paul Williams

BUDDHISM AND HUMAN RIGHTS
Edited by Damien Keown, Charles Prebish, Wayne Husted

ALTRUISM AND REALITY
Paul Williams

WOMEN IN THE FOOTSTEPS OF THE BUDDHA
Kathryn R. Blackstone

THE RESONANCE OF EMPTINESS
Gay Watson

IMAGING WISDOM
Jacob N. Kinnard

AMERICAN BUDDHISM
Edited by Duncan Ryuken Williams and Christopher Queen

PAIN AND ITS ENDING
Carol S. Anderson

THE SOUND OF LIBERATING TRUTH
Edited by Sallie B. King and Paul O. Ingram

BUDDHIST THEOLOGY
Edited by Roger R. Jackson and John J. Makransky

EMPTINESS APPRAISED
David F. Burton

THE GLORIOUS DEEDS OF PŪRNA
Joel Tatelman

CONTEMPORARY BUDDHIST ETHICS
Edited by Damien Keown

TEACHING BUDDHISM IN THE WEST
Edited by Victor Sōgen Hori, Richard P. Hayes and James Mark Shields

TEACHING BUDDHISM IN THE WEST

From the Wheel to the Web

EDITED BY

Victor Sōgen Hori
Richard P. Hayes
James Mark Shields

RoutledgeCurzon
Taylor & Francis Group

First Published in 2002
by RoutledgeCurzon
11 New Fetter Lane, London EC4P 4EE

Simultaneously published in the USA and Canada
by RoutledgeCurzon
29 West 35th Street, New York, NY 10001

RoutledgeCurzon is an imprint of the Taylor & Francis Group

Editorial matter © 2002 Victor Sōgen Hori, Richard P. Hayes, and James Mark Shields

British Library Cataloguing in Publication Data
A catalogue record of this book is available from the British Library

Library of Congress Cataloguing in Publication Data
A catalogue record for this book has been requested

ISBN 0–7007–1556–8 (hbk)
ISBN 0–7007–1557–6 (pbk)

Contents

Acknowledgments   vii

Introduction by Victor Sōgen Hori   ix

List of Contributors   xxvi

Teaching Buddhism: Past and Present

Teaching Buddhism in the Postmodern University:
Understanding, Critique, Evaluation   3
Frank E. Reynolds

Buddhist Studies in the Academy: History and Analysis   17
Charles S. Prebish

What is "Buddhism"?

Representations of Buddhism in Undergraduate Teaching:
The Centrality of Ritual and Story Narratives   39
Todd T. Lewis

Moving Beyond the 'ism':
A Critique of the Objective Approach to Teaching Buddhism   57
O'Hyun Park

Cultural Divides

Black Ships, Blavatsky, and the Pizza Effect:
Critical Self-Consciousness as a Thematic Foundation
for Courses in Buddhist Studies   71
Stephen Jenkins

An End-run round Entities: Using Scientific Analogies to
Teach Basic Buddhist Concepts   84
William S. Waldron

Skillful Means

Engaging Buddhism: Creative Tasks and Student Participation   95
Joanne Wotypka

The Peripatetic Class: Buddhist Traditions and
Myths of Pedagogy   107
E. H. Rick Jarow

Buddha Body, Buddha Mind

Buddhism and the Teaching of Jūdō   119
David Waterhouse

Introducing Buddhism in a Course on Postmodernism   141
Susan Mattis

Zen in the Classroom

Zen and the Art of Not Teaching Zen and the Arts:
An Autopsy   155
Ronald L. Grimes

Liberal Education and the Teaching of Buddhism   170
Victor Sōgen Hori

The Wheel Comes to the Web

Teaching Buddhism by Distance Education:
Traditional and Web-based Approaches   197
Mavis L. Fenn

Academic Buddhology and the Cyber-Sangha:
Researching and Teaching Buddhism on the Web   212
Brett Greider

dhism and Postmodern Philosophy. We were pleased to hear of the ingenuity displayed by teachers who had the difficult task of teaching Buddhism to students who were quite uninterested, even hostile, to Buddhism, such as Joanne Wotypka's "Introduction to Buddhism" and Jeffrey Mayer's course on Zen. Several Conference participants shared lessons learned in experimenting with different skillful means, such as William Waldron on the use of scientific analogies in explaining Buddhist concepts and Rick Jarow on the use of the "peripatetic class." Others brought accounts of quite unique courses, like David Waterhouse's course on jūdō or C. W. Huntington's course on meditation. Some, like O'Hyun Park and Todd Lewis, challenged us with presentations regarding the very nature of what we teach under the label Buddhism. And Mavis Fenn, Brett Greider and Francis Brassard presented different approaches to the impact of computer technology and the phenomenon of the World Wide Web on the teaching of Buddhism. Unfortunately for this volume, we were not able to obtain a text version of some of these presentations (Mayer, Huntington). However by compensation, this volume contains two original papers not presented at the Conference, Ronald Grimes's "Zen and the Art of Not Teaching Zen and the Arts: An Autopsy" and my own, "Liberal Education and the Teaching of Buddhism," a reflection on Frank Reynolds's keynote address.

The title of this volume, *From the Wheel to the Web*, casts as wide a net as possible to include all the themes and questions which the participants brought to the Conference. "Turning the Dharma wheel" is the traditional metaphor for teaching Buddhism. Until the modern period, the teaching of Buddhism meant the teaching of Dharma as a living practice by senior monks to junior novices within the *sangha* community itself. Within the modern college or university, teaching Buddhism means the teaching of Buddhism as a secular subject from an analytical and critical point of view. With the advent of computer technology and the creation of the World Wide Web, not only is teaching being changed by new resources and techniques but Buddhism itself is being transformed into what some people have called a "fourth *yāna*." What are the issues in teaching Buddhism from the Wheel to the Web?

Introduction

S everal years ago, the American Academy of Religion at its annual
conferences sponsored panels devoted to teaching Asian religions, panels such as the one on "Using the *Lotus Sūtra* to Teach the
Course in Buddhism" in 1992 and the panel on "Teaching the
Course on Zen" in 1993. A little while after that, the Society for the
Study of Japanese Religion similarly sponsored a panel on "Teaching
the Course in Japanese Religion." These panels proved two things.
First, the fact that they were very well-attended showed that there was
a large number of teachers in North American universities seeking to
improve the way they taught their courses; second, the quite different
approaches that panelists took showed that there was no agreement
on what were the basic issues, core texts, or best teaching techniques
for any particular course. Although many people were interested in
the question of how to teach Buddhism, there was no agreement on
the answer.

Thus, when my colleague Richard Hayes and I conceived the
Teaching Buddhism Conference, we knew we were addressing a topic
around which many people had strong interest. We knew that more
and more colleges and universities across North America were now
teaching Buddhism and the Asian religions, and we knew in a general
way, having talked with colleagues across the continent, that teachers
everywhere were concerned to teach them properly and well. But we
did not have a clear picture of the context of our topic and we did
not yet have a clear picture of the detailed issues. The Conference
itself help clarify these issues for us.

The Teaching Buddhism Conference brought together teachers of
all levels of undergraduate courses in Buddhism, from the freshman
introductory course to such specialized upper-level courses as Bud-

ple and in response to learn how to sympathize well, criticize well and personally evaluate well.

In the second keynote address, "Buddhist Studies in the Academy: History and Analysis," Professor Charles Prebish recounted the story of the birth of Buddhist Studies in North America. He first told us of the European antecedents and the several individual scholars who pioneered the study of Buddhism in North America in the first half of the twentieth century. Despite their work, however, as late as the immediate post-war period there were few universities offering courses in Buddhism. Then in the 1960s Buddhist Studies started to emerge as an identifiable discipline and during the years of the Vietnam War it experienced a boom. Using data from two surveys he conducted in 1992 and 1995, Prebish painted for us a much more precise picture of the growth of the field. One measure of the sudden growth is the number of doctoral degrees awarded in the field. In the seventy-year period between 1900 and 1971, there were just under 100 doctoral degrees awarded in North American schools with dissertation topics on Buddhism. But in the next quarter-century, there were nearly 1000 such degrees. At the same time, professional organizations for Buddhist scholars, such as the International Association of Buddhist Studies and the Buddhism Section of the American Academy of Religion, got started and grew steadily.

Aside from giving us precise measurements to chart the growth of Buddhist Studies, Prebish pointed us toward two issues of substance. First, a significant number of Buddhist scholars are also practitioners who have made a strong personal commitment to Buddhism. Second, the definition of the field, Buddhist Studies, seems to be shifting away from a narrow philological and philosophical study of classical Buddhist texts to a wider study of Buddhisms, both past and present, in their historical, social and cultural contexts. These issues—What is the relation of the teacher of Buddhism to the subject matter of Buddhism? And what is the study of Buddhism itself?—arose again and again throughout the Conference.

Where Did We Come From?

Professor Frank Reynolds, in the first keynote address, "Teaching Buddhism in the Postmodern University: Understanding, Critique, Evaluation," reminded us that not just in Buddhist Studies but in all of liberal education, questions and doubts have been raised about just what it is we are doing in university teaching. In his keynote address, against which later speakers frequently positioned themselves, he gave us a short history lesson showing that the very notion of liberal education had evolved from a curriculum based on a Renaissance humanistic study of core classical texts through a modernist curriculum emphasizing the study of Reason in both the physical and social sciences. In the present postmodern period—where even the notion of objective Reason is being criticized as just another culturally determined, politically manipulated tool—rather than fulfilling its announced role of education to liberate the mind, liberal education is being accused of cultural chauvinism and of promoting ideological agendas. In this context, how do we teach Buddhism and how do we justify our choices?

Reynolds has grown tired of the usual Introduction to Buddhism course which begins with the life of the Buddha, goes on a travel tour through Buddhist doctrinal history and ends with a snapshot of "Buddhism Today." Instead he suggests a new kind of course that is based in the present not in history, that is oriented to practice not doctrine, that takes seriously the notion that there is a Buddhist experience to which students can be introduced. He wants to expand the usual upper-level course that focuses on the reading of a primary text to include an investigation of the use of the text as a ritual sourcebook or political ideology. In all of these courses, he emphasizes the teacher's display of well-honed interpretive skills and the acquisition of the same by the student. These interpretive skills include the skills of sympathetic understanding, critical analysis and personal evaluation or judgement. The goal of teaching these courses in Buddhism is not merely to master a certain body of texts and its doctrines but to be thoroughly exposed to the lived worlds of other peo-

Acknowledgments

This volume contains proceedings of a conference on Teaching Buddhism: The State of the Art, hosted by the Faculty of Religious Studies of McGill University on October 8-9, 1999. Special thanks to the co-sponsors of the conference: the Numata Foundation, Shinnyo-en (Japan), the Social Sciences and Humanities Research Council of Canada, and the Faculty of Graduate Studies and Research, McGill University. Also thanks to Cindy Bentley and Jessica Main, for their assistance in organizing the conference.

A corresponding Web site on Teaching Buddhism can be found at http://www.teachingbuddhism.org.

What is "Buddhism"?

Although the question of just what it is that we are teaching arose in several papers, Todd Lewis confronts the issue square on in his paper, "Representations of Buddhism in Undergraduate Teaching: The Centrality of Ritual and Story Narratives." He notes that as now practiced in the West, Buddhist Studies as a research discipline has developed into the philological and philosophical study of classical Buddhist texts. But in most Buddhist societies where literacy was rare, for the greater part of history only the elite in the native population wrote and read such texts. The contents of such texts were closed to the major part of Buddhist populations for whom Buddhism meant, not philosophical scholarship, but practical teachings and daily ritual directed at pragmatic well-being, moral cultivation and seeking after *nirvāṇa*. Lewis points out that when elite scholars in the modern West define the textual work of elite scholars in the Buddhist past as the only "true Buddhism," then the popular storytelling and ritual practices which engaged the attention of ordinary Buddhists will be dismissed as "vulgarizations." There is also the danger that when Western scholars go seeking for it, their notion of "true Buddhism" may be colored by their own "Protestant" assumptions about the nature of true religion. As antidote, Lewis recommends the cultivation of a "sociological imagination of Buddhism" that recognizes that the shape of Buddhism in any society was determined not so much by philosophical ideas but by institutions such as monasteries, shrines, charities, lay associations, and so on—institutions where economics, politics, medicine, art were as important as meditation and in which lay people were as influential as ordained *sangha* members. He focuses on story narratives as the central texts in Buddhist societies and examines popular ritual to learn how Buddhist doctrine was understood and practiced by common people.

If the study of the written word is one end of a spectrum, then Professor O'Hyun Park's approach to teaching Buddhism represents the other. He argues that although Buddhism as a religious and cultural phenomenon is always historically and sociologically conditioned, nevertheless its essential core is meditation, or "ontological silence or ontological inquiring-within." In his teaching, he tries to transcend sectarian divisions between Theravāda and Mahāyāna Buddhism to get at their commonality, the "existential awareness" which is the "living reality of Buddhism." He actively engages students in the exploration of nondual reality, a reality which is not attainable through the usual academic study of religion, and encourages his students to maintain a mantra or *gong-an* throughout the duration of the course. Park is well aware that his way of teaching Buddhism is quite different from the way used in most academic courses but defends this on the ground that the nature of the subject matter requires it: "the methodology of teaching and learning has to be ontologically related to its substance. The ontological meeting of method and substance is from the Buddhist perspective nothing other than the realization of one's true selfhood." A critic could charge that Park's way of teaching Buddhism is nothing more than "dogmatic affirmation," but things are not so simple. Park is a professor of Buddhism and a Christian minister and so he cannot be accused of trying to indoctrinate students into his faith. For his part, the nonduality found in Buddhism is a welcome antidote to the rigid dualism found in both Christian theology and the traditional academic study of Buddhism.

Scholar-Practitioners

Prebish talked about what we all know but rarely discuss. Many of the people engaged in Buddhist Studies in North America are serious practitioners of Buddhism. Prebish quotes José Cabezón who cautions that practitioners of Buddhism will be perceived to lack critical distance and will be suspect for allowing individual beliefs to affect the objectivity of their judgement. Here Buddhist scholars suffer from the stereotypical accusation used against scholars of religion in general: personal commitment compromises rigorous scholarship. Scholar-practitioner is an oxymoron, it seems.

In addition to the suspicion and possible criticism which Cabezón notes, there is another issue which arises in the classroom, in my experience. Many students consider themselves Buddhists or are actively considering the possibility of declaring themselves Buddhist.

They very much want to learn Buddhism not from the detached academic perspective but from the standpoint of personal commitment and lived experience. They expect class discussion to tell them "How to Be a Better Buddhist." Far from being suspicious of the practitioner, they think that a practicing Buddhist is the only legitimate teacher of Buddhism and would like nothing better than to be a disciple to a guru.

The critical attitude to Buddhist scholar-practitioners may be softening. Prebish cites Duncan Williams's listing of institutions which offer graduate study in Buddhism, a listing which includes the category "Practitioner-Friendly Institutions." Such institutions offer courses with a practice content, programs where a student may pursue a degree while training as a priest, or a general ambiance in which Buddhism is taken normatively. A recent publication, *Buddhist Theology: Critical Reflections by Contemporary Buddhist Scholars*, edited by Roger R. Jackson and John J. Makransky (Curzon, 1999), is devoted to essays by scholar-practitioners explicitly talking about their scholarship and practice. Perhaps these developments herald a future institutional separation into two: the "theological" study of Buddhism and the academic study of Buddhism. The Teaching Buddhism Conference could not devote much attention to this issue but it did recognize that the issue was there and would continue to arise.

Cultural Divides

Many observers have noted that unlike the case of Christianity or Judaism, Buddhist Studies is a Western discipline about an Asian religion. Teachers of Buddhism in North America usually do not share the same cultural background of the people, texts and religious institutions they teach about. They worry that in their teaching they may be unwittingly distorting the subject matter by viewing it through a foreign cultural lens. Even though teachers may be sensitive to the danger of cultural distortion, there is no assurance that students will be so careful and self-conscious. Almost all of the Conference participants addressed this issue in one way or another, but Stephen Jenkins in his paper, "Black Ships, Blavatsky and the Pizza Effect: Critical

Self-Consciousness as a Thematic Foundation for Courses in Buddhist Studies," dealt with it most explicitly. At his college, Jenkins had the task of preparing students for an international studies program where they would be entering into, and living in, another culture. Some students inevitably begin by treating a foreign culture as an object and think they are doing little more than studying an exotic world view. To get students past this stage, Jenkins emphasizes the "feedback loop" (or the "pizza effect") to show students they are involved in constructing, and then misperceiving, the foreign culture they are studying. Just as it was Americans who made the elaborate pizza and then mistook it for an indigenous Italian product and just as Italians have co-opted the American pizza and now make it for American tourists, so also it was westerners who created the rational "Protestant" Buddhism of modern Sri Lanka and then mistook it for an indigenous Sri Lankan product, and so also did a Sri Lankan Buddhist spokesman, Dharmapāla, sell this protestantized Buddhism back to West when he appeared at the World Parliament of Religions in 1893. There are several other examples in Jenkins's paper. The epistemological lesson he draws is that the study of other cultures provides an opportunity whereby our own subjectivity as westerners can dialogue with the subjectivity of the culture under study. This meeting of subjectivity with subjectivity constitutes inter-religious dialogue between cultures and intra-religious dialogue within the mind of a single student or scholar.

William Waldron's paper, "An End-run round Entities: Using Scientific Analogies to Teach Basic Buddhist Concepts," starts with the problem that the usual language which teachers and students have inherited from Western religion and philosophy is not suitable for discussing Buddhism. Such language, with its substantialist and theistic presuppositions, obstructs the attempt to convey the Buddhist worldview which explicitly challenges the notions of substance and theism. Waldron finds that modern science, particularly biology, possesses working vocabulary, explanations and concepts without substantialist and theistic presuppositions and that using these allows him to do an "end-run" round the substantialist entities which students automatically expect to find and which is affirmed by the language of Western religion and philosophy. It should be noted that Waldron is not arguing the intellectual claim that there is a structural parallel between Buddhism and biology, in the way that some authors have argued for Buddhism and modern physics, implying that early Buddhism somehow foresaw modern physics. Rather his aim is heuristic; it is merely a skillful means, using familiar examples, to get students to understand the unfamiliar Buddhist ideas of dependent arising, designation, and non-self. Waldron gives a step by step description of his presentation with the usual student reactions and thus generously makes his teaching technique available to all teachers.

Skillful Means

Joanne Wotypka was faced with a class of more than eighty students who had signed up for her course, "Introduction to Buddhism," because, as she says, the other Arts option course, "Witchcraft and the Occult," was already full. Her paper, "Engaging Buddhism: Creative Tasks and Student Participation," describes with a great deal of humor the Creative Tasks which she devised to motivate eighty lethargic students whose knowledge of Buddhism consisted of having seen the movies *Kundun* or *Seven Years in Tibet*. Creative Task number two was to try to explain the concept of emptiness to another person and then to report on the attempt. Wotypka discovered that the most common victims of the students were their mothers, usually at the breakfast table. The next most popular victims were significant others, usually with some alcohol involved. Also represented were other passengers on public transportation, cab drivers and in one case, door-to-door proselytizers from the Jehovah's Witnesses. Though most students readily admitted they had failed to convey emptiness to the other, they agreed the attempt to do so made them understand it much better. (One mother however questioned the value of her daughter's post-secondary education.) Creative Task number three was to attempt to live by the Five Precepts for two full days. This meant that first the students had to define just what living by the Five Precepts meant. Is coffee an intoxicant? What is sexual misconduct? In their accounts of their attempts, students reported shock at how un-Buddhist their lives were and how difficult it was to never cause harm and never tell a lie.

Part of Rick Jarow's paper, "The Peripatetic Class: Buddhist Traditions and Myths of Pedagogy," strikes again at the question, What is the Study of Buddhism? raising issues similar to those raised in the papers by Prebish, Lewis and Park. For Jarow, the standard paradigm of university teaching—where we treat our subject matter with "disembodied objectivity," where the emphasis is on the verbal and analytic, where we try to understand religion as a "pure intellectual enterprise"—is incapable of seeing entire areas of religious experience. He focuses on the "myths" that inform present pedagogical discourse: the assumption that knowledge is acquired intellectually and not in embodied form, the focus on individuals rather than on social bodies, the assumption that we teach best in highly structured classrooms. As antidote to these strictures, Jarow has taught the "peripatetic class" in which he takes his class for a walk around the Vassar campus. He found that "the walking class complemented the text-based classroom, with embodied experiences becoming mnemonic devices that brought home a number of concepts that had previously been difficult to grasp." A walk through plowed fields (the Vassar campus is itself a farm) makes concrete the story of the Buddha cautioning a farmer not to plow up a snake and the question of nonviolence towards living things is no longer just an abstract philosophical question. The sight of a caterpillar triggers a discussion of "who transmigrates from body to body" in Buddhism. At the end, Jarow asks his students if they were aware of their feet touching the ground and initiates a discussion on mindfulness. In this experiment, the simple act of using the body to go on a walk opens up other channels of learning.

Buddha Body, Buddha Mind

The use of the body is the central feature in David Waterhouse's course on jūdō. Waterhouse has been teaching courses on Buddhism and Buddhist art for thirty years and since 1990 has been teaching a third-year undergraduate course called "Jūdō in Japanese Culture," in which two hours a week are devoted to the usual in-class lecture and two hours are devoted to actual jūdō practice in the *dōjō* (training hall). His paper, entitled "Buddhism and the Teaching of Jūdō," first begins with history, making it clear that Buddhism had little influence on the development of jūdō but that Buddhist elements can been found in jūdō and commentators have found jūdō consonant with Buddhist principles. In their weekly two hours in the practice hall, the students are introduced to, and drill themselves in, warm-up exercises, breakfalls, and a selection of techniques from each of the major groups of throws, immobilization techniques and locks. In addition to the usual academic papers, Waterhouse asks his students to write an ungraded 300-word paper on their "Impressions of Jūdō." The students report they find it a novel experience to wear the white jūdō uniform and follow the *dōjō* rituals of lining up, bowing, kneeling, and sitting in silence. They again experience physical contact with another person and experience for the first time imposing and submitting to powerful jūdō armlocks and strangles. Waterhouse's course grows out of his view of "knowledge as comprising mostly nonverbal cognition: information from the senses does not have to be reducible to, or reduced to, words in order to count as knowledge." The experience of performing itself gives one a kind of knowledge not available to one who merely watches or listens to the performance. Thus in this unique course Waterhouse deliberately tries to bridge the gap between theory and practice and to give students a glimpse of the possibilities of acquiring knowledge non-verbally.

Susan Mattis notes that despite the lip service that colleges and universities pay to the goal of learning about and from other cultures, in fact, with the exception of certain select fields, their programs of studies still often focus only on Western culture. In her paper, "Introducing Buddhism in a Course on Postmodernism," she tries to show how a course in Western philosophy can legitimately be extended to include Buddhist philosophy. The Buddhist philosophy section cannot be just arbitrarily tacked on at the end but must be integrated with the themes and concepts of the original course. Mattis begins her course by reading Nietzsche and Saussure as progenitors to Derrida, the initiator of postmodernism. For each of these authors, she emphasizes those concepts and claims which have some parallel to Madhyamaka thought which she will introduce later. For example, she starts with Nietzsche's criticism of the idea that a thing has a constitution in itself freed from all its relationships with other things. Later on in the course, she can rephrase this point in Buddhist terminology: an entity cannot possess self-essence (*svabhāva*). Several other of Nietzsche's ideas are first laid down so that later they can be rephrased in the terminology of Nāgārjuna and the Madhyamaka. There is not a complete parallel between Nietzsche and Nāgārjuna because Nāgārjuna justifies his position using arguments about the nature of language while language is less of a concern for Nietzsche. To supply the linguistic turn in postmodern thought, Mattis studies Saussure, the founder of structuralism. Saussure repudiates the traditional reference theory of language in which the meaning of a concept lies in its reference to an object outside language. Instead he sees the meaning of a word as entirely determined by its difference from other words in the language. Language is not a system of meanings which mirrors the intuited objects of the world; rather the concepts of language divide up the world determining how "objects" will be intuited. Derrida's own ideas of language which further develop Saussure's ideas do not all have parallels with Madhyamaka thought but his critique of "logocentrism"—the belief that there is a fundamental principle which exists independently and is the foundation for everything else—does. Mattis finds that on some points the prior study of postmodernism aids a better understanding of Buddhist philosophy. For example, students often misinterpret the Madhyamaka position, thinking it a kind of idealism which asserts that the things of ordinary cognition are just "fabrications" of a solipsistic consciousness, or mistakenly assume that Buddhist emptiness implies that nothing has value in life. Veterans of her postmodernism course will be inoculated against these mistakes.

Zen in the Classroom

Ron Grimes has been teaching a course called "Zen Meditation, Zen Art" for some twenty years. In the beginning (back in the '70s) it was a course which overflowed with excited students eager to get Buddhist enlightenment and thrilled to do experimental Zen course assignments. That was in the old days. In his article, "Zen and the Art of Not Teaching Zen and the Arts: An Autopsy," Grimes records his frustration at trying to teach this past year's crop of students—lethargic, incurious, incredulous, indifferent. The students also seemed to have been in the thrall of fixed ideas. Despite the fact that Grimes emphasized that in Zen monasteries, monks engaged in highly ritualized behavior, strictly obeyed orders from higher up, and did everything possible to de-emphasize individuality, the students inevitably decided that Zen was all about spontaneity, naturalness and personal involvement. The stereotype of spontaneity took firm hold on the students, who proceeded to write the most rigid and wooden papers about naturalness. As example of being present in the moment, one student submitted photographs which she had taken in high school five year previous. Grimes performs an autopsy on more than one corpse, however. At the same time as he was teaching the Zen course, he was also teaching "Writing Religion," a required course for honors students in their final year. This course, designed to develop writing skills, turned out to be a constantly bubbling pot of on-the-spot improvisation, play combined with hard work, friendship and fun. Ironically the writing course seemed to be much more Zen than the Zen course. Grimes observes that that which he would do, he did not do, and that which he would not do, he did. Perhaps that's Zen, perhaps not. But that is what happens in teaching.

My own paper, "Liberal Education and the Teaching of Buddhism," starts out as a reflection on Frank Reynolds's paper on "Teaching Buddhism in the Postmodern University." I argue that in addition to examining the intellectual content of a curriculum devoted to liberal education, as Reynolds does, one also needs to examine the institutional practices of the university—the behavior of individual teachers and instructors, administrative and curricular officers, committees, departments, student advisors, disciplinary boards, and so on. These people and offices all set policy and make many individual decisions guided by the politically correct notion of the "autonomy of the student." The institutional definition, as opposed to the intellectual definition, of "liberal education" is education to respect and enhance the autonomy of the student. Halfway through the paper, I switch position and start to describe teaching techniques which I have created in imitation of techniques I learned in a Japanese Zen monastery. Some of these are quite successful but they depend on elements which are usually considered illiberal: rote repetition and imitation, hierarchy and authority in the classroom, emphasis on groups not individuals, and so on. I defend these practices as liberal not in the politically correct sense of promoting "autonomy" but in the Buddhist sense of freedom. Rather than trying to liberate students by making them "free from" any relation with other people and their environment, I argue that liberal education ought to make them "free in" their relations with other people and their environments.

Teaching Buddhism and Computer Technology

The Teaching Buddhism Conference devoted a panel to computer technology. Francis Brassard's presentation, "Use of Interactive Software for the Learning of Classical Languages such as Sanskrit," was a progress report on "Buddhacarita," the software he is developing which will function as an interactive tutor for students of Sanskrit. Recognizing that slowness in learning a language is not necessarily a matter of intelligence (thanks Francis!) but rather of organization and discipline in learning, he has designed software which will test the student, give fast feedback and then develop further tests based on the student's strengths and weaknesses. In addition, the software uses sound to give students accurate pronunciation and also combines sound and text so that the student can select a text passage and hear how it sounds when read properly. The software will have a vocabulary function so that the student can click on a Sanskrit word and immediately get the translation. Other functions are still being added.

Unfortunately the multi-media nature of this presentation made it pointless to include just the text of Brassard's presentation.

Mavis Fenn's presentation, "Teaching Buddhism by Distance Education: Traditional and Web-based Approaches," goes beyond a discussion of distance education and gives us an overview of the entire range of issues involved in developing computer-based courses of instruction. It is clear, she reports, that most faculty are uninterested in attempting to develop computer-based courses, and this for a variety of reasons: some have concerns about course quality, universities are not supportive, most instructors feel themselves technologically untrained, many have ideological objections. In attempting to evaluate the worth of Web-based courses, Fenn found that there were few analytic studies, although there was some anecdotal evidence. The evidence did indicate that while Web-based courses are more accessible to larger populations, certain categories of people were not included—those who are sight- or hearing-impaired and those who do not have access to a computer (like the poor). The number one objection to Web-based courses is the giving up of the classroom. Teachers establish their identity as teachers in the classroom and some students prefer the camaraderie of the classroom to anonymous and individual computer learning (of course, other students prefer the security of anonymity, away from the gaze of their peers). All teachers who have developed computer-based courses agree that such courses are extremely labor intensive, both to develop and then to maintain once in operation. Furthermore, not only do most universities not provide adequate technical support, some universities are pressuring faculty into creating computer-based courses and then taking possession of them. The faculty of York University in Toronto went on strike over this issue. Despite all these negative factors, Fenn found that faculty who had actually developed distance education courses were in general quite positive about the pedagogical value of their courses. They found it exciting to have students in very distant countries and were pleased at the more active participation of the students. Though there have been few rigorous studies of Web-based distance learning courses, Fenn's paper gives a capsule summary of the issues and provides much anecdotal evidence.

Brett Greider, in his article "Academic Buddhology and the Cyber-Sangha: Researching and Teaching Buddhism on the Web," examines the manifold impact of the Internet on teaching Buddhism. The World Wide Web presents students and teachers with a wealth of resource material, much of it never before available to the average person: on-line *sūtra* texts, specialized dictionaries, access to expert scholars and teachers, discussion groups with colleagues in every part of the world, and databases of information. The information on the Web is quite different from the information that presently resides in our libraries, for Web information is predominantly organized around images rather than text, and it is tangentially (not logically) hyperlinked together. Increasingly these images are moving images rather than still images and more and more they come with an audio element allowing us to hear as well as see. Web information is interactive; it allows, even requires, input from the person browsing. To access the Web, one needs computer technology with which students are often far more familiar than are teachers. To use the Web as a teaching tool, teachers have to become the students of their students. This disparity creates the possibility of a new teaching dynamic pairing the student's expertise in Web computer technology with the teacher's expertise in content. Greider describes successful Web projects he has devised. Some projects organize students to do collaborative work with each other. Some help students overcome the barrier of accepting the "otherness" of foreign cultures. Others involve cooperating with students in a school across the continent in joint projects.

The Web is also a good symbol for Buddhist concepts. As a complex of inter-related connections, the Web is a good analogy for *pratītya-samutpāda*; as a real phenomenon without any essential core, the Web is a good symbol for *śūnyatā*. But it is more than just analogy and symbol. The Web is in fact a materialization of Indra's Net, the net of jewels in the *Hua-yen Sūtra* in which each jewel reflects every other jewel and its reflections in an infinite net of unhindered mutual interpenetration.

The phenomenon of the World Wide Web is changing Buddhism itself. Never before have all the teachers and *sanghas* of every Buddhist tradition been in communication with each other creating for the first time the possibility of a united cyber-sangha. It is now possible to talk of a fourth *kaya* or body of the Buddha, a fourth *yāna* or vehicle of the teachings. The Web thus represents not merely a new set of skillful means or symbols for teaching Buddhism, but also a new stage in the evolution of world Buddhism itself.

Outstanding Issues

Though the papers collected in this volume give a good idea of the many issues important to teaching Buddhism, there are some serious gaps. Many people think that Buddhism is based on meditation and that just as chemistry courses have lab sessions, courses on Buddhism should have meditation sessions. C. W. Huntington actually conducted a course in meditation and at the Conference gave us a report on the difficulties he encountered. Unfortunately he was not able to provide a paper for this volume. Similarly, this volume has no discussion of Buddhism and art, an extremely important topic for teaching Buddhism, nor do we have a discussion of teaching Buddhism through literature such as novels and stories, a standard option in programs of Christian studies. This first Conference was directed at undergraduate education and consequently neglected the issues involved in teaching Buddhism at the graduate level, training students in primary languages, developing specialists rather than generalists, supervision of dissertations, expansion of the field of Buddhist Studies to allow dissertations on Buddhism in the West, and more. These are questions we must postpone to another conference.

Contributors

Mavis L. Fenn
Assistant Professor of Religious Studies,
St. Paul's United College, University of Waterloo

Brett Greider
Assistant Professor of Comparative Religion,
University of Wisconsin, Eau Claire

Ronald L. Grimes
Professor of Religion and Culture,
Wilfred Laurier University

Victor Sōgen Hori
Associate Professor of Japanese Religions,
McGill University

E. H. Rick Jarow
Assistant Professor in History of Religions,
Vassar College

Stephen Jenkins
Assistant Professor of Religious Studies,
Humboldt State University

Todd T. Lewis
Associate Professor of World Religions,
Holy Cross College

Susan Mattis
Lecturer, Arts and Sciences Honors Program,
Boston College

O'Hyun Park
Professor of Religion,
Appalachian State University

Charles S. Prebish
Professor of Religious Studies,
Pennsylvania State University

Frank E. Reynolds
Professor of History of Religions and Buddhist Studies,
the University of Chicago

William S. Waldron
Assistant Professor of Religion,
Middlebury College

David Waterhouse
Professor of East Asian Studies,
University of Toronto

Joanne Wotypka
Graduate student and Lecturer in Religion,
University of Alberta

Teaching Buddhism:
Past and Present

Teaching Buddhism in the Postmodern University: Understanding, Critique, Evaluation

Frank E. Reynolds

I t is very propitious that the Faculty of Religious Studies at McGill has chosen to celebrate the establishment of its recent Numata endowment by sponsoring an international conference that focuses attention on the teaching of Buddhism. Over the years I have been involved in many excellent Buddhist Studies activities devoted to the exploration of particular textual and historical issues; I have participated in a good number of very useful meetings and publications that have had as their focus the historical development, the present state, and/or the future direction of Buddhist Studies research; and I have participated in several events that have had the essentially apologetic purpose of communicating a Buddhist message to active or potential Buddhist practitioners. However the McGill Conference on Teaching Buddhism: The State of the Art (and this correlated collection of essays) is the first major Buddhist Studies project that I am aware of that has had, as its primary focus, the teaching of Buddhism to undergraduate students. It is hard to imagine a more timely topic for Buddhist Studies scholars to consider.[1]

In what follows, I would like to sketch out an overall orientation to the topic of teaching Buddhism to undergraduate students. My hope is that this general orientation will have sufficient substance that it can be supported, extended or challenged by other contributors to this volume.

The basic claim that undergirds the approach that I will take is that, in the undergraduate context, the primary purpose of teaching Buddhism is to contribute to the liberal education of students. At first glance this basic claim may seem rather obvious and innocuous. However I will try to make the case that a serious exploration of the issues that this claim raises can generate an overall perspective within which and against which relevant deliberations can creatively proceed. I will begin with a discussion of three different ways of understanding liberal education, including a newly emerging perspective that takes our postmodern intellectual and social situation seriously into account. As my exposition proceeds, I will at various points suggest particular ways in which teaching in Buddhist Studies can contribute to the process.

How, then, can we identify the kind of approach to liberal education—particularly liberal education in the humanities and social sciences—that will be truly viable as we enter into the twenty-first century?[2] Certainly it will not be the Renaissance-oriented humanistic ideal of engaging a culturally prescribed canon of texts drawn from the so-called classical tradition of the West. To be sure, this view has had a number of very influential supporters in recent years, but I am quite certain that for most contemporary scholars (including virtually everyone who is involved in Buddhist Studies) it has long since lost its power to convince.

Serious and well meaning attempts have been made to update this classics-oriented approach by including, within the canon of privileged texts, items written by women, members of minority groups, and representatives of non-Western traditions—including in some cases representatives of various Buddhist traditions. But unfortunately, despite a number of attempts, no one has yet been able to provide convincing intellectual criteria for making the innumerable choices that must be made in order to responsibly implement this kind of reform. James Foard, one of the very few Buddhist Studies scholars who has given serious thought to issues of liberal education, has put the point very precisely. If we proceed in this way, he writes, "we justify adding things *ad infinitum*...and inevitably advocate the absurdity of unlimited limits. Our opponents know this," he continues, "and we should concede the point."[3] This certainly does not mean, either for Foard or for me, that we should avoid the teaching of texts that have been labeled as classics. Quite to the contrary. But it does mean that we cannot responsibly accept a vision of liberal education that depends on the identification of a canon of privileged texts, no matter how multicultural and forward looking that canon may seem to be.

The other really major ideal of liberal education that we have inherited from our Euro-American past is what I label the modernist ideal. This modernist ideal had its origins in the Enlightenment and is characterized by the assertion of the pre-eminence and hegemony of an Enlightenment-generated understanding of Reason (Reason with a capital "R"). In its heyday in the late nineteenth and early twentieth century this modernist approach was sometimes advocated in direct opposition to the emphasis on a canon of classical texts; on the other hand it was sometimes yoked in an uneasy alliance with it. Either way, it was an approach that dominated the intellectual scene in North America.

According to the proponents of this Enlightenment-oriented approach, the kind of Reason that was constructed and deployed by Enlightenment thinkers had thoroughly unmasked and discredited other more traditional ways of apprehending and engaging reality. These Enlightenment enthusiasts were also convinced that this kind of Reason could be utilized to generate truly objective knowledge of the one empirically accessible world in which all human beings supposedly live. The direct pedagogical corollary of this modernist understanding of Reason was the notion that liberal education should be constituted by an initiation into the various positivist sciences that were specifically developed in order to pursue this reputedly objective form of knowledge. These positivist sciences included, among others, historical sciences, social and cultural sciences, and psychological sciences.

In recent years, as the hegemony of the Enlightenment notion of Reason has been increasingly challenged by a variety of late modern and postmodern critiques, the modernist ideal of liberal education has, like the classics-oriented ideal, become thoroughly untenable.

Unfortunately the ghosts of the hegemony of the Enlightenment notion of Reason still haunt some areas of contemporary scholarship
and teaching, including some contemporary scholarship and teaching
within Buddhist Studies. However, a serious intellectual defense of
the modernist ideal is no longer possible.

Given the demise of these two major notions of liberal education
that we have inherited from our past—i.e., the classics-oriented view
and the modernist view—those of us who continue to believe that
some coherent and convincing approach to liberal education is an
intellectual and social necessity face a very serious challenge. Is it
really possible to develop a fully up-to-date approach to liberal education that takes adequate account of the new realities of globalization and pluralism on the one hand, and the consequences of the
postmodern dethronement of the Enlightenment notion of Reason on
the other? This is certainly neither the time nor the place to attempt
to provide a definitive answer to this vexing question. However, a few
positive suggestions may provide a useful orientation as we strive to
identify and explore the issues that will be basic to the teaching of
Buddhism in colleges and universities in the years that lie ahead. (To
avoid misunderstanding I should indicate at the outset that in the
discussion that follows I am using a rather conservative notion of
postmodernity. It is a view of the postmodern situation that recognizes that the hegemony of the Enlightenment notion of Reason has
been definitively undercut. But it is at the same time a view that re-
sists the tendency of many postmodern scholars to throw out the Enlightenment baby with the Enlightenment bath water.)

The most basic characteristics of the view of liberal education
that I want to affirm are the following. First, this view of liberal education presumes that human beings (including ourselves, the students
we teach and the people we study) create, discover, think within and
live within a variety of different and often competing worlds, all of
which are historically situated and engaged. Second, it affirms that a
liberal education in the postmodern era should involve the exploration of a variety of very different humanly constituted worlds. (Here I
quite intentionally leave open the question of whether such worlds
are "constructed" or "discovered.") These humanly constituted

worlds should include some that are assumed to be familiar, and others that are quite unfamiliar. They should also include some that are "life worlds" and some that are constituted or projected in texts of various sorts. Finally, it is my contention that an appropriate and up-to-date liberal education must also include the cultivation of well-disciplined interpretive skills and strategies through which significant worlds and their interactions with one another can be rationally and imaginatively engaged.[4]

The pedagogical implications of this kind of view of liberal education for the teaching of Buddhism are legion. At the most fundamental level they include the need to justify the Buddhist Studies courses that we choose to teach in at least two distinct ways. The specific courses that we teach need to be justified in terms of the intrinsic significance of the world or worlds that are taken as the object(s) of study. At the same time these courses also need to be justified in terms of the interpretive skills and strategies that the teacher deploys and that the students are encouraged to engage and to cultivate. In what remains I will provide three specific examples of the kind of Buddhist Studies courses that seem to me to focus on topics and materials that meet the criteria of postmodern relevance and interest. I will then turn to a more detailed discussion of the kind of interpretive skills and strategies that need to be identified and cultivated.

In choosing Buddhist worlds that are appropriate for exploration in a postmodern liberal arts curriculum, the teacher's own areas of specialized interest and expertise necessarily play a very crucial role. Thus I am well aware that the examples that I will provide inevitably embody components that arise out of my own personal interests and my own areas of competence. Nonetheless it will be useful to put forward, at least as illustrations, three specific possibilities that highlight, in very concrete ways, the kinds of topics and data that I have in mind.

Most college or university teachers will probably agree that the hardest course to teach well in any area of scholarship is the introductory course. (Which is, of course, the reason that in most departments this responsibility is foisted off on the youngest and most vulnerable member!) At the same time, the introductory course is the most important course in any given area of study, both because it generally involves the greatest number of students and because it provides an ideal context for the recruitment of students into courses that are more advanced and more specialized.

Over the past two decades I have given a great deal of thought to ways of teaching an introductory course in Buddhist Studies, primarily in the context of teaching graduate students and preparing and evaluating textbooks. As the years have gone by, I have become increasingly uncomfortable with the kind of introduction that I have myself taught and that has for many decades dominated the scene. I mean, of course, the kind of survey course that begins with what (in our most optimistic moods) we think that Buddhist Studies may have learned about the historical life and teachings of Gautama Buddha. It moves through a rapid-fire treatment of some 2500 years of Buddhist intellectual and social history. And it finally concludes with an equally rapid-fire survey of contemporary Buddhism in various countries around the world. Whatever usefulness that kind of pseudo-historical approach to the introductory course may have had in the past, it is my conviction that it has very little to commend it in the present or in the future.

The question that arises for those of us who have come to this kind of conclusion is whether or not it is possible to develop an alternative approach that will be appropriate and effective within a postmodern liberal arts curriculum. I believe that the answer is "yes." And I have invested a great deal of effort over the past two years in the preparation of a textbook that will—if it is successful—help to confirm my optimism. The book, which is entitled *The Life of Buddhism*, includes short introductions written by myself and my co-editor that provide crucial historical background and introduce a basic technical vocabulary. But the main body of the text is constituted by fifteen different accounts of the religious context, the religious practices and the lived experiences of a wide variety of twentieth-century Buddhist communities and practitioners situated throughout many diverse areas of Asia and North America. These essays, which have been written by a wide array of Buddhist Studies scholars from various disciplines, are divided into four segments. The first segment focuses on "Temples, Sacred Objects and Associated Rituals," the second deals with "Monastic Practices," and the third looks at "Lay Practices." The final segment is constituted by a single essay that describes the practices of an American Zen community located in Rochester, New York.[5]

The topic-oriented, data-oriented goal of a course using this kind of textbook would be to introduce students to a broadly representative variety of the real worlds of real Buddhists who are involved in real Buddhist practices that generate real Buddhist experiences. The course would be designed to convey to a wide range of students a kind of collage of vivid impressions and insights. Assuming that the essays have been well chosen and that the course is well taught, these impressions and insights should constitute a responsible and compelling introduction to significant commonalities, differences and conflicts that are characteristic of various Buddhist traditions. Hopefully, for some students, this kind of introductory course will also generate the motivation to seek out more advanced courses in the Buddhist Studies area.

But what about Buddhist Studies courses that are appropriate at the more advanced levels of the curriculum? The challenge is to select topics and bodies of data that are in tune with the topics and bodies of data characteristic of the very best courses being offered by other religious studies teachers and the kind being offered in other related humanistic and social science disciplines. Or, if the courses are not so tuned, the instructor should be prepared to make a convincing argument that the criteria of selection being used represent the exploration of a new frontier rather than the last vestige of a rearguard resistance to change.

Given the kind of practice-oriented introductory course that I have suggested, I will use as my second example a course that deals with a so-called "canonical" text. The basic assumption underlying the kind of text course that I have in mind is that it is necessary to give serious attention not only to the text itself (whatever that might mean), but also to the way in which the text in question has been appropriated and used within the Buddhist tradition. The best example that I can provide, given my own interests and expertise, is a course focused on a rather short text that has been preserved in the Pali canon under the title of *Mangala Sutta* (the Discourse of Blessings). This is a *sutta* that contains thirty-eight distinct, ethically oriented segments. Over the centuries it has been one of the most important and popular texts in the Theravāda tradition that presently holds sway in Sri Lanka and mainland Southeast Asia.

The course that I have in mind would begin with a relatively concise consideration of sub-topics that have in the past tended to occupy the total attention of most scholars and teachers who have focused on this kind of text. These sub-topics would include text-critical issues of authorship, manner of composition or compilation, and questions of canonical status. They would also include a basically literary overview of the form of the text and the content of the message or teaching that it contains. In this kind of course, however, such text-critical and literary matters, though they would be addressed, would certainly not be dominant. On the contrary, they would provide a launching pad for subsequent segments of the course that would focus on different ways in which the text has been received and put to use in the tradition that it has helped to constitute. In the case of the *Mangala Sutta* one segment of the course could focus on its incorporation into an ancient source book for ritual chants that has been used throughout Theravāda history to exorcise evil spirits and evil influences. Another segment could trace the interpretation of the text generated in the traditional commentaries that have been written over the centuries by Theravāda monastic scholars. A final segment could conclude the course by focusing on the way in which the *Mangala Sutta* is presently being employed in the on-going ideological struggle between the military rulers in Myanmar (Burma) and the democratic resistance led by Aung San Su Kyi.[6]

A third, very different kind of course that would be important to include in the Buddhist Studies component of an up-to-date liberal arts curriculum is one that would deal with the nineteenth and twentieth-century impact and establishment of Buddhism in the Western world, particularly in North America. This is a fascinating story within which many of the basic issues of modernity and postmodernity could be explored in a direct and immediate way. For example, one segment of the course could cover the development of Buddhist Studies in the United States and Canada; another could deal with the impact of Buddhism on the literary and artistic culture of the North American elite; another could highlight and analyze the fascinating representations of Buddhism in films and the media; another could focus on the establishment and development of Buddhist immigrant communities; and still another could consider the establishment and development of various indigenous Buddhist communities. One primary question that could be posed is why, in the nineteenth and twentieth centuries, the United States and Canada have provided such extremely fertile ground for the reception of Buddhist approaches to life. An intriguing and appropriate counterpoint question would be how Buddhism has been adapted and transformed as it has become engaged with the modern and postmodern environments that these North American countries have provided.

Since other papers in this volume will suggest other possible topics and correlated sets of data, I will turn now to the second major component that in my judgement needs to be present in really useful and up-to-date Buddhist Studies courses. This second major component, which is seldom discussed in Buddhist Studies circles, is the very explicit display of well honed interpretive skills by the teacher, and the closely correlated formation and cultivation of those skills in the students. As Mark Taylor has written in his "Introduction" to a collection of essays recently published under the title *Critical Terms for Religious Studies*, "it is no longer sufficient to think about different religions; now [and Taylor is quite explicitly taking account of the present postmodern context] it is necessary to consider how one thinks about these religions."[7] As the title of my paper suggests, the three very basic kinds of interpretive skills that I believe it is important to highlight are the skills of sympathetic understanding, the skills of critical analysis, and the skills of personal evaluation or judgement.[8]

Though in the actual process of interpretation sympathetic understanding, critical analysis and personal evaluation are intimately interrelated and interdependent, there is an obvious heuristic value in beginning with sympathetic understanding. What I really want to emphasize here is that those of us who teach Buddhist Studies courses cannot be satisfied with simply presenting some aspect of Buddhism in a sympathetic and appealing way. We do need to do that, but in addition we need to be very explicit about the theories and methods that scholars have used in generating this kind of understanding; we need to be very explicit about the problems and possibilities that are associated with the application of these theories and methods; and we need to be very explicit about the way in which these ways of proceeding can be justified in contemporary intellectual terms.

Obviously this kind of epistemological self-consciousness becomes more feasible and more necessary as one moves from entry level courses to courses designed for more advanced students. However, at all levels, from the most elementary to the most sophisticated, students should come away from Buddhist Studies courses having acquired a sympathetic understanding of some interesting and important aspect of Buddhism. At least equally important, they should also have learned something important about the skills of understanding that they will be able to utilize in many other contexts, both within and beyond the walls of the academy.

Sympathetic understanding is a primary aspect of the interpretive process. But (and I am convinced that this is an absolutely crucial point that is missed by many Buddhist Studies teachers) it is by no means sufficient. In the academic context sympathetic understanding needs to be complemented and supplemented by critical analysis. There are various relevant forms of critical analysis that have been developed. Some have been generated within the Buddhist tradition itself. (One of the most interesting is being propounded by a highly respected group of contemporary Japanese Buddhist scholars who are putting forth the explicitly normative claim that "Buddhism is criticism.")[9] There are also the quite different modes of critical analysis that are being developed and widely deployed in the postmodern academy. These include post-positivist modes of critical analysis that are central to historical, social, cultural and psychological sciences. They also include the newer forms of so-called critical theory that focus on the dynamics of power, particularly as these dynamics of power are played out in the hierarchies of ethnicity, class and gender.

It is obvious that in different Buddhist Studies courses the extent of the critical component will vary and the modes of critical analysis that are deployed will differ. However, I am convinced that in virtually all Buddhist Studies courses some emphasis on the cultivation of critical skills is crucial. In each case students should at least be introduced to the relevant critical scholarship that is being carried forward within contemporary Buddhist communities. In each case students should also be exposed to the relevant critical scholarship that is being generated within the secular academy. Hopefully, as students proceed through the various segments of the liberal arts curriculum, they will gradually acquire for themselves the kinds of intellectual and imaginative expertise that various forms of critical analysis require.

Thus both sympathetic understanding and critical analysis are necessary components within the interpretive process that teachers in the liberal arts should seek to encourage in their students. However, even taken together, they are not sufficient. The third component that must be added to the mix is the cultivation of well-disciplined judgements and evaluations. So far as I am aware, the best exposition of the importance of this third component of the interpretive process, and of the best means for cultivating it in students, appeared recently in a multi-authored essay entitled "Rhetoric, Pedagogy and the Study of Religions," published in the *Journal of the American Academy of Religion*. In this article the authors propose what they call a "rhetorical paradigm." Within this paradigm the chief goal of undergraduate teaching, particularly but not exclusively in the Religious Studies area, is "neither to improve technique nor to make students more knowledgeable, but to empower individual voices and to provide a space for practicing critical skills and reflective inquiry about matters of personal and public importance."[10]

The key point that I want to emphasize here is that within this rhetorical model the formation and cultivation of well-disciplined judgements and evaluations becomes an integral and culminating segment within the interpretive process itself. The role of the teacher is certainly not to convince students to adopt his or her position on the issues that may arise. On the contrary, the art of teaching within this paradigm consists in helping students to develop, alongside the skills of sympathetic understanding and the skills of critical analysis, the rhetorical skills of articulation and argumentation that facilitate the cultivation and expression of their own personal commitments. These are, it is important to add, the very same skills that will ultimately facilitate an effective engagement in the kind of serious and rational public dialogue that is absolutely essential for the future health of a democratic society.[11]

It is quite evident that up-to-date, well taught courses in Buddhist Studies will raise issues that are of serious personal and social importance. Therefore these courses provide one of the very best contexts within which to help students cultivate the skills that are involved in generating and expressing well disciplined, rationally formed evaluations and judgements.

By way of conclusion let me simply reiterate the basic normative claim that I made at the very outset—namely the claim that the primary purpose of teaching Buddhism to undergraduates in North American colleges and universities should be to facilitate and implement the process of liberal education. I am convinced that if this purpose is taken seriously, and if textbooks, courses and classroom teaching methods are self-consciously oriented toward that goal, the results will be very positive. On the one hand, liberal education will benefit from a distinctive Buddhist Studies contribution. On the other, Buddhist Studies will be able to secure and expand its still very tenuous presence within the North American academy.

Notes

[1] The timeliness of the topic is directly related to recent very rapid developments in Buddhist Studies research. For a review of the research situation in North America see Reynolds 1999 and an unpublished paper by Bruce Matthews entitled "Buddhist Studies in Canada: 1970–1998."

[2] I am keenly aware that any full understanding of liberal arts education must include a strong natural science component. However, given the concerns of this conference, I will focus my attention on issues that arise in the humanities / social science context.

[3] Foard 1990a, 170.

[4] My reflections on this topic began to develop in a serious way in the context of a project sponsored by the U.S. National Endowment for the Humanities in the late 1980s. The book that was generated by that project—*Beyond the Classics? Essays in Religious Studies and Liberal Education*—contains a number of essays that are still useful for those interested in pursuing the topic further. The most relevant are the following: Judith Berling, "Religious Studies and Exposure to Multiple Worlds"; Sheryl Burkhalter, "Four Modes of Discourse: Blurred Genres in the Study of Religion"; James Foard, "Beyond Ours and Theirs: The Global Character of Religious Studies"; Robin W. Lovin, "Confidence and Criticism: Religious Studies and the Public Purpose of Liberal Education"; Frank Reynolds "Reconstructing Liberal Education: A Religious Studies Perspective"; and Lawrence Sullivan, "'Seeking an End to the Primary Text' or 'Putting an End to the Text as Primary'."

[5] This book, which I have co-edited with Jason Carbine (an advanced graduate student specializing in Buddhist Studies within the History of Religions program at Chicago) will be published by the University of California Press in the fall of 2000.

[6] The kind of Buddhist Studies research that is correlated with this kind of course development was the topic of a conference on "Pali Texts in New Contexts" held at the University of Chicago Divinity School in May 1998. For two superb and highly relevant papers presented at that conference see Walters 1999 and Blackburn 1999.

[7] Taylor 1998, 12.

[8] In the discussion that follows I am self-consciously referring to the cultivation of interpretive skills that presume that students have already acquired basic college-level abilities in reading, writing, conceptualization and argumentation. For a suggestion for a very basic introductory course that focuses on the cultivation of the really primary skills that many students have not yet acquired, see James Foard's superb essay entitled "Writing Across the Curriculum: a Religious Studies Contribution" (Foard 1990b). Though the specific course that Foard describes deals with "Religions of the World," the pedagogical strategies that he sets forth could easily be adapted to a course focused on Buddhism.

[9] See Hubbard and Swanson 1997.

[10] Miller, Patton and Webb 1995, 820.

[11] For an earlier presentation of this same kind of view see Lovin 1990.

References

Blackburn, Anne. 1999. "Magic in the Monastery: Textual Practice and Monastic Identity in Sri Lanka." *History of Religions* 38 (4): 354–72.

Burkhalter, Sheryl, and Frank Reynolds, eds. 1990. *Beyond the Classics? Essays in Religious Studies and Liberal Education*. Atlanta: Scholars Press.

Foard, James. 1990a. "Beyond Ours and Theirs: The Global Character of Religious Studies." In *Beyond the Classics? Essays on Religious Studies and Liberal Education*, edited by
Sheryl Burkhalter and Frank Reynolds. Atlanta: Scholars Press.

———. 1990b. "Writing Across the Curriculum: A Religious Studies Contribution." In
Beyond the Classics? Essays on Religious Studies and Liberal Education, edited by Sheryl
Burkhalter and Frank Reynolds. Atlanta: Scholars Press.

Hubbard, Jamie, and Paul L. Swanson, eds. 1997. *Pruning the Bodhi Tree: The Storm Over
Critical Buddhism*. Honolulu: University of Hawaii Press.

Lovin, Robin W. 1990. "Confidence and Criticism: Religious Studies and the Public Purposes of Liberal Education." In *Beyond the Classics? Essays on Religious Studies and Liberal Education*, edited by Sheryl Burkhalter and Frank Reynolds. Atlanta: Scholars
Press.

Miller, Richard B., Laurie L. Patton and Stephen H. Webb. 1995. "Rhetoric, Pedagogy
and the Study of Religions." *Journal of the American Academy of Religion* 62 (3): 819–50.

Reynolds, Frank. 1999. "Coming of Age: Buddhist Studies in the United States 1972–
1998." *Journal of the International Association of Buddhist Studies* (fall).

Taylor, Mark, ed. 1998. *Critical Terms for Religious Studies*. Chicago: University of Chicago
Press.

Walters, Jonathan. 1999. "Suttas as History: Four Approaches to the Sermon on the Noble Quest." *History of Religions* 38 (3): 247–84.

Buddhist Studies in the Academy: History and Analysis

Charles S. Prebish

There can be little doubt that both the practice and study of Buddhism in the Western world have grown enormously in the last quarter-century. Fueled by a dramatic increase in ethnic Asian Buddhist communities in Western countries since 1965, and the continued expansion of various convert Buddhist communities, many million Buddhist practitioners now reside in the Western world. Although the expansion of the Western Buddhist movement is likely not surprising to observers of the modern religious landscape, the surge of scholarly interest in Buddhism in general was surely unexpected. In the years between 1900 and 1971 (when I received my Ph.D. in Buddhist Studies from the University of Wisconsin), there were just under 100 Ph.D./Th.D. degrees awarded in North American colleges and universities with dissertation topics related to Buddhism. In the next quarter-century, nearly 1,000 doctoral degrees—with Buddhist-related dissertation topics—were awarded in those same institutions.[1] Moreover, at the Twelfth Congress of the International Association of Buddhist Studies—the flagship professional organization for the discipline of Buddhist Studies, founded in 1976—held in Lausanne in August 1999, there were more than 200 papers presented, with the overall conference being attended by over 300 individuals. In view of the explosive growth of the discipline of Buddhist Studies, at least a small amount of historical reflection is useful.

European Antecedents

Recently, the important volume *Curators of the Buddha: The Study of Buddhism under Colonialism* has attracted much attention. It was the topic of a panel at the 1995 annual meeting of the American Academy of Religion and the subject of a review article, "Buddhist Studies in the Post-Colonial Age," by Jan Nattier. The book is a careful exercise in self-reflection, and Nattier is correct when she begins her article by observing, "This is a provocative book in many senses of the word. By exploring not just the ideas but the attitudes conveyed in the writings of several founding fathers of Buddhist Studies in the West...*Curators of the Buddha* will provoke its readers into seeing these figures in a new light."[2] However, the book is not the first attempt to contextualize and comment upon the discipline of Buddhist Studies in the West.

Although there was very little reliable information in the West pertaining to Buddhism prior to the nineteenth century, Henri de Lubac's *La rencontre du bouddhisme et l'occident*, published in 1952, is especially useful in summarizing this early literature. Of course one can find such landmark works as Simon de la Loubère's *Du royaume de Siam*, published in 1691, but it was not until the early nineteenth century, with the appearance of Michel François Ozeray's *Recherches sur Buddhou* (1817), that the picture began to brighten. Soon, the pioneering efforts of Henry Thomas Colebrooke, Brian Houghton Hodgson, Alexander Csoma de Körös, and Eugène Burnouf, followed by their intellectual heirs, brought the reliable study of Buddhism to Europe.

To a large extent, this interest in Buddhism was philological, converging on the increasing availability of Sanskrit and Pali manuscripts that were appearing on the European continent. Perhaps the most thorough examination of this development is Russell Webb's "Pali Buddhist Studies in the West," serialized in the now defunct *Pali Buddhist Review*, which systematically reviews the developments of Pali and Buddhist Studies in virtually all European countries, as well as Canada and the United States. Webb continues this work, having updated these early studies, in "Contemporary European Scholarship on Buddhism," published in 1989. But the interested scholar should also examine William Peiris's *The Western Contribution to Buddhism*, which contains much historical detail and interesting character sketches of the early scholars of Buddhism. Jan W. de Jong's *Brief History of Buddhist Studies in Europe and America*[3] also offers valuable information, although, despite its title, America is virtually absent from the volume.

Early Buddhist Studies in America

Thomas Tweed's *The American Encounter with Buddhism 1844-1912: Victorian Culture and the Limits of Dissent* is a wonderful and complete introduction to the early pioneers of the American Buddhist movement. For those unwilling to wade through more than 200 pages of Tweed's meticulous prose, a pleasant narrative can be found in Rick Fields's chapter on "The Restless Pioneers" in *How the Swans Came to the Lake*.[4] Unfortunately, there are no such books or chapters documenting the development of the discipline of Buddhist Studies in America,[5] and the existence of such work remains a desideratum. Here we can only begin to sketch a very short overview of Buddhist Studies in America.

Although some might consider Eugène Burnouf the founding father of Buddhist Studies as a discipline,[6] the beginning of Buddhist Studies in the United States seems inextricably bound to three primary individuals: Paul Carus, Henry Clarke Warren, and Charles Rockwell Lanman. Carus arrived in America in the 1880s with a Ph.D. from Tübingen, eventually becoming the editor of *Open Court* journal and later of Open Court Publishing Company. His career and relationship to American Buddhist Studies are chronicled in an interesting new article by Martin Verhoeven, "Americanizing the Buddha: Paul Carus and the Transformation of Asian Thought." Although he wrote more than a dozen books of his own, including the still widely read *Gospel of Buddhism* (1894), Carus is probably best known for bringing D. T. Suzuki to America and employing him at Open Court for many years.

Henry Clarke Warren and Charles Rockwell Lanman were more scholarly in their approach than Carus, and worked diligently to establish the Buddhist literary tradition in America. Lanman studied Sanskrit under William Dwight Whitney, earning his doctorate in 1875 before moving on to Johns Hopkins and eventually becoming Professor of Sanskrit at Harvard University in 1880. Warren, though horribly deformed as a result of a childhood accident, studied Sanskrit with Lanman at Johns Hopkins, and followed his learned master back to Harvard, where the two struck up an alliance that culminated in the creation of a new publication series known as "The Harvard Oriental Series." Hendrik Kern's edition of the *Jātakamālā*, or collection of Buddhist birth stories, was the first edition, with Warren's famous *Buddhism in Translations* becoming the third volume in 1896.

Following Warren's death in 1899, and with Lanman moving on to other studies in the Indic tradition, the development of Buddhist Studies was left to others. One of these early trailblazers was Eugene Watson Burlingame, who had studied with Lanman at Harvard before shifting to Yale, where he worked industriously on a variety of Pali texts. By 1921 he had published a three-volume translation of the *Dhammapāda* commentary in the Harvard Oriental Series. Burlingame was followed by W. Y. Evans-Wentz, a 1907 Stanford graduate, who studied extensively in Europe, and is best known for his collaborative compiling of the translations of his teacher, Kazi Dawa-Sandup. By the time of Evans-Wentz's death in 1965, a new group of buddhological scholars had developed on the American scene, including such committed scholars as Winston King, Richard Gard, and Kenneth K. S. Ch'en.

Despite the work of these early educators, it was not until after 1960 that Buddhist Studies began to emerge as a significant discipline in the American university system and publishing industry. During the Vietnam War years and immediately thereafter, Buddhist Studies was to enjoy a so-called "boom," largely through the efforts of such leading professors as Richard Hugh Robinson of the University of Wisconsin, Masatoshi Nagatomi of Harvard University, and Alex Wayman of Columbia University. No doubt there were many reasons for the increased development of Buddhist Studies, not the least of which were the increase in Area Studies programs in American universities; growing government interest in things Asian; the immense social anomie that permeated American culture in the 1960s; and the growing dissatisfaction with (and perhaps rejection of) traditional religion. During the 1960s, a formal graduate program was instituted at the University of Wisconsin, offering both an M.A. and a Ph.D. in Buddhist Studies. Interdisciplinary programs emphasizing the study of Buddhism were soon available at Berkeley and Columbia as well. As other programs arose, such as the program at the Center for the Study of World Religions at Harvard University, and the History of Religions program at the University of Chicago, it became possible to gain sophisticated training in all aspects of the Buddhist tradition, and in all Buddhist canonical languages as well. As a result, a new generation of young buddhologists was born, appearing rapidly on the campuses of many American universities, and rivalling their overseas peers in both training and insight.

This picture of expanding American buddhology is perhaps not so rosy as one might think, rapid growth notwithstanding. As interest grew, funding for graduate education did not keep pace, and would-be buddhologists no longer had the luxury of being able to spend six or eight or even ten fully-funded years in preparation for the Ph.D. As a result, the breadth and scope of their training was compromised, resulting in an accelerated urgency for specialization. The consequence was that very few new buddhologists were appearing with the complete philological training and geographical comprehensiveness of their teachers. Thus, it became usual to find individuals focusing on *one* tradition, such as Indian or Tibetan or Chinese or Japanese Buddhism, but rarely *all* of the traditions. And if the distinctions that characterize the Anglo-German, Franco-Belgian, and Leningrad schools are accurate, the "American" school is equally divided within itself.

Current Buddhist Studies

More than fifteen years ago, I titled a review article on recent Buddhist literature "Buddhist Studies American Style: A Shot in the

Dark," explaining at the outset that the conjured image of Inspector Clousseau "falling through banisters, walking into walls, crashing out of windows, and somehow miraculously getting the job done with the assistance of his loyal Oriental servant,"[7] was not an accidental choice on my part—Buddhist Studies in America was just as erratic as poor Clousseau.

Lately, as noted above, Buddhist Studies in America has begun to engage in the useful process of self-reflection, and the results of that inquiry are fruitful and inspiring. Following David Seyfort Ruegg's insightful "Some Observations on the Present and Future of Buddhist Studies," the *Journal of the International Association of Buddhist Studies* devoted an entire issue (Winter 1995) to the topic entitled "On Method," providing the occasion for scholars to reflect on various aspects of the discipline. José Cabezón, in a careful, brilliant article, summarizes the critical question:

> Although the academic study of Buddhism is much older than the International Association of Buddhist Studies and the journal to which it gave rise, the founding of the latter, which represents a significant— perhaps pivotal—step in the institutionalization of the field, is something that occurred less than twenty years ago. Nonetheless, whether a true discipline or not—whether or not Buddhist Studies has already achieved disciplinary status, whether it is proto-disciplinary or superdisciplinary—there is an apparent integrity to Buddhist Studies that at the very least calls for an analysis of the field in holistic terms.[8]

One must be aware, too, that there is a vast chasm between Buddhist Studies and other disciplinary studies in religion, such as Christian Studies. In the same forum, Luis Gómez notes,

> The difference between Christian and Buddhist Studies is perhaps in part explained by the fact that Buddhist Studies continues to be a Western enterprise about a non-Western cultural product, a discourse about Buddhism taking place in a non-Buddhist context for a non-Buddhist audience of super-specialists, whose intellectual work persists in isolation from the mainstream of Western literature, art, and philosophy, and occasionally even from the mainstream of contempo-

rary Buddhist doctrinal reflection. The audience to which Christian Studies speaks shares with the Judeo-Christian tradition a more or less common language. It is possible, if not natural, for members of the audience to accept the conceit that they belong to the tradition and the tradition belongs to them.... Furthermore, whereas Christianity and Christian Studies as we know them are the fruit of a continuous inter-action with Western secularism, rationalism, and the modern and postmodern Western self, most of our Buddhist materials and many of our Asian informants belong to a very different cultural tradition. The methods and expectations of our scholarship and our audiences have been shaped by a cultural history very different from that of Buddhist traditions.[9]

The homogeneity that a "common pattern of institutional sup-port provides" is simply lacking in Buddhist studies, as buddhologists invariably find their academic homes in religious studies departments, Area Studies centers, language institutes, and even schools of theol-ogy, as Cabezón straightforwardly points out.[10] Thus, when he goes on to identify Buddhist Studies as a "hodge-podge," signalling its het-erogeneity, this is no surprise. Nor should it be when he proclaims, "Now that the cat is out of the bag, what will guarantee the stability and longevity of the discipline is not the *insistence on homogeneity*, which in any case can now only be achieved through force, but in-stead by *embracing heterogeneity*."[11]

To this point, what has also been ostensibly lacking in the discus-sion is a consideration of that portion of the community of North American buddhologists which falls into a category that is most prop-erly labelled "scholar-practitioner."

Virtually everyone who begins an academic career in Buddhist Studies eventually pours through Étienne Lamotte's exciting volume *Histoire de Bouddhisme Indien des origines à l'ère Śaka*, either in the origi-nal French or in Sara Webb-Boin's admirable English translation. That Lamotte was a Catholic priest seems not to have influenced ei-ther his understanding of, or respect for, the Buddhist tradition, al-though he did worry a bit from time to time about the reaction of the Vatican to his work. Edward Conze, arguably one of the most colorful Buddhist scholars of the century, once remarked: "When I last saw him, he had risen to the rank of Monseigneur and worried about how his 'Histoire' had been received at the Vatican. '*Mon professeur*, do you think they will regard the book as *hérétique*?' They obviously did not. His religious views showed the delightful mixture of absurdity and rationality which is one of the hallmarks of a true believer."[12] Although there have been only a few scholarly studies chronicling the academic investigation of Buddhism by Western researchers, and fewer still of the academic discipline known as Buddhist Studies, until quite recently the issue of the religious affiliation of the researcher has not been part of the mix. Almost exclusively, the founding mothers and founding fathers of Buddhist Studies in the West have had personal religious commitments entirely separate from Buddhism.

As a novice graduate student in the prestigious "Buddhist Studies Program" at the University of Wisconsin in the Fall of 1967, the very first "in-group" story I heard from the senior students was about the recent visit of Edward Conze, conclusively acknowledged as the world's foremost scholar of that complicated form of Mahāyāna literature known as *prajñāpāramitā*. The narrative, however, had nothing whatsoever to do with Professor Conze's great scholarly passion. Instead, it concerned a question, playfully put to the rather blunt and outspoken scholar during a seminar session: "Dr. Conze, do *you* actually meditate?" Conze's simple reply: "Yes." But the student pressed on: "Ever *get* anywhere?" The brusque response: "First trance state." The dialogue abruptly ceased and the issue was never broached again. Upon hearing that story as a naïve fledgling buddhologist, I was utterly and absolutely astounded to learn that any scholar of Buddhism actually *did* anything Buddhist. Now, barely a quarter-century later, it is rather ordinary for individuals teaching Buddhist Studies in universities throughout the world to be "scholar-practitioners," involved in the practice of training associated with various Buddhist traditions and sects. The back cover of Georges Dreyfus's new book *Recognizing Reality: Dharmakīrti's Philosophy and Its Tibetan Interpretations*, for example, mentions his academic affiliation *and* the fact that he earned the monastic Geshe degree following fifteen years of study in Tibetan Buddhist monasteries in India.[13] Nonetheless, it is not always easy for these academics to reveal their religious orientation in an environment that is not uniformly supportive of such choices. Thus this chapter will serve the dual purpose of describing not only the development of the academic study of Buddhism in America, but also some of the ways in which that development has affected the personal lives of those scholars who have made formal religious commitments to the Buddhist tradition.

In an interesting article entitled "The Ghost at the Table: On the Study of Buddhism and the Study of Religion," Malcolm David Eckel writes in his conclusion:

> It is not just students who are attracted to religious studies because they "want to know what it is to be human and humane, and intuit that religion deals with such things." There are at least a few scholars of Buddhism who feel the same way. For me the biggest unsettled question in the study of Buddhism is not whether Buddhism is religious or even whether the study of Buddhism is religious; it is whether scholars in this field can find a voice that does justice to their own religious concerns and can demonstrate to the academy why their kind of knowledge is worth having.[14]

In a recent issue of *Tricycle: The Buddhist Review*, Duncan Ryūken Williams, an ordained Sōtō Zen priest and Ph.D. candidate at Harvard University, compiled a short list of institutions which offer graduate study in Buddhism. Although Williams's listing includes the expected sorts of categories ("Most Comprehensive Programs," "Institutions with Strength in Indo-Tibetan Buddhist Studies," and so forth), he also includes a category called "Practitioner-Friendly Institutions." About these he says, "Nevertheless, there are a number of degree programs that encourage or support Buddhist practice and scholarship among students. These 'practitioner-friendly' programs generally offer one of three things: the ability to pursue a degree in the context of Buddhist priestly training, courses in the practice of Buddhism that complement academic study, or an emphasis on Buddhism from a normative point of view."[15]

Williams comes right to the edge of the scholar-practitioner pond when he notes, "At most universities, faculty members in Buddhist studies tend to be far fewer in number than their Christian or Jewish counterparts,"[16] but he chooses not to jump into the issue. Cabezón and Gómez elect to take the leap, both dramatically and insightfully. In advancing his comprehensive discussion of the discipline of Buddhist Studies, Cabezón suggests: "One of the best entries into the identification of the variant kinds of scholarship is not through their sympathetic depiction, but through their caricature in stereotypes. These stereotypes are associated with specific racial/ethnic, national, religious and gender characteristics. Like all stereotypes, they are falsehoods: racist, sexist, and generally exhibiting the type of intolerance to which we as human beings are unfortunately heir. But exist they do."[17]

While Cabezón lists nine specific stereotypes, each of which is interesting in its own right, it is the first of these that informs this enterprise:

> Critical distance from the object of intellectual analysis is necessary. Buddhists, by virtue of their religious commitment, lack such critical distance from Buddhism. Hence, Buddhists are *never* good buddhologists. Or, alternatively, those who take any aspect of Buddhist doctrine seriously (whether pro or con) are scientifically suspect by virtue of allowing their individual beliefs to affect their scholarship. Good scholarship is neutral as regards questions of truth. Hence, evaluative/normative scholarship falls outside the purview of Buddhist Studies.[18]

Without undervaluing the critical goals implicit in all buddhological scholarship, Gómez adds yet another dimension to the conversation, arguably the most critical. He says,

> Contemporary Buddhists, wherever they might be, are also an audience for our scholarship.... They can be a source (however maligned and deprived of authority they may sometimes appear) because, inevitably, they speak to us and make demands on us.... But in our field the object is also a voice that speaks to us and hears us. It is present not only as object but as a set of voices that demands something from us. In fact our "object" has had a biographic presence in all of our lives—*especially on those of us who can remember moments in our life narra-*

tives in which we have "felt Buddhists" or "have been Buddhists" or have *"practiced," as the contemporary English expression has it.* I would venture more, even for those who at one time or another have seen in some fragment of Buddhist tradition a particle of inspiration or an atom of insight, Buddhism is an object that makes claims on their lives. For those who have failed even to experience this last form of interaction with the object, there must have been at least moments of minimal encounters with seeking students or, after a dry and erudite lecture, one of those emotional questions from the audience that makes all scholars nervous.[19]

Of course the above places the contemporary buddhologist squarely between the proverbial rock and hard place. If one acknowledges a personal commitment to the tradition being studied, the suspicion Cabezón cites so clearly is immediately voiced; but if one remains silent, how can the demands Gómez outlines be fairly confronted? These are issues not confronted by the American scholar of Judaism or Christianity, and they are a powerful impetus for the silence among buddhologists.

Survey Results

In the Winter 1991 issue of the *Journal of the American Academy of Religion*, former editor Ray L. Hart was afforded 112 pages to present the results of a survey entitled "Religious and Theological Studies in American Higher Education: A Pilot Study." Thirty-five pages of his "report" were devoted to a presentation of the statistical evidence gleaned from a questionnaire distributed to 678 faculty members at eleven types of institutions; the rest of the space was devoted to Hart's interpretive narrative.

Curiously, Hart's findings were nearly chronologically coincident with a five-year administrative review of the Buddhism Section of the American Academy of Religion, arguably the largest academic arena for buddhologists in North America (if not the entire world). American Academy of Religion's external evaluator for that review, Professor Malcolm David Eckel of Boston University, noted in his December 1991 report: "The most important achievement of the Buddhism

Group and Section at the AAR in the last 10 years has been to create a safe and reliable forum for Buddhist scholars who represent a wide variety of approaches, disciplines, and geographical orientations to exchange views and build bonds of cooperation and understanding that create an active and imaginative scholarly community."[20] In a later article, Eckel reveals that in the five years between 1986 and 1991, attendance at the Buddhism Section's annual business meeting grew from 60 to 140, and the mailing list expanded from 106 to 600![21]

With interest piqued by the data included in Hart's report and the suppositions inherent in Eckel's, in October 1992 I set out to gather materials from the North American community of buddhologists that would afford this community data similar to Hart's upon which to conduct a second level of self-reflection. It was clear from the outset that the 600-member mailing list mentioned above contained, in addition to so-called buddhologists, a large number of scholars of other Asian religions, many non-specialist comparativists, and a profusion of "others." After careful sorting and synthesis, a list of 125 scholars whose primary teaching and research work fell within the discipline of Buddhist Studies was compiled, and these individuals were sent requests soliciting both data and narrative statements about the discipline. Following two additional requests, and with a rather surprising response rate of 69.6 percent (compared with Hart's 64 percent), the received material was collated. Later a second survey was conducted, beginning in Fall 1995. In the intervening years, the list was updated, revised, and refined, reflecting the arrival of new scholars into the buddhological community, the death of others, and shifting interests. Thus, the initial list of requests in the new survey numbered 140, with 106 responses received (or 75.7 percent). On an individual level, the results collected provide an ample look at the demographics of Buddhist Studies in America.

My sample seems to suggest a young discipline, with the 1995 data showing 1980 as the average year for earning the Ph.D. The earliest doctoral degree recorded was 1948, and the most recent 1996. In decades, the breakdown yields:

Decade Ph.D./Th.D. Granted	Number of Respondents
1990s	21
1980s	45
1970s	25
1960s	12
1950s	1
1940s	1

In terms of specialization, any comparison between samples would be incongruous because, for the 1993 sample, only one primary specialization was recorded, while in the 1995 sample, it became clear that in many cases, multiple specializations were emphasized. As such, in 1993, 37.0 percent of the sample reported specializing in Japan/East Asia, while 29.6 percent reported India/South Asia, 23.5 percent Tibet/Inner Asia, 6.2 percent China/East Asia, 2.5 percent Korea/East Asia, and 1.2 percent indicated other choices. Bearing in mind that multiple listings were allowed in the 1995 sample, yielding a total in excess of 100 percent, the survey showed:

Area	Number of Respondents	Percent
Japan/East Asia	39	36.8
India/South Asia	37	34.9
Tibet/Inner Asia	22	20.8
China/East Asia	16	15.1
Korea/East Asia	2	1.9
Other Areas	3	2.8

The sample has shown a remarkably high level of activity in presenting scholarly papers at the annual meetings of professional societies. Additionally, those sampled have been very active in presenting scholarly papers (not simply "lectures") in other professional settings such as international conferences, regional professional meetings, and thematic conferences sponsored by various institutions. Adjusting the results to reflect those who did not respond with information on this item, the findings show:

Papers at Annual Meeting	4.4 per respondent
Other Scholarly Papers	12.2 per respondent

Thus, the average respondent has made 16.6 professional presentations during their academic career. That this figure is slightly lower than the 19.8 figure reported in the 1993 sample reflects the earlier supposition that the 1995 sample is slightly junior to the previous group of respondents.

Although it has never been clear how to report scholarly publication data with precision, Ray Hart's study utilizes three categories: (1) Books, (2) Articles, Essays, Chapters, and (3) Book Reviews. Hart is only concerned with the immediately past five-year period. In other words, Hart presents no career publication data, a statistic which may well be more revealing than his five-year information. Thus, in this study, I have confined myself to presenting *only* career data. The categories are at once problematic in that Hart does not distinguish between refereed and non-refereed publications, a distinction now made in virtually all colleges and universities. Equally, Hart makes no distinction between books authored and books edited, another distinction that is part of the politically correct protocol of the American system of higher education.

In an attempt to address the exigencies of that system, I have sought to refine Hart's categories somewhat in favor of presenting more meaningful statistics. In so doing, I have separated the Book category into two sub-categories: (a) Books Authored/Co-Authored and (b) Books Edited/Co-Edited. I have also pared Hart's Articles, Essays, Chapters category into Refereed Articles and Chapters (taking the stand, not shared in all university evaluations, that chapters are indeed refereed, often bringing to bear a higher standard than many refereed journals). In my schema, the following career results can be reported:

Category of Publication	1993 Sample Average (No.)	1995 Sample Average (No.)
Books Authored/Co-Authored	2.4 (209)	2.3 (239)

Books Edited/Co-Edited	1.7 (148)	1.1 (116)
Refereed Articles & Refereed Chapters	7.3 (769) 16.8 (1462)[22]	6.5 (689)
Book Reviews	12.7 (1105)	12.9 (962)[23]

Interestingly, none of the material included in Hart's religious studies survey or in the narrative responses to mine offered any information about teaching Buddhism in the college or university setting. In addition, of the 25 panels and 75 individual section papers of the recent Twelfth Congress of the International Association of Buddhist Studies, including more than 200 speakers, no single paper addressed the issue of teaching Buddhism. The September 3, 1999 issue of *The Chronicle of Higher Education*, however, does deal with teaching in an item entitled "Faculty Attitudes and Characteristics: Results of a 1998–99 Survey."[24] There it was revealed that 98.0 percent of its sample reported being a good teacher to be a very important personal goal while only 54.1 percent of the sample reported becoming an authority in one's own field to be a very important personal goal. In determining "primary interest," 72.8 percent responded "leaning toward teaching" (37.1) or "very heavily into teaching" (35.7) compared with 27.1 percent who responded either "leaning toward research" (23.8) or "very heavily into research" (3.3). The additional statistics in the survey amplify this point. In the sample, 83.8 percent had published less than three books, manuals, or monographs; 87.8 percent had published fewer than five chapters in edited volumes; 55.7 percent had published fewer than five articles in academic or professional journals; and 67.9 percent had fewer than three professional writings published or accepted for publication in the last two years. On the other hand, 71.6 percent of the sample had developed a new course in the last two years; 59 percent had participated in a teaching enhancement workshop in the last two years; and 67 percent spend more than eight hours per week preparing for teaching. Surprisingly, 35.9 percent had even placed or collected course assignments on the Internet.[25]

Conclusions

Like all disciplines, Buddhist Studies is continually changing, primarily as a result of faculty relocation, altered interests, retirement, and new hires from the continually increasing number of newly minted scholars entering the field. José Cabezón accurately points out: "For about a decade or so, buddhologists in North America have found employment in increasing numbers in departments of religious studies and schools of theology. Often this has meant that we have had to expand our pedagogical repertoire beyond courses in Buddhist Studies to accommodate the curricular need of these institutions."[26] After surveying a number of issues having impact on Buddhist Studies, Cabezón goes on to conclude:

> All of these factors have contributed to what we might call the diversification of the buddhologist: a movement away from classical Buddhist Studies based on the philological study of written texts, and toward the investigation of more general, comparative and often theoretical issues that have implications (and audiences) outside of Buddhist Studies. Some colleagues have resigned themselves to this situation: a set of circumstances that must be tolerated for the sake of gainful employment. Others—and I count myself in this camp—have found the pressure to greater diversification intellectually stimulating, affording an opportunity to enter into broader conversations where Buddhist texts are one, but not the only, voice.[27]

Thus it is no longer completely clear what constitutes a full-time buddhologist, and when one factors in the movement in the opposite direction—scholars from other disciplines incorporating Buddhist materials into their work—the entire issue of listing the number of full-time buddhologists in any unit becomes quite murky.

In collating the data in my surveys, and evaluating the narrative statements submitted, two clear sentiments emerged. The first, which was quite obvious, reflected the number of colleagues who came to the study of Buddhism, and to academe, as a result of their strong personal commitment to Buddhism as a religious tradition; or those who cultivated a commitment to the personal practice of Buddhism as a result of their academic endeavors. For many in this first group, this has created a powerful tension between scholarship and religious commitment, between buddhology and personal faith. The second sentiment seemed to signal a shift away from Buddhist texts and philosophy (the Buddhist "theology" which some of us have been accused of propagating), toward an investigation of Buddhism's contextual relationship with culture. Or, as Cabezón puts it,

> There is today a call for the increased investigation of alternative semiotic forms—oral and vernacular traditions, epigraphy, ritual, patterns of social and institutional evolution, gender, lay and folk traditions, arts, archaeology and architecture.... The critique is really a call for greater balance and holism within the field; it is not only a demand that equal recognition be given to new areas of research, but a call for an integrated and mutually interpenetrating research program aimed at the understanding of Buddhism as a multi-faceted entity.[28]

At the outset of this paper, reference was made to the volume *Curators of the Buddha: The Study of Buddhism under Colonialism,* along with a number of comments about the book from a review article by Jan Nattier. To be sure, Nattier is correct when she outlines some of the issues still lacking in the volume: a consideration of the difference in outlook and methodology between specialists in Tibetan Buddhism and those of Chinese Buddhism, variations in the training and perspective between Buddhist Studies scholars trained in religious studies departments and those who were trained in Area Studies programs, those who have had a personal dialogue with a Buddhist community and those not so involved, and a consideration of the "rifts" in North American Buddhist Studies.[29] Yet, after praising Lopez for his frankness and willingness, as an American buddhologist, to discuss his own encounter with Buddhism, she concludes by saying, "If there are difficulties here, they are not with the keen and self-critical eye with which Lopez reflects on his own experience as a student of Buddhism but with the degree to which he generalizes from that experience to characterize prevailing attitudes in the Buddhist Studies field at large."[30]

Considering that the data collected in my two Buddhist Studies surveys is consistent with the publication figures reported in Ray Hart's 1991 survey and the recent *Chronicle of Higher Education* survey, it is not unreasonable to conclude that the majority of Buddhist Studies scholars surveyed are equally involved in teaching as their primary enterprise. As such, this volume, emerging out of the McGill Conference on Teaching Buddhism, becomes a most important resource for an academic discipline that rarely, if ever, finds the time to acknowledge and affirm pedagogy as a critical component of its mission. Whether these generalizations are correct or not remains to be seen. At least the question has now moved beyond Father Lamotte's concern with being *hérétique*.

Notes

[1] Williams 1999.

[2] Nattier 1997, 469.

[3] Jong's *Brief History* originally appeared as two articles in *The Eastern Buddhist*. The first carried the same title as the eventual book and appeared in NS 7 (1974); the second was titled "Recent Buddhist Studies in Europe and America 1973–83" and appeared in NS 17 (1984). It is curious that of the roughly 400 individuals listed in the Index under "Names of Scholars," less than 5 percent are primarily associated with North America. Like nearly all of Jong's publications, this one bristles with his trenchant editorializing and brutal evaluations. In the foreword, he mentions Guy Welbon's engaging *The Buddhist Nirvāṇa and Its Western Interpreters* (Chicago: University of Chicago Press, 1968), based on Welbon's doctoral dissertation at the University of Chicago, concluding that "The usefulness of his book is diminished by the fact that the author was not sufficiently equipped for this difficult task" (Jong 1987, 2), and citing the reference to his even more acerbic review in the *Journal of Indian Philosophy*.

[4] See Fields 1992, 54–69.

[5] I am not the only one to make this point. José Cabezón, in "Buddhist Studies as a Discipline and the Role of Theory," says as much: "No comprehensive history of Buddhist Studies as a discipline exists" (1995, 236 n. 8).

[6] See, for example, Gómez 1995, 193 n. 8.

[7] Prebish 1983, 323–30.

[8] Cabezón 1995, 236.

[9] Gómez 1995, 190.

[10] Cabezón 1995, 236–38. The quoted phrase is Cabezón's as well.

---

[11] Cabezón 1995, 236, 240.

[12] Conze 1979, 43.

[13] See Dreyfus 1997. It is interesting to note that Dreyfus lists his Geshe Lharampa degree (earned in 1985) on his *curriculum vitae* along with his M.A. (1987) and Ph.D. (1991) from the University of Virginia.

[14] Eckel 1994, 1107–8.

[15] Williams 1997, 68.

[16] Williams 1997, 68.

[17] Cabezón 1995, 243.

[18] Cabezón 1995, 243. To his credit, Cabezón cites Jacques May's alternative view in "Études Bouddhiques: Domaine, Disciplines, Perspectives," *Études de Lettres* (Lausanne), Serie III. Tome 6, no. 4 (1973), 18.

[19] Gómez 1995, 214–15 (italics are mine).

[20] Eckel 1991, 2.

[21] Eckel 1994, 1088.

[22] This category was not separated in the first survey, but redesigned in the second.

[23] Only 72 respondents listed book reviews, and this is reflected in the statistical average.

[24] The figures reported were based on survey responses of 33,785 faculty members at 378 colleges and universities. It was conducted in the Fall and Winter of 1998–99. Only full-time employees were queried, and only those who spent at least part of their time teaching undergraduates were included. The response rate was 43 percent.

[25] "Faculty Attitudes and Characteristics," A-20, A-21.

[26] Cabezón 1995, 255.

[27] Cabezón 1995, 255–56.

[28] Cabezón 1995, 262–63.

[29] Nattier 1997, 484.

[30] Nattier 1997, 480.

Bibliography

Cabezón, José. 1995. "Buddhist Studies as a Discipline and the Role of Theory." *Journal of the International Association of Buddhist Studies* 18 (2).

Conze, Edward. 1979. *The Memoirs of a Modern Gnostic, Part II*. Sherborne, U.K.: The Samizdat Publishing Company.

Dreyfus, Georges B. J. 1997. *Recognizing Reality: Dharmakīrti's Philosophy and Its Tibetan Interpretations*. Albany, NY: State University of New York Press.

Eckel, Malcolm David. 1991. "Review and Evaluation of the Buddhism Section of the American Academy of Religion." Photocopy.

———. 1994. "The Ghost at the Table: On the Study of Buddhism and the Study of Religion." *Journal of the American Academy of Religion* 62 (4).

Fields, Rick. 1992. *How the Swans Came to the Lake*. 3rd edition, revised and updated. Boston: Shambhala.

Gómez, Luis. 1995. "Unspoken Paradigms: Meanderings through the Metaphors of a Field." *Journal of the International Association of Buddhist Studies* 18 (2).

Hart, Ray L. 1991. "Religious and Theological Studies in American Higher Education: A Pilot Study." *Journal of the American Academy of Religion* 59 (4).

Jong, Jan W de. 1987. *A Brief History of Buddhist Studies in Europe and America*. 2nd, revised and enlarged edition. Delhi: Sri Satguru Publications.

La Loubère, Simon de. 1952. *Du royaume de Siam*. Paris.

Lamotte, Étienne. 1988 [1958]. *Histoire de Bouddhisme Indien des origines à l'ère Śaka*. Translated by Sara Webb-Boin. Louvain: Institut Orientaliste of the Université de Louvain.

Lopez, Donald S., ed. 1995. *Curators of the Buddha: The Study of Buddhism under Colonialism*. Chicago: University of Chicago Press.

Lubac, Henri de. 1952. *La rencontre de bouddhisme et de l'occident*. Paris: Aubier.

Nattier, Jan. 1997. "Buddhist Studies in the Post-Colonial Age." *Journal of the American Academy of Religion* 65 (2).

Ozeray, Michel François. 1817. *Recherches sur Buddhou*. Paris.

Peiris, William. 1973. *The Western Contribution to Buddhism*. Delhi: Motilal Banarsidass.

Prebish, Charles S. 1983. "Buddhist Studies American Style: A Shot in the Dark." *Religious Studies Review* 9 (4).

Ruegg, David Seyfort. 1992. "Some Observations on the Present and Future of Buddhist Studies." *Journal of the International Association of Buddhist Studies* 15 (1).

Tweed, Thomas. 1992. *The American Encounter with Buddhism 1844-1912: Victorian Culture and the Limits of Dissent*. Bloomington: University of Indiana Press.

Verhoeven, Martin. 1998. "Americanizing the Buddha: Paul Carus and the Transformation of Asian Thought." In *The Faces of Buddhism in America*, edited by Charles Prebish and Kenneth Tanaka. Berkeley: University of California Press.

Webb, Russell. 1976-80. "Pali Buddhist Studies in the West." *Pali Buddhist Review* 1 (3): 169–80; 2 (1): 55–62; 2 (2): 114–22; 2 (3): 162–67; 3 (1): 35–36; 3 (2): 84–87; 3 (3): 146–53; 4 (1–2): 28–31; 4 (4):86–90; 5 (1–2): 39–41; 5 (3): 89–92.

———. 1989. "Contemporary European Scholarship on Buddhism." In *The Buddhist Heritage*, Vol. 1 of Buddhica Britannica, edited by Taedeusz Skorupski. Tring: The Institute of Buddhist Studies.

Williams, Duncan Ryūken. 1997. "Where to Study?" *Tricycle: The Buddhist Review* 6 (3).

———. 1999. "North American Dissertations and Theses on Topics Related to Buddhism." In *American Buddhism: Methods and Findings in Recent Scholarship*, edited by Duncan Ryūken Williams and Christopher S. Queen. Surrey, U.K.: Curzon Press.

What is "Buddhism"?

Representations of Buddhism in Undergraduate Teaching: The Centrality of Ritual and Story Narratives

Todd T. Lewis

In teaching Buddhism, as in many other fields of cross-cultural inquiry, there has been a natural propensity for intellectuals to be drawn to the worldviews of other intellectuals. In the undergraduate classroom, I share the goal of showing how Buddhist philosophers meet high standards of logical-intellectual rigor and that Buddhist meditation masters explore compelling arenas of human spiritual experience. Most students who take Buddhism courses wish to acquire deeper understanding of Buddhist philosophies, philosophers, and forms of meditation and it is important to broaden and deepen their spiritual imaginations. But I also want students to emerge from my classes capable of contextualizing these noble ideals and connecting with typical Buddhists, past and present.

To focus solely on literate elites and their texts, however, makes the latter goal impossible as it leaves students uninformed about the fundamental socio-cultural realities in Buddhism's history. Elite-focused presentations in textbooks and Western classrooms that privilege philosophical texts frequently ignore the central role of institutions and the cultural evidence from archaeological and epigraphic sources.[1] Modern anthropological demonstrations of the scarcity of monk-scholars in the transmission of tradition have likewise made little impact on the predisposition to assume the normative centrality of *nirvāṇa*-seeking literati in portraying Buddhism. Thus, elite text-based representations of Buddhist tradition in history remain skewed toward the intellectuals and in the modern imagination Buddhism is reduced to philosophy. In the process, too, Buddhist history contracts to be the outcome of contending ideas and the humanity of Buddhist devotees is reduced to intellect. Both are naive, ivory tower misconceptions. The growing library of publications directed to interested or converted westerners has also been quite friendly to this idealizing and simplistic portrayal.

This reductive appropriation of Buddhism is a continuation of the early Western investigators and exponents of Buddhism who were hoping to find in the tradition an antidote to (in their view) the blind ritualism and irrational monotheisms of Europe, and they often imported Protestant assumptions and categories about true religion in the process.[2] It was also convenient for scholars to dismiss modern practices as distortions or degenerations of a "true Buddhism," a discovery that Europeans alone were equipped to make.[3]

The cost of elite bias among Buddhist scholar-teachers remains great, however, as the older paradigms endure and "academic fossilizations" reproduce the earlier biases in the classroom. As a result, there has been very slow progress in understanding how and why Buddhist institutions and cultures evolved across Asia. Textbooks still purvey a propensity to ill-founded discussions about who "true Buddhists" are (or were) on such issues as Buddhism's alleged "atheistic" or "anti-caste" ideology; they privilege belief over practice in defining Buddhist identity, fail to make intelligible the 95 percent of Buddhists who were householders, and ignore the idealistic and inclusive utopian vision that Buddhism held for entire societies. I suspect that even the Western construction of the small sector of Buddhist virtuosi as resolutely isolated from the popular traditions is, as well, a distortion.

Students still encounter Buddhism and Buddhists with naive, elitist biases. If one of the first principles of comparative religion methodology is "to compare like with like" and carefully match level to level, modern representations of Buddhism relying on elite texts still do not convey socio-culturally informed renderings of the tradition.

These distortions in representing the tradition also give no foundation on which to build an understanding of the vicissitudes faced by contemporary rank-and-file Buddhists and Buddhist institutions in modernizing Asia.

Towards a Sociological Imagination of Buddhism

A "sociological imagination of Buddhism" must recognize that economic resources and political alliances have been as crucial to the tradition's successful global domestications as ideas. The teaching of Buddhist history must also focus greater attention on institutions. Buddhism in any social context cannot be understood as based upon unified philosophical schools in isolation; nor was the *sangha* centered on a singular doctrinal orthodoxy but on conformity to discipline. Monasteries of course varied but their leaders were most commonly concerned with the practical perpetuation of the faith's material and spiritual culture in a manner that could dominate the socio-religious life of the surrounding community. The institutions that maintained Buddhism—monasteries, temples, *stūpa* shrines, charities, lay associations—did so via interlocking economic, ritual, educational, medical, artistic, political, and meditation activities. Service to the local society was essential to institutional survival, prior to any philosophical or scholarly pursuits.[4]

The historical re-imagination of Buddhist societies should be built upon the textually-defined norm of religious pluralism within Buddhist cultures, noting that all societies are composed of a broad spectrum of individuals pursuing different spiritual regimens. Monastics and laity, and even followers of other religious schools, were all seen as converging "on the path" heading through rebirth levels toward eventual *nirvāṇa*-realization. It is thus time to abandon a misbegotten legacy of early anthropological theory that was merged with the curatorial text/literati bias: the use of a two-level model for Buddhist communities that divides the "true ordained followers" from everyone else.[5] This "reductive orthodoxy" model has been so singularly adopted in both academic and popular accounts that "popular" literature and ritual practices are routinely dismissed as being mere "vulgarizations" of proper Buddhist thought, or as concessions to the masses.[6]

The two-tier imagination of Buddhism finds little support from epigraphic or anthropological accounts pertaining to monastic roles or institutions. It also defies the tradition's own early and textually-located notion of *anupūrvīkathā*, "the gradual path." The specific progress of a typical Buddhist is charted as:

Dāna/punya→ *śīla/svarga*→ evils of *pāp/kāma*→ value of renunciation→ Four Noble Truths[7]

George Bond draws out the importance of this understanding very explicitly:

> The notion of the path links all diverse persons, stages, and goals. Although these manuals define some *suttas* as mundane and others as supramundane, and though they identify some *suttas* as applying to ordinary persons and others applying to adepts, the manuals do not regard these as distinct religious paths; they do not separate the kammic from the nibbanic path. Though the path has many levels and applications, the *Dhamma* is one and the path one. This...is the secret to understanding the logic and meaning of the Buddha's teachings.[8]

This gradual path doctrine envisions society as a multi-point hierarchy of beings who are different according to their *karman* and spiritual capacities. In the "gradual path," too, we find the central ideal of all Buddhists interdependent and linked through ritual and patronage, connecting advanced practitioners with others moving up along the "gradual path." It has been these relationships that have shaped and sustained Buddhist communities. Such inclusivity applies as well to Mahāyāna contexts, with the appreciation of teaching and ritual performance as *upāyas*, expressions of a bodhisattva's skillful assistance to the community.

Thus, the presentation of the elite as "the sole norm" is an ethnocentric notion, a distorted projection doubtless agreeable to Western converts, but ahistorical and not even based upon textual authority. This idealizing paradigm of Buddhism dominated by aloof, meditating ascetics and controlled by intellectuals is unsuitable for portraying the typical Buddhist monk or nun, as Schopen has pointed out;[9] and it certainly can no longer stand scrutiny as a model for the history of Buddhism's doctrinal or institutional evolution.[10]

Taking philosophy texts as most representative of Buddhist understanding has led many westerners—including our students—to view "typical Buddhists" who do not conform to the modern construction of the elite ideal with derision or condescension.[11] It makes it extremely problematic for students to encounter immigrant Buddhists as "true Buddhists."[12] To overcome the over-idealizing and disembodied philosophy-centered imagination of Buddhism, I suggest that our teaching extend to include ethnographic accounts[13] as well as the most widespread texts and practices in every Buddhist society: story narratives and rituals.

Story Narratives as the Central Texts in Buddhist Societies

Evidence for the centrality of narratives in Buddhism comes from their early collection and the vast accumulation of story collections, indicating popular interest in these parables and the universal need for monk-scholars to redact them for use in sermons. It also comes in a quite straightforward way from the record of sculpture and painting at *stūpas* and monasteries. This wealth of cultural evidence implies that from the earliest days onward it was the story narratives that shaped the spiritual imaginations and fixed the moral landmarks in the minds of most Buddhists, including the great majority of monks and nuns.

To understand the sources of doctrinal definition, moral guidance, or popular rituals in the history of Buddhism in any locality, then, one must look to the popular narratives, not just the "classics" of the intellectual elite.[14] (A tough-minded cultural historian's approach might even decide: better to assume that the latter literature was marginal in Buddhist societies unless proven otherwise.[15]) These narratives include the collections of *jātaka* and *avadāna*, as well as the stories integrated with ritual manuals. A large number of narratives come from the *vinaya* compilations themselves, indicating again that it was typical monks and nuns who were concerned with orthopraxy, ritual performances, patronage, and storytelling.[16] That these "popular" stories were taken seriously and read carefully by the literati is confirmed by their use in the legal systems of Southeast Asia.

In the Newar case studies that I have studied for my forthcoming book on the most popular narratives that have been told and retold in public storytelling,[17] Buddhism in practice was quite different from what the virtuosi-level texts might have led us to expect: much less individualistic, anti-woman, and anti-family; quite at home with the norms of Brahmanical society in respecting caste privilege, acquiescing to the logic of widow immolation, accepting the deities of the local pantheon (albeit demoting their superior status); and focused primarily on merit-making and pragmatic "this worldly" goals. Rituals aimed at fostering prosperity, health, and wealth are regarded as powerful and central to the "true Buddhist's" religious identity and lifestyle.

As in modern Nepal, story narratives have from ancient times performed very important roles within Buddhist polities. These include envisioning the society's moral imagination, tracing the realm of karmic retribution, and providing a venue for entertaining Buddhist utopian scenarios. Buddhist stories in Nepal illustrate these functions abundantly: husbands and wives are reunited in subsequent lives, demonesses are removed from the scene by a merchant-king, rulers find rituals and fierce protectors to pacify their realms, monks alleviate their fears and gain support in their practice, and Buddhas bestow *dhāranī* recitations linked to ritual practices that can redress all forms of suffering. The *dharma* includes the teachings that lead elites to realize *nirvāṇa*; it also includes the means of merit-making to progress in *saṃsāra*. But the narratives and ritual texts also convey a more widespread and pragmatic notion of the *dharma* in Buddhist communities: the distilled words designated by the Buddha that can repel evil and create good, protecting those who take refuge in it. As the *Mahāvastu* states, "For verily *dharma* protects the one who lives by *dharma*, as a large umbrella protects us in time of rain."[18]

The Pre-eminent Buddhist Ideology: Merit-Making

The dominant religious orientation in Buddhist communities throughout history has been merit accumulation. The logic of Buddhist institutional history in every locality has been shaped by those householders and monastics seeking to make merit for current happiness and better rebirth either as a human being or as a god.[19]

Surprisingly, early canonical texts dealing with merit and the practical ethos of proper human striving have been downplayed or ignored in Western accounts of Buddhist doctrinal tradition. Yet there are many passages that cover this territory with subtlety and insight. One notable Pali text is worth careful consideration—and course inclusion—as it is mirrored in the themes and concerns found in the popular Mahāyāna culture of Nepal. This passage from the *Anguttara Nikāya* treats the issue of merit and the householder life directly, as Śākyamuni instructs the good Buddhist to seek "The Four Conditions":

> Housefather, there are these four conditions which are desirable, dear, delightful, hard to win in the world. Which four?...
> [1] Wealth being gotten by lawful means...
> [2] Good report gotten by me along with my kinsmen and teacher...
> [3] Long life and attain a great age...
> [4] When the body breaks up, on the other side of death may I attain happy birth, the heaven world!...[20]

The text then proceeds to specify how the moral and wealthy Buddhist householder should attain these goals by doing the "The Four Good Deeds":

> Now, housefather, that same Aryan disciple, with the wealth acquired by energetic striving, amassed by strength of arm, won by sweat, lawful and lawfully gotten, is the doer of four deeds. What are the four?
> [1] [He] makes himself happy and cheerful, he is a contriver of perfect happiness; he makes his mother and father, his children and wife, his servants and workmen, his friends and comrades cheerful and happy. This...is the first opportunity seized by him, turned to merit and fittingly made use of.

[2] Then again, the...disciple...with that wealth makes himself secure against all misfortunes whatsoever, such as may happen by way of fire, water, the king, a robber, an ill-disposed person.... He takes steps for his defense and makes himself secure....

[3] Then again...the disciple...is a maker of the five-fold offering (*bali*), namely: to relatives, to guests, to departed hungry ghosts, to the king, and to the gods (*devatā*)....

[4] Then again, the...disciple...offers a gift to all such recluses and brahmins as abstain from sloth and negligence, who are bent on kindness and forbearance, who tame the one self, calm the one self...to such he offers a gift which has the highest results, a gift heavenly, resulting in happiness and leading to heaven.[21]

This teaching passage ends with the praise of one whose wealth has been used fittingly, who has "seized the opportunity," and who has "turned wealth to merit."

The provisions and actions articulated here are congruent with the popular Nepalese texts that echo similar householder concerns for family, wealth, rituals, and protection. Thus, in the laity's spiritual imagination shaped by popular narratives and ritual, Buddhist merit-making "cheats death" by reuniting couples after death and reuniting the rich with their wealth. Merit-making is also not strictly individualistic, as actions by husbands and wives, patrons and shipmates, monks and kings may affect the destinies of others. Finally, heavenly rebirth was recognized in numerous passages as an exalted religious goal for good Buddhists to strive for as well. In short, householder practice across the Buddhist world is centered on merit-making (often collective in practice and effect), showing respect for local deities, and heaven seeking. To focus on elite texts designated to guide the rare meditation master or philosopher is to miss the center of Buddhism in society.

Householder texts like this and Buddhist rituals concerned with less than *nirvāṇa*-seeking have been consistently discounted as sources for understanding the "true Buddhist" in the Western historical imagination. So many false assumptions and ridiculous socio-cultural assertions about Buddhism, ancient and modern, could have been avoided by comprehending the worldview and ethos of the Buddhist householder tradition. In the *Anguttara* summary above and in the Nepalese texts, we see that Buddhism fosters family ties, encourages an "energetic striving" after economic success, promotes the worship of hungry ghosts and local gods, justifies the rightful seeking after worldly happiness and security, applauds the religious virtues of faith and heaven-seeking, and underlines the virtue of being a donor and patron. This pragmatic conception of the *dharma*, however nuanced in every local community, shaped the domestication of Buddhism from Sri Lanka to the Himalayas, from Central Asia to Japan.

I suggest that by broadening focus beyond the elite to include householders, committing to memory (and analysis) "The Four Good Deeds" alongside "The Four Noble Truths" as distillations of normative Buddhism, we can convey how Buddhist tradition developed three interlocking tracks of legitimate spiritual striving:

PRAGMATIC WELL-BEING	MORAL CULTIVATION	NIRVĀṆA SEEKING
ritual/merit-making	merit-making	meditation

This coexistence is evident in the narrative realm, seen in the juxtaposed images of *mithuna* couples and pragmatic deities (e.g., Hārītī and *nāgas*) at early *stūpas*, and made clear from the content and development of Buddhist ritualism.

Buddhist Ritual: Dharma Applied with Compassion

Whatever else we might surmise about the faith's variegated history, Buddhism in every society ritualized spiritual ideals and incorporated pragmatic traditions into monastic iconography and ritualism, textual chanting, *stūpa* devotions, the festival year, and the life-cycle rites of specific communities.[22]

The neglect of ritual in the understanding of Buddhism (and Buddhists) has also obscured the application of Buddhist doctrinal constructs to the events of "real life," especially childhood, marriage, old age, and after-death contingencies. Far from being a "vulgarization" or a "concession" to the masses, ritual in all Buddhist societies has been the fundamental means of applying *dharma*-analysis to acculturate the young or, to use Buddhist terms, to shape consciously and beneficently (*kushala*) the *skandhas*—body, sensations, perceptions, habit energies, consciousness—of individuals, ultimately pointing them toward spiritual maturity and awakening.

To have studied a living Buddhist community is to know that children come to understand the teachings by questioning the meaning of rituals, through practical examples conveyed in stories, and by listening very intently to the doctrinal testimony that swirls around them when death rituals are being conducted in the family circle. In Nepal, Mahāyāna rituals are carefully constructed to work on multiple levels, too: many act and impart meanings differentially for those all along the "gradual path," from beginners to advanced tantric practitioners, from little children to elder adepts. Recognizing this (in Nepal) means to discern the *upāya* of the collective Mahāyāna tradition.[23]

Students need to understand ritual in its premodern setting as we are prone to forget two facts about the context of Buddhism at that time. First, literacy was rare. Only a very few individuals could read texts to learn the *dharma*; most had to learn through oral accounts and the experience of ritual. Buddhist ritual, thus, was developed and sustained by those wishing to shape human experience consciously.[24] Second were the simple realities of public health in the urban Eurasian world.[25] Epidemics that premodern medicines could not alleviate periodically moved across the trade routes; when at their worst, pandemics wiped out 10 to 50 percent of a settlement's population, often within weeks. More constant was the fact of infant mortality. Only roughly 50 percent of children reached the age of five.[26] Such an existential baseline of life in the premodern world must inform the modern imagination of such basic Buddhist notions of suffering, the emphasis on the rarity of human life, and the attraction of Buddha, Dharma, Sangha as refuges for vulnerable humanity. To describe and analyze rituals in this light can help students see how Buddhist doctrines are applied to real life circumstances and how ritual traditions have been critical in explaining the faith's historical success.

Several individuals at the Teaching Buddhism Conference asked me to specify an inventory of Buddhist rituals. This is no easy task to do comprehensively given the diversity of regional and sectarian traditions. It is emblematic of the philological-philosophical dominance of our discipline that there has never been a history written of Buddhist ritual, nor much interest by textual scholars in translating the multitude of ritual texts or vernacular guidebooks, despite their importance to the monastic communities that composed them. The paucity of information on ritual is especially true for the various Mahāyāna societies. Despite these shortcomings, the following list marks a first step for defining a survey of Buddhist rituals.[27]

A List of Major Buddhist Ritual Practices

Householders and Monastics: Going for Refuge; Taking the Precepts; Merit Making and Transference; Establishing *stūpas* (permanent and ephemeral); Worshipping *stūpas*; Establishing Images; Worshipping Images; *Uposadha* Rituals (extra precepts, fasting, etc.); Śākyamuni's Birthday/Enlightenment/*Parinirvāna* (e.g., "bathing the infant Buddha image"); Chariot Festivals; Pilgrimage; *Pañcavarsika* (Five-year Donation Festival); "Freeing living beings."

Ordained Monastics: Monastic Ordination (novice and full); *Uposadha* (Pratimoksha Recitation; Preaching Rituals); Begging Round; Rituals at *stūpas* and Images; *Varsha* ("Rain-Retreat") Rituals (beginning and end: *Pavarana*); *Kathina*: Robe Donations; *Paitta* Recitations; Healing Rituals using Blessed Water; Making and Empowering Amulets; Rituals of Meditation Hall; Adopting Optional Ascetic Practices; Death Rituals and Post-Cremation/Burial Rituals; Transferring Merit to the Dead.

Mahāyāna Developments: Bodhisattva Vow Taking; *Anuttara* ("7-part") *Pūjā*;[28] Guru Mandala *Pūjā*;[29] Buddhist Homa; Rituals of Feeding Hungry Ghosts; Life Cycle Rites (Nepal);[30] Death Rites; Cult of the Book *Pūjā*;[31] *Vratas* to Bodhisattvas (Nepal and Tibet);[32] *Dhāranī* Recitations; Tantric *Abhiseka*.

For the multitudes who have performed rituals associated with specific narratives or have integrated pragmatic texts into their practice of Buddhism (like the *paritta* in the Theravāda world or the *rakshā* literature in the Mahāyāna), taking refuge in Buddha/Dharma/Sangha meant following a tradition that had demonstrated that the Buddha's words and the faith's saints could exert control over the powers of the universe and thus could resist disease and chaos while promoting worldly prosperity. As Jan Yun-hua has noted, there is a similar strong focus on spiritual power in the Chinese Buddhist storytelling traditions: "The claim of supernatural power of recitation may be disputable among scholars as well as sectarians, yet one point has clearly emerged... From an insider's viewpoint, the power of recitation is extremely powerful, and in certain cases, it is claimed to be even more powerful and preferable than either a philosophical understanding or the excellence in moral disciplines."[33]

Thus, I would argue that it was ritual practice that created and defined Buddhist identity and it was faith in the pragmatic powers of the Buddhas and bodhisattvas accessed via ritual that held the center of Buddhist tradition. Lofty moral values and blissful fruits of meditation certainly must have impressed and converted some; but the *dharma*'s control over the powers that insure health, wealth, progeny, peace—even overcoming bad *karman*—certainly would have had the widest appeal in securing the faith's success in contexts as different as nomadic pasturelands, urban enclaves, or subsistence farming villages.

Conclusion: A Parable

One hundred years ago, William James wrote of being in the mountains of North Carolina and seeing what at first appeared to be pure squalor: settlers had killed all the trees, planted their crops around the stumps, and erected rough cabins and crude fences, thus marring the landscape. "The forest," James observed, "had been destroyed; what had 'improved' it out of existence was hideous, a sort of ulcer, without a single element of artificial grace to make up for the loss of Nature's beauty..." But greater acquaintance with the people of the area taught him his error. "When *they* looked on the hideous stumps, what they thought of was personal victory. The chips, the girdled trees and the vile split rails spoke of honest sweat, persistent toils and final reward. The cabin was a warrant of safety for self and wife and babes. In short, the clearing, which to me was a mere ugly picture on the retina, was to them a symbol redolent with moral memories and sang a very paean of duty, struggle, and success.... We of the higher classes (so called)...are trained to seek the choice, the rare, the exquisite, exclusively, and to overlook the common. We are stuffed with abstract conceptions, and glib with verbalities and verbosities; and in the culture of these higher functions...we grow stone-blind and insensible to life's more elementary and general goods and joys."[34]

Privileging the elite's texts as the central sources for imagining typical Buddhists or constructing Buddhist history fixates students on high philosophy and ascetic esoterica, exaggerates (even if unintentionally) the importance of the intellectual traditions, and skews the historical understanding of the religious tradition's institutions. It has also impoverished the treatment of the *dharma* itself as it has been understood in Buddhist communities.

Attention to the content of locally-domesticated vernacular texts and pragmatic ritualism is needed to hasten the development of the post-Orientalist teaching of Buddhism free of idealization, "protestantization" (especially an assumption of ritual practices as superstition), and the overestimation of the role philosophical elites played in shaping Buddhist history. To survive and to achieve the Buddha's missionary call to spread the faith with insight and compassion, Buddhists created institutions and crafted a wealth of pragmatic practices alongside its soteriological traditions.

By performing rituals, Buddhists have taken refuge with powers identified by the Buddha as eminently suitable for securing both temporal and spiritual benefits. This was a development that small circles of Buddhist philosophers throughout history might have found disconcerting. But my guess is that most Buddhist scholars have carried amulets into their study rooms and placed them down alongside their learned *sūtra* commentaries. By reconfiguring our imaginations to include pragmatic rituals and the ideology of merit-making expressed in the narrative traditions, we can awaken students to Buddhism's contributions to "life's more elementary joys" and convey the full religious meaning of the faith's triple refuge.

Notes

[1] Schopen 1991.

[2] See, for example, Gombrich and Obeyesekere 1988, 202-40.

[3] Arguing for a more socio-cultural approach to Buddhism, Donald Lopez writes of the field's "curatorship" as follows: "But the Buddhism that largely concerned European scholars was an historical projection derived exclusively from manuscripts and blockprints, texts devoted largely to a 'philosophy,' which had been produced and had circulated among a small circle of monastic elites. With rare exception, there was little interest in the ways in which such texts were put to use in the service of various ritual functions. Buddhist studies has thus been to a great degree the history of master texts, dominated by scholastic categories it seeks to elucidate, what Said has called a 'paradigmatic fossilization' based upon the finality and closure of antiquarian or curatorial knowledge" (Lopez 1995, 7).

[4] The practical foundation to missionization is indicated in a Chinese text giving instructions on how to establish the faith in a locality: 1. Build monastic halls and temples; 2. Plant fruit trees, shade trees and then excavate bathing pools; 3. Freely supply medicines to heal the sick; 4. Construction of sturdy boats; 5. Safe placement of bridges suitable for the weak or ill; 6. Dig wells near roads for the thirsty and weary; 7. Enclose sanitary toilets (According to the Chinese *Tripitaka* [Taisho 16, #683]).

[5] See Cabezón 1995, 262; Dargyay 1988.

[6] Hallisey and Hansen 1996, 309.

[7] Note how a class beginning with the "Four Noble Truths" defies the tradition's own understanding of how to present the faith and puts our students, in their first exposure, right up in the position of the most advanced adherent.

[8] Bond 1988, 42.

[9] "The actual monk, unlike the textual monk, appears to have been deeply involved in religious giving and cult practice of every kind from the beginning. He is preoccupied not with *nirvāṇa* but above all else with what appears to have been a strongly felt obligation to his parents, whether living or dead. He is concerned as well, for example, with the health of his companions and teachers" (Schopen 1988-89, 167).

[10] Tambiah 1973.

[11] I have found it useful to counter this elitist view among my Catholic students by suggesting a disconfirming analogy to expose their misconception: would they accept that only

celibate priests and nuns were "true Christians"? Are they as Catholic householders "slacker Christians"?

[12] Further, this misconstruction has been one reason that Western converts and immigrant Buddhists have remained isolated from one another in North America and Europe (Nattier 1995).

[13] The scarcity of anthropological texts in print is a serious obstacle for teachers who wish to include case studies of Buddhism in context. Undoubtedly the best village study, S. J. Tambiah's *Buddhism and the Spirit Cults of Northeast Thailand* (Cambridge: Cambridge University Press, 1970), has been out of print for over a decade, as has his *Buddhist Saints of the Forest and the Cult of Amulets* (Cambridge: Cambridge University Press, 1984). Richard Gombrich's *Precept and Practice* (Oxford: Clarendon, 1971) has also gone into retirement, as has Manning Nash's *The Golden Road to Modernity* (New York: Wiley, 1965). Yes, Melford Spiro's *Buddhism and Society* (Berkeley: University of California Press, 1970) still remains in print and contains a wealth of ethnographic information, but in my experience it inevitably imparts to students the idea of great separation between different Buddhisms and faulty views about Buddhism and the spirit cults; both problems reinforce attitudes of condescension toward typical lay Buddhists. My students without Asian studies backgrounds have felt it too difficult to follow the welter of detail in Donald Swearer's *The Buddhist World of Southeast Asia* (Albany: State University of New York Press, 1996). Frank Reynolds at McGill's Teaching Buddhism Conference recommended the recent work by Nicola Tannenbaum, *Who Can Compete Against the World? Power-Protection of Buddhism in the Shan Worldview* (Ann Arbor: Association of Asian Studies, 1995). Martin Southwold's *Buddhism in Life: The Anthropological Study of Religion and the Sinhalese Practice of Buddhism* (Manchester: Manchester University Press, 1983), like B. J. Terwiel's *Monks and Magic: An Analysis of Religious Ceremonies in Central Thailand* (Bangkok: White Lotus, 1994) is not readily available in North America. On Tibetan Buddhism, the late Stan Mumford's *Himalayan Dialogue* (Madison: University of Wisconsin Press, 1989) is a brilliant account of Tibetan Buddhism in interaction with Tibeto-Burman shamanism, yet the subject matter is difficult for introductory undergraduate courses. Part of the problem of anthropological Buddhist studies remaining in print has been the lack of their use in introductory classrooms. I hope to assemble a sourcebook of anthropological accounts from Buddhist societies. Suggested readings are welcome!

[14] Two fine course books are a selection of the Pali *jātakas* (Rhys-Davids 1988) and Aryasura's *Jātakamālā* (Khoroche 1990).

[15] Could it be that the philosophical discourse among the virtuosi in Buddhist monasteries was as peripheral to the history of the faith as are the debates in modern philosophy departments to the history of academic institutions?

[16] The potential results from focusing on texts that we know were connected with householders should prove salutary: "Attention to the worklike aspects of the texts may help us to educate our imaginations, such that we do feel that we have a reasonable idea about

what subsequent Buddhists might have learned from a story" (Hallisey and Hansen 1996, 311).

[17] Todd T. Lewis, *Popular Buddhist Texts from Nepal: Narratives and Rituals of Newar Buddhism*. (Albany: State University of New York Press, forthcoming in 2000).

[18] Jones 1952, II: 77.

[19] See Schopen 1985, 1991, 1993; Lopez 1995a, 15. This last point, made in a key article by Gananath Obeyesekere for Theravāda contexts (1968), has been noted for other culture areas where Buddhism was domesticated (e.g., for Tibet [Gombo 1985; Samuel 1993]; Nepal [1992]; China [Gernet 1995]).

[20] *Anguttara Nikāya* IV, VII, 61 (Woodward 1992, 74, with numbering added).

[21] *Anguttara Nikāya* IV, VII, 61 (Woodward 1992, 75–76, with numbering added).

[22] As David Ruegg has noted, "Buddhism is indeed not only philosophy and/or religion but also a way of living and being, a cultural and value system permitting Buddhists in vast areas of the world to construct so much of their mundane as well as spiritual lives" (1995, 104).

[23] Lewis 1994.

[24] As Southworth has noted, "Buddhists themselves are very aware of this effect, and they stress that just as it is true that having a right or good state of mind leads to right or good conduct, so too does good conduct tend to produce good states of mind" (1983, 199).

[25] Diamond 1997.

[26] Reynolds and Tanner 1995, 110.

[27] For references on some these practices, see the section on rituals in Lewis 1997.

[28] See Crosby and Skilton 1996, chapter 3, 9-22.

[29] See Gellner 1992.

[30] See Lewis 1994.

[31] See Schopen 1975.

[32] See Locke 1987; Lewis 1989.

[33] Yun-hua 1977, 299.

[34] Quoted in Levine 1996, 145.

References

Bond, George. 1988. "The Gradual Path as a Hermeneutical Approach to the *Dhamma*." In *Buddhist Hermeneutics*. Honolulu: University of Hawaii Press.

Cabezón, José. 1995. "Buddhist Studies as a Discipline and the Role of Theory." *Journal of the International Association of Buddhist Studies* 18 (2): 231-68.

Dargyay, Eva K. 1998. "Buddhism in Adaptation: Ancestor Gods and their Tantric Counterparts in the Religious Life of Zanskar." *History of Religions* 28: 123-34.

Diamond, Jared. 1997. *Guns, Germs, and Steel: The Fates of Human Societies*. New York: W. W. Norton.

Gellner, David N. 1992. *Monk, Householder and Tantric Priest: Newar Buddhism and Its Hierarchy of Ritual.* Cambridge: Cambridge University Press.

Gernet, Jacques. 1995. *Buddhism in Chinese Society: An Economic History from the Fifth to the Tenth Centuries.* New York: Columbia University Press.

Gombo, Ugen. 1985. "Belief in Karma and its Social Ramification in Samsara." In *Soundings in Tibetan Civilization*, edited by Barbara N. Aziz and Matthew Kapstein. New Delhi: Manohar.

Gombrich, Richard, and Gananath Obeyesekere. 1988. *Buddhism Transformed: Religious Change in Sri Lanka.* Princeton: Princeton University Press.

Hallisey, Charles and Anne Hansen. 1996. "Narrative, Sub-Ethics, and the Moral Life: Some Evidence from Theravāda Buddhism." *Journal of Religious Ethics* 24 (2): 305-25.

Jan Yun-hua. 1977. "The Power of Recitation: An Unstudied Aspect of Chinese Buddhism." *Studi Storico Religiosi* 1: 299.

Jones, J. J. 1949-56. *The Mahāvastu.* 3 vols. London: Luzac and Co.

Khoroche, Peter. 1990. *Once the Buddha Was a Monkey: Arya Sura's "Jātakamālā."* Chicago: University of Chicago Press.

Levine, Lawrence. 1996. *The Opening of the American Mind.* Boston: Beacon Press.

Lewis, Todd T. 1989. "Mahāyāna *Vratas* in Newar Buddhism." *Journal of the International Association of Buddhist Studies* 12 (1): 109-38.

———. 1994. "The *Nepāl Jana Jīvan Kriyā Paddhati*, a Modern Newar Guide for Vajrayāna Life-Cycle Rites." *Indo-Iranian Journal* 37: 1-46.

———. 1996. "Patterns of Religious Belief in a Buddhist Merchant Community, Nepal," *Asian Folklore Studies* 55 (2): 237-70.

———. 1997. "The Anthropological Study of Buddhist Communities: Historical Precedents and Ethnographic Paradigms." In *Shamanism, Altered States, Healing: Essays in the Anthropology of Religion*, edited by Steven Glazier. Westport: Greenwood Press, 319-67.

Locke, John. 1987. "*Uposadha Vrata* of Amoghapasha Lokeshvara in Nepal." *l'Ethnographie* 83 (100-1): 159-89.

Lopez, Donald S., ed. 1995a. *Buddhism in Practice.* Princeton: Princeton University Press.

———. 1995b. *Curators of the Buddha: The Study of Buddhism Under Colonialism.* Chicago: University of Chicago Press.

Nattier, Jan. 1995. "Visible and Invisible." *Tricycle: The Buddhist Review* (fall): 42-49.

Obeyesekere, Gananath. 1968. "Theodicy, Sin, and Salvation in a Sociology of Buddhism." In *Dialectic in Practical Religion*, edited by Edmund Leach. Cambridge: Cambridge University Papers in Anthropology 5: 7-40.

Reynolds, Vernon and Ralph Tanner. 1995. *The Social Ecology of Religion.* New York: Oxford University Press.

Rhys-Davids, Caroline A. F. 1988. *Stories of the Buddha.* New York: Dover.

Ruegg, D. Seyfort. 1995. "Some Observations on the Present and Future of Buddhist Studies." *Journal of the International Association of Buddhist Studies* 15 (1): 104-17.

Samuel, Geoffrey. 1993. *Civilized Shamans: Buddhism in Tibetan Societies*. Washington: Smithsonian Institution Press.

Śāntideva. 1996. *The Bodhicaryāvatara*. Translated by Kate Crosby and Andrew Skilton. New York: Oxford University Press.

Schopen, Gregory. 1975. "The Phrase '*sa prthiviprades`ascaityabhuto bhavet*' in the *Vajracchedika*: Notes on the Cult of the Book in Mahāyāna." *Indo-Iranian Journal* 17: 147-81.

_____. 1984. "Filial Piety and the Monk in the Practice of Indian Buddhism: A Question of 'Sinicization' Viewed from the Other Side." *T'oung Pao* 70: 110-26.

_____. 1985. "Two Problems in the History of Indian Buddhism: The Layman/Monk Distinction and the Doctrines of the Transference of Merit." *Studien zur Indologie und Iranistik* 10: 9-47.

_____. 1987. "Burial '*ad sanctos*' and the Physical Presence of the Buddha in Early Indian Buddhism: A Study in the Archaeology of Religions." *Religion* 17: 193-225.

_____. 1988-89. "On Monks, Nuns and 'Vulgar' Practices: The Introduction of the Image Cult into Indian Buddhism." *Artibus Asiae* 49 (1/2): 153-68.

_____. 1991. "Archaeology and Protestant Presuppositions in the Study of Indian Buddhism." *History of Religions* 31(1): 1-23.

_____. 1993. "Stupa and Tirtha: Tibetan Mortuary Practices and an Unrecognized Form of Burial *Ad Sanctos* at Buddhist Sites in India." In *Buddhist Forum II: Papers in Honour of D. S. Ruegg*, edited by T. Skorupski. London: School of Oriental and African Studies, University of London.

Southwold, Martin. 1983. *Buddhism in Life: The Anthropological Study of Religion and the Sinhalese Practice of Buddhism*. Manchester: Manchester University Press.

Tambiah, Stanley J. 1973. "Buddhism and This-Worldly Activity." *Modern Asian Studies* 7 (1): 1-20.

Woodward, F. L., trans. 1992. *The Book of Gradual Sayings*. Volume 2. Oxford: Pali Text Society.

Moving Beyond the 'ism': A Critique of the Objective Approach to Teaching Buddhism

O'Hyun Park

For some time now, Buddhism has been entering the conscious-ness of occidental people, with ever-increasing interest on the part of teachers, scholars and laypersons. A vast scholarship on Bud-dhism has arisen through the translation of texts and the proliferation of commentaries, and for a number of decades now Buddhist Studies has been taught in North American colleges and universities. Fur-thermore, the influence of Buddhism is discernible in modern art, poetry, popular culture, counter-culture as well as in modern and postmodern philosophy. In other words, there are now many writings which are either directly or indirectly about Buddhism as a religious and cultural phenomenon. Nevertheless, it is strange to see that there are comparatively few books focused on "the one who is enlight-ened." The importance of the Buddha, and, correspondingly, the *inwardness* of Buddhism, has been greatly neglected.

Teachers of Buddhism frequently see Buddhism as historically, sociologically or otherwise conditioned; they concern themselves with Buddhist philosophy, ethics, sociology, anthropology, psychology, and aesthetics, and tend to analyze Buddhism from these and other perspectives separately. Of course, one cannot simply ignore objective data; Buddhist traditions do have these conditions and consequences, the study of which is a valid and important enterprise. However, teaching Buddhism as one of the world religions should not merely duplicate what can be done in other academic departments. It is certain that the *raison d'être* of teaching Buddhism must be something other than these objective studies. Otherwise, teachers, putting the cart in front of the horse, will remain in the deplorable condition described by Holmes Welch in *The Buddhist Revival in China*. During his trip to Hong Kong, Welch recalls a Buddhist monk who had possession of an important Buddhist document. The monk allowed him to make a copy of it. Playing down Welch's enthusiasm for the manuscript, the monk earnestly urged him to meditate on enlightenment for a year. After Welch's departure, the monk wrote a letter to him saying: "You should not go to Treasure Mountain and then come home empty-handed." As Welch relates: "My suitcases were full of material on Chinese Buddhism, but I know what he meant."[1]

This incident indicates the predominant practice in which many teachers deny or set aside Buddhist meditation ("Treasure Mountain") as one of those mysteries about which nothing can be said or done. Although meditation (Skt. *dhyāna*, Ch. *ch'an*, Jp. *zen*) can be viewed from many angles, this paper takes it as nothing "special." In other words, meditation is not a special possession of a particular sect of Buddhism, nor a special activity distinguished from other activities, nor is it limited to a special time or place. "If anyone starts to think of doing meditation, it is not meditation but delusion."[2] One's original mind can be deluded, if one seeks stillness as the goal or result of the practice of meditation. A truly meditative person can live, move and exist in the world without being attached to any place or any time. "The greatest meditation is to maintain the original and true mind."[3] So long as one separates teaching, research, or any living task from one's original mind, one remains external to meditation. Meditation as such is an internal centrality, which escapes through the meshes of a purely objective method of teaching or research. It is this innermost meditation that I have undertaken to explore and discuss in my class. I propose that inattentiveness to such has characterized—and limited—most of Buddhist teaching in the past several decades. Historically, the teaching of Buddhism has sought objectivity, an approach which may have been motivated either by a wish to evade confrontation with Buddhist reality, by a premature despair of finding that reality, or by a fear of violating the law.

As an alternative way of teaching Buddhism, I usually begin the class by reminding the students of the importance of the Buddha and of meditation; that is, I remind them of the significance of ontological silence or ontological inquiring-within. One must first *be still* in order to teach and learn Buddhism. In no other way can its essence truly be known or shown. Seen from this point of view, teaching and learning Buddhism, if it is not filtered by meditation, is not worthy of attention. The *Sūtralamkara* says: "The truth indeed has never been preached by the Buddha, seeing that one has to realize it within oneself."[4]

In the class, no particular form of Buddhism is advocated or set up as archetypal, whether Theravāda, Māhāyana, or Vajrayāna. Although my class is concerned with these Buddhist traditions, I attempt to transcend sectarian differences, in order to try to get at the commonality of the Buddhist traditions, which is, I believe, to be found in the Buddha's spiritual awakening.

As I see it, the direction in which the study of Buddhism should be heading in the new millennium necessitates the development of a proper alternative to merely external and objective teaching. The proper alternative, I think, is not a relapse into sheer subjectivity, but rather the adoption of an enlarged and more flexible approach to Buddhism, which would not limit itself to one side of the subject-object dichotomy. In other words, the "objective" perspective is, like the "subjective," only one ingredient. In the end, one must confront the large (ontological) mystery of the relation of the objective to the subjective. An enlarged and more flexible methodology for teaching Buddhism is inseparable from the question of human reality, and it cannot be based on the separate duality of teacher and student, subject and object, or substance and method. Robert Bellah has recognized this crucial point: "One of the special opportunities in teaching Buddhism at the present is that it is one of the few fields concerned with integration, with problems of the whole. Perhaps it is the only such field now that philosophy at so many universities is given over to narrow technicism."[5]

Such a non-dual approach, which must be distinguished from a non-dualistic approach, may creatively aspire to contribute to the "comparative study" of religious thought by clarifying the uniqueness of Buddhism over against other world religions. In order to offer students a non-dual study of human reality which is inseparable from a realization of the importance of one's own Buddha-nature, I begin by talking about the name "Buddhism." I let them know that it was occidental scholars who coined this nominative, which is in fact incompatible with the central Buddhist term, *dharma*.

In south Asian religions, the term *dharma* has an infinite variety of meanings. In Hinduism, it can be understood as a general term for the Hindu religion, as "way of life." Considered in terms of moral law, it can be taken to mean the rules for a higher life which is not given over to sexual or material desire. As one of the Three Jewels of Buddhism: Buddha, Dharma, and Sangha, it refers specifically to the teachings of the Buddha. When it is used in the plural, *dharmas* refer to sense objects or events. Furthermore, it can be understood as the unchanging and absolute Buddha-nature cherishing the cosmos. Seen from the last point of view, Buddha-nature is the normative truth, which transcends individual truths in the sense that it cherishes and enhances individual truths.

As the class focuses on the Buddha himself, I must discuss the teachings of Siddhartha Gautama Buddha. I contrast the Buddha and his teachings to: a) those Hindu monists or brahmins who tended to abstractly wallow in God by creating a pantheistic, monistic or polytheistic potpourri; b) Mahāvīra, founder of Jainism, who tended towards extreme asceticism; c) Guru Nānak, founder of Sikhism, who tended towards external syncretism; d) Jesus. Unlike Jesus, who was (in human if not theological terms) the son of a carpenter, the Buddha was the son of a king, and thus endowed with virtually everything people ordinarily seek. Objectively viewed, he lacked nothing. And yet, after enjoying himself for a period of nearly three decades, his life finally became a burning problem, and he was driven to inquire into its secret. His quest and subsequent finding (the "Middle Path") made Buddhism fundamentally different from other world religions, which tend to be either moralistic or theistic. To understand his ontological inquiring-within and the whole meaning of Buddhism, I challenge students with the Buddha's own paradoxical question, which serves as the mantra for the whole semester: What do I lack when I have everything? The answer is enlightenment or awakening (*bodhi*), which is not an externally-gained possession. For that reason, I express it as fundamental human reality. By necessity, it has many different names such as "Reality," "Truth," "Mind," "Buddha," "Normative Principle" or "Living Things." However, I suggest to the students that they should not cling to names when seeking explanations.

One of my objectives in teaching Buddhism is to let students know that the Buddha's own quest was not merely a personal quest but more fundamentally a human quest—an attempt to comprehend this unique question and to enter into a reality which is not to be owned, but which, when it is lacking, leaves all possessions ultimately unsatisfying. In other words, I do my best to offer students the Buddha's world, that is, *nirvāṇa*, in order to enlarge their view of reality. Although *nirvāṇa* cannot objectively be proven to exist, I do press hard upon them to realize the spiritual truth that the absence of an objective proof is not always proof of a thing's absence. The modern mind has led the students to be unnecessarily attached to the scientific outlook stretching from Descartes in the seventeenth century through Kant, Darwin, Marx and Comte in the nineteenth century. I ask them to go beyond this modern mind-set which puts everything to the rack for objective proof, simply because the Buddha's inner search for reality cannot be objectively proven to exist (it culminates, after all, in a realization of emptiness, or *śūnyatā*). In spite, or perhaps because of this, the Buddha's search became, for lack of a better term, "ontologically contagious" for others in his time as well as for many—including an increasing number of westerners—today. I interest my students in the further exploration of this non-dual reality. Such a contagious truth or reality is an important aspect of Buddhism, and one that is simply not attainable through a mere academic study of Buddhism.

Therefore, my procedure in the class setting from the beginning of the semester to its end is to elucidate the nature of non-dual reality. I provide some documentation (a conclusive validation by objective documentation being ruled out by the very nature of the reality) and evaluate some recent interpretations of Buddhist thought in light of this reality. I invite students to look into my book, *An Invitation to Dialogue Between East and West: A Critique of the Modern and the Post-Modern Thought*, in which I elucidate this non-dual reality in full detail. I also mention this book in order to further their understanding of both oriental religious concepts and basic Buddhist concepts such as the Middle Path, Three Refuges, *karma, anitya, anātman, duḥkha, nirvāṇa*, Buddhahood, and *śūnyatā*. Throughout the entire semester, my students, keeping the mantra or *gong'an* in mind, are asked to remember that the official stance of the teaching of Buddhism is the examination of that non-duality, which has far-reaching ramifications. At times I am informed that my lectures suggest a dogmatic affirmation; this is only because I have temporarily been carried away by my deeper bias in the area. However, that this discussion of non-duality may lead students to re-examine their own approach to their lives and to enlarge their world is for me a sufficient justification for teaching it. A fair number of students have been very appreciative. For these reasons, my way of teaching Buddhism at Appalachian State University can be taken as a possible alternative method, one which delineates itself from both the methods of the natural sciences and the social sciences.

The non-dual aspects of Buddhism come as a surprise or revelation to many students. Specifically, they are surprised to discover that their dissatisfaction or disenchantment with their own dualistic religious traditions need not be the end of religiosity but may in fact serve as the beginning of their religious quest. One of my recent students visited me in my office and said: "This class is incredibly powerful." Having absorbed the spirit of the class made him quit taking drugs and smoking cigarettes. This incident suggests that students may learn from Buddhism to tranform themselves into new persons and develop a new society appropriate for the new millennium. I am, however, not operating under the naïve presumption that I have presented the actual essence of Buddhist spirituality to the students. The living substance of Buddhism may be likened to a mountaintop. I have not undertaken to reproduce the view from the mountaintop. I have only attempted to point to the mountain which needs to be climbed by any student wishing to enjoy the view, and to call the students' attention to paths which lead in other directions. In truth, there seems to be only one prerequisite for taking this course of mine. That is, one must be willing to find a spiritual companion whom one can love and who merits one's love. When one's companion wants to climb the mountain, both may climb together. Then everything in one's life is very easy.

In short, the inwardness of the Buddha's human quest is not to be acquired by mere hermeneutic virtuosity or the scrupulous decoding of texts alone, but by the encounter with it as a living thing and with living representatives and authentic teachers. Buddhism, in what I have called its ontological contagiousness, has always transmitted itself not primarily through the written word but through the personal mode of Buddhist apprenticeship. Texts are in the end externalizations, formalizations, and codifications of something more intimately living which the text at its best can point to but cannot directly convey.

For a text as a proverbial finger pointing to the moon, I have chosen my own translation of a sixteenth-century Buddhist text written by Xishan, a Korean Zen master. His book, entitled *Chanjia Guijiam* in Chinese, might be literally translated "A Paragon of Zen House." It is only a text, and like all texts, it is limited. However, it is defensible as a basic teaching text on the grounds of being broad, variegated, multi-scriptural and multi-national and therefore, hopefully, representative of certain tendencies in Buddhist thought. Xishan made a substantial effort not only to grasp the essence of Buddhism, but also in most cases to make it relevant to the breadth of human existential awareness. In my judgement, this text warrants use as an alternative to most current texts that are based upon a widespread unawareness of the central thrust of Buddhist religiosity, a deficiency which may be related to long engrained patterns of dualistic thought.

For the rest of the semester, I creatively repeat the importance of the life of non-duality by juxtaposing such with dualistic patterns of thought. For example, dualistic patterns of thought characterize the methodology of those who choose to limit themselves to linguistic, objective, external, scientific, cultural and purely conceptual treatments of Buddhism as a package of doctrines and practices which have been geographically and historically conditioned. Such treatments refuse to confront Buddhism as a living reality, to meet it on its own grounds and to understand it in its own terms. They grasp these specific elements as intellectually controllable commodities and view them from the perspective of the external spectator rather than from the perspective of the living participant. Such an approach is often based on the metaphysical bias that reality is sheer objectivity and that the more objective is teaching, the closer it will be to reality. But my bias and the bias of Buddhism in my judgement is that reality is encountered in the life of non-duality, that is, within wholeness; that what excludes subjectivity can never be wholeness; and that the dualism of subject-object must be broken through before the living truth may be known.

Buddhism, which is concerned with the problem of the whole, requires the wholeness of the teacher as well as the students. It will not reveal its totality when it is approached with partiality. In other words, a teacher must be a seeker, one who is not divorced from that which is sought. The seeker must go beyond merely teaching Buddhist concepts and the moral discipline found in Buddhist texts to find "that before which all words recoil." In other words, what I am suggesting to my students is that one's interest in finding or knowing the truth should progressively diminish, even as one must become more interested in finding enlightened people and associating with realized people who are full of truth. I encourage my students to "collect" saints as their goal. Such a vision of spiritual companionship is, as I have noted, the prerequisite for students to take my course. In other words, the methodology of teaching and learning has to be ontologically related to its substance. The ontological meeting of method and substance is from the Buddhist perspective nothing other than the realization of one's true selfhood. For Buddhism: "Being is not to be grasped speculatively but is only to be entered into existentially. One knows reality to the extent that one is real, and the problem is not to formulate an objective and formal criterion of reality, but to be real oneself...; the question...is not: What is *Being qua Being?* but *How do I contact my own true being?*"[6]

This suggestion may contribute to religious anthropology, insofar as it may broaden the perspective of discussion of the human situation by directing students to one of the great *gong'ans*: Who am I? To Buddhism, this question is not merely anthropological or psychological but is fundamentally religious or cosmic. All other serious questions of human existence, including the Buddha's own quest, involve this question. Without an ontological answer to the question, Who am I? all answers to other questions are abstract (suspended in midair), simply because the questioner herself remains questionable. Questions like, How can I teach or learn about Buddhism? What ought I to teach or learn? What is my objective? are to the Buddha abstract and thus unreal and dead questions. These questions are put objectively and seek objective answers and thus do not confront the *I* who puts the questions. The ultimate and fundamental question, that is, Who am I? will not be answered at the dualistic level where question and questioner are separated and the question is merely considered rationally. In an academic setting, the subjects of anthropology, theology, philosophy, ontology, phenomenology, psychology, science and ethics are pursued separately. For the Buddha, they are all spokes of one wheel whose hub is the true self (Buddha-nature). Without the hub, the spokes have no point of unity and the wheel must crumble. Hui-nêng says, "To search for the Buddha-nature while separating from one's true self is to search for a rabbit's horn." These insights will hopefully help form a new orientation towards teaching Buddhism, as an alternative to the traditional methods.

To review, the main objective of my class has been to clarify the original intent of the Buddha and to show that at least a large number of influential evaluations of Buddhism misconstrue his intent and operate from premises which he did not share. It can be said that many of those who clamor most loudly for a traditional critical methodology seem to be uncritical in regard to their own objective methodology. This is to say they seem unconscious of the unproven assumption on which this criticality rests.

Buddhism, as I see it, does not share this critical view, but it need not be ruled out of court for that reason. All that needs to be said is that if traditional studies of Buddhism are correct, then the alternative way of teaching Buddhism I am presenting here is the pursuit of a fantasy. On the other hand, if my way of teaching Buddhism is right, then the traditional academic study of Buddhism is doomed to an increasingly devitalized irrelevancy. The question of which one is correct is not to be decided by the arbitrary and pontifical proclamation of a simple methodology suitable for serious learners. Methodology, if it is to disclose reality, must be adapted to the nature of reality; otherwise it becomes tyrannical and Procrustean. The fundamental question then is whether studies of Buddhism should be limited to academic studies of the formal dimensions of Buddhism, or whether they should also involve the effort to confront the realities of Buddhism. The forms of Buddhism can be studied or known externally and objectively, but reality can only be known by reality. And to enter into the reality of Buddhism, one must also enter into one's own reality.

On that note, let me say a few words about my own "non-dual" experience as both a professor of Buddhism and a Christian minister. Buddhist religiosity seems to me to be in some respects antidotal to Western forms of Christianity. It may in fact supply the needed way out of the cul de sac of Christian theologies today. Christian theology is grounded in the belief in a transcendental deity. According to this view, God is something which is other than or beyond ordinary reality, and thus religious reality differs from what is immediately given in this world. This notion has been theologically formulated as the dualism of creator and creature. In contrast to this perspective, the postmodern consciousness rejects any sort of theistic transcendental God, and has tried to annihilate any distance between the two.

Traditional Christian theology has not been friendly to any easing of the distinction of creator and creature, of transcendence and immediacy. As a consequence, the intrinsically dualistic nature of traditional Christian theology has been responsible for human alienation from reality. Believing that one should conform to the will of the divine, many people find themselves unable to do so. The unbrigeable gulf between faith and practice forces the modern consciousness in its search for authenticity into the rejection of the traditional theistic belief in a transcendental God. Recognizing, along with postmodern thought, that it is indeed this entrenched dualism which is the fatal flaw of theistic Christianity, I seek a correction of it not through postmodern atheism or secularism but through Buddhist spirituality. Buddhist spirituality stands neither for theological speculation about the divine transcendence nor for humanistic affirmation of life in the world, but for the total reality which is non-duality of the human and the divine.

Hopefully, these suggestions taken together may also serve as something of an antidote to a good deal of modern and postmodern ways of teaching Buddhism, insofar as I have tried to clarify the extent to which teachings of Buddhist traditions are conditioned by occidental or provincial patterns of thought and arbitrarily limited methodologies. It is typical of occidentals as well as of many contemporary Buddhists to wish to teach Buddhism by means of scientific understandings of Buddhist ideas. These objective studies of Buddhism fail to transmit the living essence of Buddhism, and in consequence, those whose approach is purely of this sort may conclude that Buddhism at its best is merely a form of psychology and has little to do with religious life. Of course, there is a considerable similarity between Buddhism and psychology, and there has been a general rapprochement between Buddhists and those who work in the various fields of psychology and psychiatry. As a matter of fact, the goal of my way of teaching Buddhism is one which is common to the area of psychology, because Buddhism is also deeply concerned with human adjustment to life. However, I am drawing hard on the difference between the two by characterizing Buddhism as a religion, and thus expressive of what we might call a "cosmic psychoanalysis."

Among the differences between traditional Buddhist thought and contemporary "objective" Buddhist scholarship is this one: Buddhist thought is existentially oriented in the sense that its aim is to direct one to the full possession of one's humanity (Buddhahood). Hence, if it is true, it is not just pointing to a truth but to the "pearl of great price." Objective scholarship has no such intention. If it is true, it is simply *artificially* true, and still leaves one with one's spiritual needs unsatisfied. One's spiritual thirst will not be quenched at the fountain of objective learning and if that is all there is, then one would be doomed to remain thirsty. In that case, we should be left with the mystery: How is it that the human species is endowed with this thirst which nothing in this world can quench?

To sum up, the goal of my teaching of Buddhism is to introduce students to the Buddha's world and to help them be engaged in the process of moving in that direction themselves. In the process, the spirit of Buddhism may rub off on them. I personally do not know what in the process of teaching Buddhism has rubbed off on me, but I can only hope that whatever it is can be passed on to my students.

Notes

[1] Welch 1968, 268.
[2] Xishan 1999, 111.
[3] Xishan 1999, 111.
[4] Quoted in Huxley 1968, 6.
[5] Bellah 1970, 6.
[6] Phillips 1968, 16.

References

Bellah, Robert. 1970. "Confessions of a Former Establishment Fundamentalist." In *Council on the Study of Religion* 1 (3). Hanover: The American Academy of Religion.

Huxley, Aldous. 1968. *The Perennial Philosophy*. New York: World Publishing Company.

Park, O'Hyun. 2000 [1996]. *An Invitation to Dialogue Between East and West: A Critique of the Modern and the Post-Modern Thought*. New York: Peter Lang.

Phillips, Bernard. 1968. "Reflection on Zen and Humanism." *The Humanist* 28(6).

Welch, Holmes. 1968. *The Buddhist Revival in China*. Cambridge: Harvard University Press.

Xishan. 1999. *A Paragon of Zen House*. Translated by O'Hyun Park. New York: Peter Lang.

Cultural Divides

Black Ships, Blavatsky, and the Pizza Effect: Critical Self-Consciousness as a Thematic Foundation for Courses in Buddhist Studies

Stephen Jenkins

The Conference on Teaching Buddhism that sponsored these papers is part of a general trend in Buddhist Studies toward a heightened sense of critical self-consciousness. I want to argue here that it is not only crucial, but exciting, to bring this critical self-consciousness directly to students in the classroom. Most of the focus in this trend has been on our ways of knowing and representing Buddhism. As most would now agree, in studying Buddhism we are not treating a static external object. What we perceive is powerfully conditioned and contextualized by our own culturally defined ways of seeing. Our minds are like instruments of observation that have their own characteristic modality and calibration. The object of our study arises within our own subjectivity; it is necessary therefore for us to engage in self-examination before and in the process of engaging another culture or religion. This requires attention not only to the development of the academic study of Buddhism, but also to the study of Buddhism in Euro-American cultures, and the history of the encounter between Asia and the West.

In practical terms, I started with this approach as a response to the task of preparing undergraduates for an international studies program. I needed both to prepare them to engage a foreign culture with sensitivity and to deal with the intense self-transformation that confrontation with an alternate reality generates. I began by asking them to consider who they were as Americans and how this effected their responses, interpretations, and impressions. Furthermore, they needed to be aware of the impact of their presence in a foreign world, and for this they should know some of the sad, sometimes bizarre, history of Euro-American treatment of Asian cultures. When I prepared to teach again in the traditional classroom, I realized that I was leading the students into a similar encounter with similar, although less intense, potentials for transformation and violation. As we are increasingly aware, not only our direct intervention in foreign cultures but our ways of knowing have the potential for violation. It is also important to note that, since there is no safe distance at which to study Buddhism, the potential for self-transformation is there in the classroom as well as in the field.

I was concerned from the first use of this approach that students, excited perhaps by the prospect of studying Zen, would be unwilling to engage in the apparently secondary methodological issues of professional academics, but it is consistently one of the most exciting parts of my courses. Before they look at another world, they must begin by asking what are the causes and conditions that have delivered them up into a moment of consciousness such as they experience. How do those preconditions dispose them to respond to the traditions they are about to encounter, to react like American students? Beginning from within, having them question who they are and what they bring to the dialogue, "gets them where they live." It also breaks down the artificial barriers between themselves and the process in which they are engaged, that is, the whole institutionalized classroom experience. They learn to see themselves and the class as part of a larger historical process and a distinctive historical moment that their parents, and certainly their grandparents, could not have experienced. The course becomes more than a study of an exotic worldview, it becomes as well a course about them.

The heuristic examples are extraordinarily interesting and compelling. I have used, among others, the art of spitting, the penis of God, ritual cannibalism, a hard-swearing cigar-smoking Russian medium, and the so-called pizza effect. In short, there are a wonderful variety of things one can use to capture students' attention. My primary examples for Buddhism are the early encounters of Europeans and the Japanese, and the feedback loop that resulted in the representation to Euro-American culture of "Protestant" Buddhism as a reflection of our and their biases and preconceptions.

The new self-consciousness in Buddhist Studies is intimately connected to the study of Buddhism in America. For better or worse, and intentionally or unintentionally, we participate in the transmission of Buddhism to America in the classroom and it is through the study of Buddhism in America that we reach an understanding of our student audience and ourselves. Without a deep consideration of American religious preconceptions and tendencies and their effect on the evolution of our interaction with Buddhist ideas and cultural phenomena, we do not know who we are or what we are doing. Even for undergraduate concentrators in the study of religion this should be a foundational element, not to speak of graduate students.

Directly connecting historical critical awareness to the understanding of their immediate experience generates a positive attitude to theoretical issues and dramatically raises the level of class discourse. Examining the history of the transmission and interpretation of Buddhism in Euro-American culture sets up the discussion of the reciprocal transformation of Buddhism and Tibetan or East Asian cultures. Beginning with the fact that the same processes are active here in the West, and that they themselves are indeed part of those processes, makes such issues seem far more interesting in distant ancient worlds.

Raising doubts about the modality of their experience of Buddhism interweaves elegantly with the introduction of Buddhist systematic thought. As Frank Reynolds noted in his keynote speech to this conference, in at least one modern formulation, Buddhism *is* criticism. As Nishitani would put it, the fundamental Buddhist problem is the unexamined presentation of the self to itself. The ideas that we create and the world we claim to describe are figments of our own imagination, and the framework of the conceptions of subjectivity and collective intersubjectivity can be taught fully in terms of Buddhist thought.

A Methodological Argument

This dual attention to both the subjectivity of those whose culture we study and our own subjectivity suggests a dialogical model. I want to argue here that both individual scholarship and classroom study can be profitably viewed as modes of interreligious dialogue. If so, then it follows that teaching that fails to address our own subjectivity is seriously impoverished. The kind of sensibility I would extend to the classroom has been presented by Raimundo Pannikar in the discussion of interreligious dialogue. He writes: "I would like to begin by stressing the often neglected notion of an *intrareligious* dialogue, i.e. an inner dialogue within myself, an encounter in the depth of my personal religiousness. If *interreligious* dialogue is to be real dialogue, an *intrareligious* dialogue must accompany it, i.e. it must begin with my questioning myself and the relativity of my beliefs (which does not mean their relativism), accepting the challenge of a change, a conversion and the risk of upsetting my traditional patterns."[1]

These thoughts take on broader significance when intrareligious dialogue is seen, not only as an optional part of a certain mode of discourse, but as a necessary and unavoidable part of the process of engaging other religions. For the Buddhists of brutally colonized Sri Lanka, or the average person in Japan, all these components, profound inner encounter, self-questioning, and the challenge of change and conversion, are not optional. It is only from a position of power, enhanced by the American illusion of geographical isolation and the abstracted space of the classroom, that such processes can be mistaken as optional. A person of non-Western cultures has only to look around him to see a world transformed by intercultural dialogue. Perhaps this is why a man from a India, like Pannikar, describes the aspects of that dialogue so well.

José Cabezón, in the context of interreligious dialogue, recently put forth the related suggestion that the consciousness of any individual scholar is the locus of an interreligious encounter. "The scholarship of a single scholar, even when not self-consciously cast as interreligious dialogue, can be considered as the site or locus of an interreligious encounter...not only in written forms, but also within other modes of activity that are more intimately connected to the subjectivity of the scholar."[2]

Even for scholars who regard themselves as committed Buddhist practitioners, the study of Buddhism is an instance of intercultural, if not interreligious, dialogue. It is a moment when a person of one collective intersubjectivity attempts to comprehend and explicate another intersubjectivity, most often through their intentional acts of communication. Our private scholarship can be regarded as an act of interreligious dialogue, as can, by extension, the whole historic endeavor of Buddhist Studies. If interreligious dialogue is a natural and unavoidable aspect of the study of religion, then we should consider Pannikar's analysis as more than an authentic way to engage in a certain mode of conversation. It becomes relevant to our private scholarship and especially to our classroom teaching. For better or worse, we facilitate an *intra*religious dialogue for our students, as surely as if we were leading a study group abroad. Each student becomes the locus of an encounter between worldviews. If so, we should lead our students in giving the same attention to their own subjectivity as we do for Asian cultures.

It is critical for us to know something of American religious history in order to understand what our students bring to this process and most particularly to know the prior history of the encounter of the West with Buddhism, both in terms of academic study and broader cultural developments. Otherwise, we cannot really know and take responsibility for what we are doing in the classroom. The dynamics of the "real world" interface between Buddhism and Euro-American culture directly parallel the dynamic of the students' encounter with Buddhism in the classroom. We must take care not to ask our students to develop sophisticated ways of analyzing intercultural dialogue and transformation, as in Buddhism's spread from India to China to Japan, while blind-siding them to the fact that they are involved in a similar process themselves. We must begin by asking who we are, how we construct the other, and how our imagination of others effects them. Raising the student's awareness in this regard breaks down the subject-object split. On a personal level, it means recognizing their encounter with Buddhism as a transformative dialogue unfolding from within their own subjectivity. On a cultural level, it makes them aware of the incredible damage we have done to others and that worlds may be at stake in our choice of ways of know-ing.

Following Pannikar's model, we must also acknowledge that we are facing the students with "the challenge of a change, a conversion and the risk of upsetting...traditional patterns." There is no safe ob-jective distance from which the student can engage Buddhist thought. This is particularly a problem when teaching students who are "fundamentalists" of various faiths or have strong evangelical Chris-tian beliefs. Fundamentalists, of whom we so often have naïve and intolerant expectations, instinctively recognize Pannikar's risks. They know, perhaps through their own faith in the word, that listening is transformative and therefore dangerous, because transformation is not always good. It can be difficult to honor the beliefs of these stu-dents when teaching Buddhism from a methodology informed by Buddhist thought.

It may seem that not only the content, but the method of teach-ing advocated here, violates these students. Too often we invite these folk onto a neutral or middle ground which is really our own home ground. One should have sympathy and respect for fundamentalists and evangelicals who attempt to cover their ears with the Bible, rather than listen to relativistic teachings. Relativity can appear to be, and often is, little more than the saw that we use to cut off the limb that they are standing on. But listening and the risk of transformation are not optional here. It is not just that these are my issues, they are the issues of our times and they are raised by Buddhist analysis and the study of the cultural transformations of Buddhism. I can honor these students, who believe that truth is objective or in a literal in-terpretation of scripture, by not pretending that there is no danger here and by helping them work on the key problems that are pre-sented to their beliefs.

Practical Examples

I recommend moving from playful examples that draw from the students' everyday experience to examples drawn from the historical encounter of Buddhism and the West. Thanks to all the recent work on Buddhism in America, the base of examples and the literature to draw on has become quite rich.

My approach is to engage students in a number of thought experiments to prepare them for the question of who we are, how we are calibrated and preprogrammed to respond in certain ways to Buddhism, and finally to describe the so-called "pizza effect" as it has played out with "Protestant" Buddhism. The examples here are sketchy for two reasons. One is that I am not really interested in the students retaining the details of the examples; I want to engage them in a certain kind of self-questioning. The other is that I cannot argue here at length for the presentation of the cases and that is not the point. Readers will no doubt have their own set of examples to draw from.

I first ask the students to consider that when we study the religions of others, we bring one vision of reality up against another. We are looking out of the dream in which we live and into the dreams of others. They threaten to transform one another; it is a dangerous moment. The transformation is not always good, one dream can swallow another one or destroy it. Whoever is the final dreamer in all these dreams within dreams, worldviews within worldviews, is the ultimate arbiter of reality. The harshest form of imperialism, using this role as arbiter, deprives the victim of their right to claim their own vision of reality, to dream their own dream, to present themselves to us, and even to mediate their own self-understanding.

To help them understand what it means to have a worldview, a dream, or an intersubjectivity to abide in and to have that violated, I ask them to consider the popular culture of their school. On virtually every campus there are various groups, from Goths to Rastafarians, that use a certain style of dress, music, dance, and so forth, to present a certain identity. Coming from the '60s, it is easy to draw on examples from my own past that they find quite amusing. I ask them to

consider why oppressed groups often strongly manifest these styliza-
tions in making their claim on a private reality that evades scrutiny
and understanding by those whose dream threatens to destroy their
own. Undergraduates, for whom identity construction is such a delicate and difficult matter, intuitively understand the pain of cultural
humiliation.

An even more valuable exercise is to consider their own exotic
selves from the outside. Here I use accounts of the first Japanese encounters of westerners emerging from their strange black ships as
hairy, Pinocchio-nosed, extremely tall, bat-winged, wide-eyed, un-
clean, smelly, crude, pushy, and obsessed with shiny stones. Slides of
the visual representation of westerners are also helpful. It is also useful to have them consider how truly exotic a religion it must be which
has ritual cannibalism at its center, and in which, whether magically
or symbolically, the adherents drink the blood of their God and eat
his body. Students often do not know what religion I speak of even
after this description. Furthermore, one can give them a feeling for
how strange it is, from the perspective of most cultural contexts, for
the central symbol to be an instrument of torture, sometimes with
the divine victim bloodily hanging from nails. The focus here is on
White Christians, particularly Protestants, as they are the ultimate
arbiters of reality in America. Students of other races and religions,
even Catholics, are far less in need of learning what it feels like to be
exotic or to have their worldview threatened.

Another useful experiment is to imagine reverse westernization.
Imagine Hillary Clinton and the entire White House staff in kimo-
nos. Imagine an America in which only those who are unable to fi-
nancially manage it fail to appear in traditional Japanese dress and
where some even seek plastic surgery to appear more Asian.

The difficulty of knowing the other can be taught by pointing out
to the students that, even should they stay in their university community, they will never be "townies." My own primary example is the
art of spitting. In the mountainous dairy country to which I am native, spitting has developed into a particularly nasty art that has held
on since the days of chewing tobacco. An old friend has been coming
from New York City to the Catskills for most of his life and despite

endless efforts, unlike the heroine in the movie *Titanic*, he will certainly die before he has mastered it. Beginning with everyday examples prepares the way for discussion of cases from the Western encounter with Asia. The early history of Christianity in Japan and the story of the Portuguese in Sri Lanka are excellent for this purpose. Letters, journals, and accounts of debates are especially effective.

It is important for students to know how little time it has been that a course such as they are taking has been possible and that it is quite likely that in fifty years our present understanding of Buddhism will be considered primitive. I also ask them to consider that it took hundreds of years of effort for the Chinese and Japanese to grasp Buddhism and what they eventually came up with was very much their own. Like those cultures before us, what crystallizes as Buddhism for us will not be something transported from afar, but something "in between."

If it is something in the middle that we know, something conditioned by our own ways of seeing and constructing, then it is crucial for us to evaluate the calibration of our own minds as instruments of observation, and to ask how it is that they have been thrown up into such a moment of consciousness that gives rise to our ways of questioning and knowing. If we should start by asking who we are, then the next step is to ask what characterizes the dominant American religious predispositions, to evaluate the dream against which, or within which, all other dreams must struggle for validation, not only nationally, but increasingly on a global level. In describing those predispositions, I hope for the students to have a sense of self-recognition and to prepare them to later recognize feedback loops in the presentation of Buddhism to the West.

I dramatize the development of Protestant sensibilities by describing Martin Luther as a German monk in a thunderstorm, some five hundred years ago, who felt the wrath of God thundering down on him. He was spiritually tormented by the fact that he could find no way to justify himself, and his personal crisis acted as the catalyst for an age in a way that still powerfully shapes the American experience. Luther had two main ideas. First, his idea of salvation through grace alone, rather than works, indicates that there is no way to make oneself more holy in the eyes of God. Protestant sensibilities tend to be anti-ritualistic and anti-ascetical to the extent that there may never be a true American monasticism. The second idea is that through the Holy Spirit anyone can receive the message of God from scripture. This gave an enormous impetus to individual literacy and creative thought and further to individualism and denominationalism. The centrality of scripture gave words primacy over images and the rational dominance over the mythological. Because it removes the need for any intermediary between oneself and the divine, except scripture, it is also anti-clerical and anti-hierarchical.

As Catholics warned, this led to an explosion of sects. Today there are thousands of them in America, many of them descended from groups who came to establish, not religious freedom, but their own brand of religious authoritarianism. Out of this incredible diversity, which eventually included all the world's religions, a reluctant pluralism developed. Pluralism required a number of adjustments that inform American religiosity. Americans generally de-emphasize doctrine. They tend to be iconoclastic and informal. They want substance, not form. They emphasize ethics. It is common to hear that it is not important what church you belong to, as long as you are a good person; this fits a basic pragmatism. So in addition to being White, male, Protestant, and heterosexual, the dominant American worldview could be described as rationalistic, pragmatic, self-reliant, individualistic, denominational, anti-formalistic, anti-ritualistic, iconoclastic, anti-hierarchical, and anti-ascetical. I do not mean to characterize America without reference to non-Protestant religions, but to point out the predispositions that dominate. It is no easy thing, for instance, to be a Catholic or Hindu in a nation whose dominant sensibility is represented by the bare white Protestant church. I realize that the conclusions and causality here regarding American sensibilities are endlessly debatable and that this is something that needs to be taught with special awareness to the make-up of each student body. However, the idea here is not to give a course in American religion, but to raise certain questions.

To illustrate the effects of not paying attention to who we are in the process of engaging Buddhism, I give the students examples of a hermeneutical feedback loop characterized as the "pizza effect." Although pizza has some old Italian antecedents, American pizza as we know it was largely a product of Italian-American cooking. However, pizza-loving American tourists, going to Italy in the millions, sought out authentic Italian pizza. Italians, responding to this demand, developed pizzerias to meet American expectations. Delighted with their discovery of "authentic" Italian pizza, Americans subsequently developed chains of "authentic" Italian brick-oven pizzerias. Hence, Americans met their own reflection in the other and were delighted.

I use several personal examples before moving to the Buddhism of Olcott, Dharmapāla and Rahula. I describe my own experience with physically rigorous yoga training in India, whose extreme rigor I regarded as a mark of authenticity, after which my teacher commented that Americans always want a workout. Another example was when a guide in India, pointing to a *liṅgam*, proclaimed to my students, who had just read Purāṇic accounts of Śiva's ejaculate forming sacred lakes, "No Hindu will say this is the penis of God." Where had this sensitivity come from and why was it important to say this to us? It is interesting for them to consider this moment as one in which the two parties, coming from two of humanity's most exquisite religious traditions, might view each other respectively as ritual cannibals and penis worshippers.

Colonel Olcott and Madame Blavatsky can be well characterized as the original Scully and Mulder of *The X-Files*: one a recognized government investigator and the other an occultist seeking the Celestial Masters. They came together to Sri Lanka in search of Buddhist wisdom. After hundreds of years of brutalization and humiliation by Western powers, Sri Lankan Buddhists were visited by the amazing spectacle of westerners paying homage to their religion. Their presence gave an aggressive edge to a budding Buddhist revival. Anagārika Dharmapāla, formerly David Hewivitarne, was their long time protégé and one of the first Buddhist missionaries to the West. Like most foreigners, he knew us and our world much better than we knew him, through missionary schools, study of Western literature, Blavatsky and Olcott, and the general effects of colonialism. Students should consider how many South Asians play cricket, speak

English, or watch Western movies and television. This is even more true today, when *Baywatch* is the most watched television program in the world.

At Chicago's World Parliament of Religions in 1893, Dharmapāla quoted Christian scripture in excellent English. He opened his address by citing Western scholars of religion, giving a whole summary of their attempts to understand Buddhism. He knows he has caught the Western religions under the shadow of the doubt of science, particularly in intellectual circles, and finds himself in a position to present to his arrogant listeners a tradition that does not suffer the same vulnerabilities. Suddenly Christians were the ones caught in a seemingly untenable theistic cosmology challenged by Darwin and the whole thrust of modern science. Under the influence of Olcott, who saw the present Buddhism of Sri Lanka with its rituals, monastic hierarchy, and supernatural beings as degenerate, he presented the original Buddha as a rational philosopher free from supernaturalistic beliefs and cosmology.

This vision of Buddhism came to be called "Protestant" Buddhism, often in contrast to "Catholic" Mahāyāna Buddhism which was characterized by its apparently contrary enthusiasm for images and ritual. It is certainly as valid a modern buddhological development as any other, but it is quite problematic from a historical critical viewpoint to identify it with the early tradition's memory of the Buddha. In a text with the title *What the Buddha Taught*, Walpola Rahula presented a Buddha who was rational, scientific, pragmatic, self-reliant, individualistic, and who disavowed ritual, hierarchy, priesthood, and gods. Hopefully, after listening to the previous discussion, the students are prepared to recognize this list of characteristics as one that might be tailor-made to fit the predispositions of Westerners disaffected with Abrahamic religions, regardless of whether it is an accurate depiction of the Buddha. Rahula's Buddha, as in Olcott's Buddhist Catechism, is above all a man like any other.

Again and again, over the many years I taught with this book as a Harvard teaching assistant, I saw the students' shock and dismay as we moved to the Mahāyāna and the sudden apparent corruption of Rahula's Buddhism with magic, ritual, heavens, hells, saviors and supernatural beings. This moment provides a beautiful teaching opportunity to show that the very origins of this dismay, their American predispositions, are also an important originating cause of the view of Buddhism presented to them by Rahula. In his foreword to the book, Paul Demiéville describes Rahula, after eight years in France, as "wearing the yellow robe, breathing the air of the occident, searching perhaps in our old troubled mirror [for] a universalized reflection of the religion which is his."[3] Surely then, before interpreting his message, we must consider that "old troubled mirror" in which Rahula considered and crafted his own reflection and lead our students to do the same.

Notes

[1] Pannikar 1978, 40.
[2] Cabezón 1998, 93.
[3] Rahula 1959, ix.

References

Cabezón, José. 1998. "Scholarship as Interreligious Dialogue." *Buddhist Christian Studies* 18.
Pannikar, Raimundo. 1978. *The Intra-Religious Dialogue*. New York: Paulist Press.
Rahula, Walpola. 1959. *What the Buddha Taught*. London: Gordon Fraser Gallery.

An End-run round Entities: Using Scientific Analogies to Teach Basic Buddhist Concepts

William S. Waldron

Students bring with them to the classroom assorted sets of assumptions, however implicit or inchoate they may be, about the world, about causal relations, about personal identity, linguistic reference, and so on. Since so many aspects of the early Buddhist view radically differ from commonly held assumptions, students are often perplexed in their initial encounter with Buddhist thought. This reaction is exacerbated, I think, by the standard presentation of the Buddhist catechism with its time-honored stock formulas—the Four Noble Truths, the Three Marks, and so forth. I have therefore tried to introduce key Buddhist perspectives without using Buddhist jargon. Instead, I have found it expedient to initially present Buddhist concepts in terms of current scientific explanations rather than in those inherited from, for example, traditional Western religion or philosophy. This paper will outline the purpose of using scientific analogies to present basic Buddhist concepts and briefly describe some practical procedures.

Purpose

Because so many of our persisting modes of thinking and expression are derived from substantialist Greek philosophy or from theistic religion, it is often difficult to extricate ourselves from terms of substance, essence, souls, and identity, and to find skillful ways to express the Buddhist worldview. There is a disjunction between the aims and assumptions of the Buddhist worldview and the means of expression most readily available to present and explain that world-view. In other words, our working vocabulary for discussing religion and philosophy is so imbued with substantialist assumptions that the vocabulary itself obstructs rather than edifies the very worldview we are attempting to explain. Hence, if we are to adequately convey the radically different perspective provided by the Buddhist worldview, we need a different vocabulary, a different set of categories based upon a different set of assumptions.

Fortunately, such terms, categories and assumptions are already available in some of the overlapping worldviews comprising our modern age, particularly in the general principles of various scientific disciplines. It is possible to exploit these pre-existing scientific notions of interdependent causality, drawn from a variety of fields and used in a variety of applications, as an effective means of breaking down the a priori assumptions students typically bring with them regarding the reality of entities, essences and active agents—the very assumptions that typically prevent students from understanding the Buddhist notions of interdependence and selflessness. Scientific analogies therefore provide explanations, a working vocabulary and a useful set of categories that are more commensurate with the Buddhist worldview than those derived from cultural traditions which are so irrevocably at odds with that worldview. By providing a bridge to Buddhist concepts that is based upon familiar conceptual frameworks and is couched in commonly understood terms and categories, scientific analogies can provide an "end-run" around the entities and essences assumed in traditional Western worldviews. (Needless to say, this process neither attempts any comprehensive comparison of Buddhist and scientific worldviews, nor aims to accrue the credibility of one field onto another; it is used strictly heuristically.)

Practice

Although quantum physics may be the most obvious area for analogies with Buddhist thinking—with the wave/particle nature analogized to the non-duality of Emptiness and Form perhaps the most famous—

nevertheless, I think the Indian Buddhist worldview is much better served by analogies derived from biology, as the vegetative metaphors and similes used in Buddhist texts would readily suggest: trunks and roots, seeds, fields and fruits, and so on. Hence, I have found it useful to initially engage in modes of inquiry that draw upon students' (my students at least) pervasive concern with environmentalism and basic understanding of biology, evolution and ecology.

Because my purpose is to use general scientific principles primarily as heuristic devices rather than to suggest potentially specious point-by-point analogues, I use a Socratic method of bringing out certain foreseeable conclusions through classroom participation. I begin by inquiring into the constitutive conditions of an inanimate object, usually a river, and then proceed with the same deconstructive method to animate objects, a tree, a frog and finally, to humans (severely straining the forbearance of those for whom this is their first chance to develop *anutpattika-dharma-kṣanti*).

Dependent Arising

I ask the students to describe as the constitutive conditions of a river: how it came to be, how it persists, and what exactly the term "river" refers to. Students generally enjoy demonstrating their environmental and ecological literacy (as, I suppose, do I) and we hastily make headway toward a variety of "Buddhistic" conclusions:

- That because the term "river" refers to the continuous flow of water bound by the river bed and riverbanks, and fed by tributaries that were themselves fed by rainfall that was in turn produced by evaporation from the oceans into which the rivers themselves ultimately fed (i.e., the widely understood "water cycle"), we readily reach the classic Buddhist position that the term "river" is merely a useful designation for a selected part of a complex set of processes that come about through a long history of interaction and that persist only as long as the conditions that enable it also persist (with the important corollary that the processes that brought about the river were themselves products of complex conditions).

- That because it was the flow of the water itself through gravity and friction (i.e., erosion) that initially carved out the river bed that thereafter directed the subsequent flow of water, which in turn carved out a deeper bed, and so on, it is easily understood that the river current and the river bed mutually shaped and influenced each other, building upon the formations carved out by their own previous interaction; from this, the notion that structures or patterns arise through a history of interaction of distinct yet inseparable processes is clearly and almost viscerally understood.
- That because our understanding of the persisting interaction of gravity, friction, the water cycle, and so forth, is sufficient to account for the origins of the river without reference to any controlling or directing force external to the relations between these nor inherent within any single factor among them, we readily come to the conclusion that it is nonsensical (given a naturalistic frame of reference) to ask the question: "Who made the river?" This point is so obvious, students usually laugh when I ask it.

It takes but a few minutes to extend this line of questioning to plant life, using a tree as an example. This complicates the process considerably of course, because of the necessary antecedent condition of seeds, the metabolic processes of organic growth and development, the complex chemical processes of photosynthesis, and so on. This line of inquiry necessarily engages evolution as well. But the complexity here strengthens rather than weakens the aforementioned conclusions, especially the point that the patterns of natural phenomena come about without any external or internal agent or force. So we have now painlessly reached, through biology alone, three strong points indispensable to the Buddhist worldview, all without referring to anything outside of the student's previous range of knowledge:

1. That complex processes come about through long histories of interaction and persist only as long as the conditions that enable them also persist.

2. That interaction and mutually reinforcing feedback mechanisms create and build upon structures that are fabricated by their own previous interaction (more on this below).

3. That natural phenomena come about without any external creator, nor by means of any internal agent or force. Who *makes* the cells photosynthesize? Who *makes* cells reproduce, absorb and process nutriments, et cetera? In fact, who *grows* the tree? Does it *grow* itself, as an active agent? If so, which exact part of it grows itself?

Their now pleasantly puzzled faces indicate that they find these questions predictably absurd and silly. They have reached that quintessentially Buddhist sentiment expressed in the *Zenrin kushū*: "the grass grows by itself."

This exercise skillfully sidesteps the implicit and widespread assumption that entities are fixed "things" somehow isolated from their surrounding environment, knowable without reference to their own developmental histories, and singular or unitary despite any internal differentiation. By simply avoiding such assumptions, scientific analogies are actually *more* useful that traditional (i.e., cultural) language in conveying the sense of many Buddhist concepts—for the very reason that they break down, rather than reinforce, the sense of the world as comprised of isolated entities bumping up against each other in billiard ball Newtonian universes. That "things" arise conditioned by their systemic relations with a complex of other factors is an underlying assumption of virtually every modern scientific discipline, and the students implicitly know this. We are already firmly in the groundless realm of dependent arising.

Designation

The concept of "designation" was also alluded to in the above passages, for in the analysis of a river or tree students readily understood that these terms focused on only certain parts of a much larger complex of related processes, a focus that is somewhat arbitrary depending upon one's interests. A tree can be but an insignificant part of a forest to an ecologist, a total environment to an entomologist, a natural resource to a businessman, or a source of inspiration to a mystic or poet.

This point then can be extrapolated from the designation of objects to a critique of theoretical discourses by asking a simple question. Which discipline is the really correct way of understanding human life: anthropology, psychology, sociology, biology, religion? This will be greeted with a laugh and a shrug, so commonsensical is the Mahāyāna idea of conventional truth, that technical discourses are skillful means designed to meet specific, contingent needs. The acknowledgment that each field has its own models that might not map onto one another undermines claims to an exclusively valid discourse and hence relativizes discursive thinking altogether, a point that Nāgārjuna would find congenial, I think. How one cuts up the pie, then, is determined by a collective agreement based upon the specific pragmatic purposes it is designed to serve, not by some incorrigible correspondence with Reality. Again, I have found the scientific analogies for this critique of linguistic reference far more accessible to students than similar formulations found in traditional Western thinking. At the very least, they serve as an efficient way to prime them for deeper reflections.

Non-self

We are all familiar with the difference between technical scientific discourses and the well-nigh necessity of speaking colloquially in terms of entities, essences, egos and agency. We anthropomorphize weather and so-called "computer memory"; we use allegories, similes, synecdoches, to express complex patterns of interaction that are otherwise difficult to grasp. There is thus a radical disjunction between most scientific explanations based on complex multicausality and our everyday language which either refers to or implies the existence of entities and agents. This disjunction is brought out most clearly by extending the kind of deconstructive analysis previously applied to rivers and trees even closer to home—to us.

Extrapolating from the analysis of trees and their seeds, we now analyze how animals with rudimentary nervous systems, like frogs, came to be and to "do." Like the river and the tree, animals are also the result of countless transformations that were, in each and every step, built upon structures already created by their own previous developmental history. The mutually reinforcing feedback mechanisms called evolution (again, assuming a naturalistic worldview) operates without any external creator or internal, directing force. Once again we may ask, who *grew* the frog? Does it actively *grow* itself? But these questions are similarly ill-formed.

Even the frog's behavior, such as abruptly capturing a fly with its sticky tongue, can be understood as a natural and "automatic" functioning of its primitive nervous system, whose structures and capacities came about through complex evolutionary developments, and which operates, like the metabolic processes of photosynthesis, without the need for any central controlling agent. Who, after all, *makes* the neuron respond the way that it does? If the chemical processes in plants operate "by themselves," then so do neurons in the nervous systems, which engage only the stimuli they have evolved to engage. There is no need to impute higher cortical functions of conscious intention to each and every cell, nor, perhaps, to anything at this stage of life. Like the river, the tree, and its individual neurons, can't the frog's simple activities also be thought to "just happen"? Assenting students have unwittingly crossed a conceptual Rubicon.

We are now but a short step from some cold, slimy frog, whose nervous system "functions by itself" without any central controlling agency, to our warm cuddly neonate whose potentially complex nervous system is still too undeveloped to speak unequivocally of agency or intention: when a baby is hungry it cries, when it is happy it coos. The language of agency, identity or intentionality is still premature. In the growth and maturation from the neonate to an adult, however, a personality, a personal identity, is forged through the complex and countless interactions between nervous system, environment, experience, memory, and so forth. But we must analyze the construction of personality in the same fashion as before. Who made the personality? Who is in charge of its growth? Who, in short, made us who we are?

Propelled by the inertia of the previous analyses of the river, the tree and the frog, we are forced to conclude that the personality is the end result of the development of neural and cognitive structures created through previous actions and experiences, an endless interaction between one's internal, physical and social worlds, all of which came about without an external or internal controlling agent. So *who* experiences moment to moment? *Who* desires, gets hungry, passes water, and so on? Like the Zen grass, like the river, the tree, the frog's nervous system, whatever we "are" came about, matured and continues to operate "by itself."

We have no *explanatory* need for an internal director in charge of it all, a hidden puppet master pulling all the strings, in order to account for either the genesis of personality or the moment-to-moment processes of body and mind. A naturalistic account of who we are requires no real "we" behind it all, only a conventional designation. Whatever the sense of self may be or refer to, it clearly seems added on to the basic metabolic and cognitive processes of human life, and its adventitious nature is painfully but inescapably demonstrated.

Students' smiles give way to gasps of inchoate objection as they viscerally register the implications of this basic Buddhist perspective. We know that they have come to understand the concept of attachment to self by that fact that they react to this last round of deconstructive analysis, demonstrating the basic Buddhist idea of non-self, not with the elation elicited at the outset but with despair at the dénouement.

Once contextualized in this fashion, the presumed primacy of narrative agents, of beings in charge of their own story, is irredeemably challenged; it loses its status as self-evident truth. Narrative agents may now be seen as products of a kind of myth-making, with no myth claiming as strong a hold on our imagination as that of a self within, our homunculus watching the movie at home. Some judicious reference to the congruent conclusions of cognitive scientists at this point may stir the pot even more.

This short exercise in scientific analysis and analogy has altogether bypassed the detours of essentialist and substantialist thinking and taken students to the threshold of Buddhist thought. Where you go from there is up to you.

Skillful Means

Engaging Buddhism: Creative Tasks and Student Participation

Joanne Wotypka

I come to you with a story—a tale of woe and a tale of joy. Picture it: a chemistry lecture theater, Edmonton, 1998. Before me were eighty-plus people in various states of attentiveness, ranging from total unconsciousness to caffeine-induced hyperactivity. The class: "Introduction to Buddhism," or as one colleague has chosen to name it, "Mission Impossible."

Impossible, you ask?

Well, let me tell you.

In this group of eighty-seven people (75 percent female), there were representatives of almost every discipline offered at the University of Alberta, except Religious Studies. Only one major in this area, no minors, and 95 percent of the class had taken no other courses in which Buddhism was discussed. They all, however (with two or three exceptions), had seen either *Kundun* or *Seven Years in Tibet* (or both), and stated that they were all taking the class strictly out of interest.

The truth, however, could not be suppressed for long.

On the index cards filled out by each student were names, majors/minors, e-mail addresses, and the usual bureaucratic information. These cards also revealed that approximately 90 percent of the students were in the class to fulfill their Arts Option, and "Witchcraft and the Occult" was full. Both these courses have the reputation of being easy, as evidenced by one brave soul who indicated on his card that he was taking this Buddhism class for the purpose of raising his GPA.

None of this was unexpected, so I decided to experiment. How could such a group get interested in the subject of Buddhism, and not just in their grade? How could I get them to actively participate? I racked my brains, and soon my own dubious past offered an idea.

During the previous year I had sat in on a class on Classical Japanese Poetry, taught by Professor Sonja Arntzen of East Asian Studies. Before my classmates and I knew what was happening, she had us writing poetry and staging our own poetry contests. We were terrified at first, but soon discovered that we were poets! Oh, how we learned, and oh, how I remembered.

So what if I had my class write a haiku on a Buddhist concept? A nice idea, but not enough to justify a participation mark. What else could I have them do? After much brainstorming with myself, the Creative Tasks were born.

On that first day of class, as the syllabus was handed out, the students noticed something different. Along with the usual information about papers and essays was a small entry:

Creative Tasks (5 at 2%=10%): Five tasks of a low-stress and creative variety. They will be marked on participation, not artistic merit. This isn't figure skating.

I did not give them the exact tasks at this point, but explained that they would relate to what they were learning about in class, and stressed that handing *anything* in would get them their 2 percent. As one of my favorite TV characters would say, "if you can make a mark on a piece of paper, you're my kind of people."

Their reaction? The various states of attentiveness galvanized into a single state of near panic. They weren't creative, they argued, they were university students. After many assurances on my part that there would be no part marks, and the only way they could lose marks was to not hand in anything, I sent them on their way. To my surprise, everyone showed up the next day, looking somewhat grim, but determined.

After a week, I decided to reveal what the tasks were. More panic ensued. I assured them that they could do them in any order, do them all at once or separately, and hand them in whenever they liked, as long as the were in to me on or before the last day of classes. In short, the students had 10 percent of their mark completely in their own hands, and none of them liked it. Over the next four months, each of them had to complete the following tasks:

1. Pick a contemporary figure who might be the future Buddha, and tell his/her life story, using the life stories of Gautama in our texts as examples.
2. Pick any person (as long as he/she is not in this class), and attempt to explain the concept of emptiness to them. Report on your success or lack of success.
3. Pick any forty-eight consecutive hours during the term, and live them according to the Five Precepts of the Buddhist laity.
4. Write a haiku about a Buddhist concept (e.g., *nirvāṇa*, ego, no-self).
5. Identify a problem in contemporary society, and create a Bodhisattva to be appealed to for guidance. Draw a picture of this being.

Happily, once the initial shock wore off, and the course was a few weeks in, most students settled down and began to enjoy the dreaded tasks. Many questions were voiced in class as to the interpretation of the tasks, but I gave them free rein to do whatever they wanted. Could a cartoon character be the future Buddha? Of course! Could a collage substitute for a drawing? Marvelous! I assured them that I would happily mark whatever they handed in. The result was an unexpected deluge of creativity.

Creative Task #1: The Future Buddha

We had read many versions of the life of Gautama Buddha, so I directed the students to pick a contemporary figure and have that person go through the steps of renunciation. During the term we had the Grinch Who Stole Christmas practicing the obscure austerity of climbing up and down all the chimneys in Whoville on a single night, as well as Ronald McDonald getting the better of Grimace, the Guru with the Purple Tinge. What we didn't have were duplicates. Out of the entire class, no two students selected the same figure. President Clinton and his family (including First Cat Socks) were represented, plus all the Simpsons, Jimi Hendrix, Garfield, Princess Diana, Papa Smurf, fitness guru Susan Powter, Pope John Paul II, and many more.

The modern world presented problems for these figures that Gautama Buddha certainly didn't have to deal with: Homer Simpson found himself pursued for child support, and the daughters of Māra were embodied in the paparazzi who pursued Princess Diana. The background of the students also played a role—a rural student had Mr. Potato Head renounce the world, while a Political Science major gave the nod to Boris Yeltsin.

Some students wrote one page, some wrote five to ten pages, and one student even submitted a comic strip of her Buddha-to-be. This task led to an interesting discussion about cults, gurus, and what would happen if the future Buddha *did* manifest him/herself in today's society.

Creative Task #2: Explaining Emptiness

This was a rather worrisome task for the students, for even after several classes of discussion on this topic, none felt confident enough to explain the concept to anyone. Perfect! I cried, so go try it and see what happens!

Oh, the interesting conversations that were had. The most common victims were mothers, and usually at the breakfast table. The next most popular were significant others and friends, usually with alcohol involved to some extent. Also represented were passengers on public transportation, cab drivers, and in one memorable case, door-to-door religious people. One student, a Chinese Buddhist exchange student, was being frequently visited by the Jehovah's Witnesses, and decided to invite them in and attempt to explain emptiness to them. As the student diplomatically put it, they all eventually agreed to disagree.

Most students felt that they had failed to adequately explain the concept, but admitted that having to try forced them to explain it to themselves as well. They were forced to think and reason and be articulate when faced with the task of relaying information to another person. The other person was also welcome to report on this task as well: one mother questioned the value of her daughter's post-secondary education, and a cab driver was uneasy that the fare, being empty, would not be paid. As an unlooked-for bonus, many students encountered friends and total strangers who knew quite a lot about Buddhism.

Creative Task #3: Living the Precepts

This was by far the favorite task, after the Precepts had been explained. They had to refrain from harming other living beings, lying, stealing, committing sexual misconduct, and taking intoxicants. A lively discussion was held as to what exactly these things meant. Was coffee an intoxicant? Did they all have to become vegetarians? What was considered "sexual misconduct"? In the case of the latter, I told them that this wasn't *Penthouse Letters*, and they could keep the details to themselves.

I informed the class that it would be up to them to interpret the Precepts, and then monitor their behavior accordingly. I warned them that depending on what interpretations they chose, and which forty-eight hours were selected, this task could be very simple, or very challenging. A few students chose a time when they were studying for exams, but most chose a weekend, which for a student and temporary Buddhist layperson, is a time fraught with danger.

Having to do this task forced the students to choose an interpretation and live every moment of the forty-eight hours in awareness of what they had decided, and in the results of their actions. Sometimes rationalizations were given: one student reported that she was still drinking coffee (an intoxicant) in order to avoid breaking the First Precept by harming another living being. Another student admitted to lying when his girlfriend asked if he liked her new shirt, in order to prevent *his* living being from becoming harmed.

Two hardy souls decided to try living by all Ten Precepts, which required a lot of creative interpretation on their part (credit cards aren't money, right?). Unfortunately, both were undone by one night of sleeping on the floor. High and luxurious beds strike again!

Most students kept a diary of their forty-eight hours, and some were exceptionally detailed. Most students were shocked at how "un-Buddhist" their lives were, and the Precepts got them thinking about many issues: vegetarianism, celibacy, the merits of absolute truth-telling, and so on. One student experienced a moral crisis over having to feed live crickets to her pet lizard. Which suffering was greater, that of the crickets or that of the lizard? Should she have a pet that required live food? Should she have a pet? The solution, I recall, was to release the crickets in the cage and let nature take its course.

Creative Task #4: Haiku Very Much

The thought of writing poetry did not sit well with the class, especially with those members who considered it to be a less-than-masculine pursuit. To encourage them, I gave them a few examples of haikus that I had written for Professor Arntzen's class, and I explained the basic form to them. Reassured with a syllable count which supposedly made the task less creative and more mechanical, they began. Given their reluctance, I did not expect the same enthusiastic response that the Precepts were given, but I was wrong. Many students turned in more than one haiku, and many were superb: "Emptiness is relative / Coke without a label / is only pop;" "writing a great paper / can of coke spills on keyboard / the file disappears;" and the Gameboy Tetris Haiku "placing blocks in rows / random pieces meet / shapes and lines vanish—empty".

Aside from revealing that the students were drinking too many carbonated beverages, this task helped them focus on a concept and relate it to an image that was meaningful to them. As might be expected from university students, suffering and emptiness were the two most popular subjects, but a number of them also produced inventive haikus relating the recycling industry to rebirth. Most importantly, this task showed them that poetry wasn't that scary after all.

Creative Task #5: Modern Bodhisattvas

After talking about manifestations of popular Buddhism, and debating whether or not Buddha and the Bodhisattvas were being worshipped, I gave the students a chance to develop a Bodhisattva figure in response to a modern problem. My goal was simply to get them to draw something, but many in the class were taken by the colorful pictures of Avalokiteśvara, Mañjuśrī, and others that were passed around. Instead of merely producing a simple picture (stick figures would do nicely—after all, they had seen me draw), many students got in touch with their inner child/artist in a big way.

I received a collage depicting Caribini, the Bodhisattva of Tropical Vacations (see Appendix A). This being aids those suffering from long, dreary work-weeks, giving them an opportunity to relax and meditate. His portly stature reveals that one should not obsess about body image when confronted with a bathing suit. Another submission was the Bodhisattva of Bureaucracy, a fine example of the stick-figure bodhisattva, who offers guidance and solace for those left on hold for hours (see Appendix B). Anyone abandoned for more than eight hours will be granted admittance to his Pure Land, where phones, faxes and forms are forbidden. Those people responsible for the bureaucracy will be destined for the most horrible of rebirths. Also submitted was a wonderful color drawing of Pamprin, the Bodhisattva of Water Retention (see Appendix C). As the class was largely female, most could relate to a being who could relieve monthly suffering.

I received submissions in the form of paintings, computer cut-and-paste, a macaroni picture, and a play-dough tableau that was duly admired and then returned to the student's three-year-old for a new rebirth. For the most part, the students enjoyed the opportunity to be artistic with no fear of being judged, and many undiscovered talents were revealed.

Conclusion

At the end of the day, what did these tasks reveal? At least two things: (1) Even students who hated the rest of the course stated (in their course evaluations) that they learned a lot from the tasks, as they helped make strange concepts more familiar and meaningful to them. A few grudgingly admitted that they were also forced to complete their assigned readings in order to complete the tasks. (2) University students are starved for creative assignments. Almost all the students stated that they hadn't done any creative writing or artwork since Junior High, or even Elementary school. The tasks showed them that they were and could be creative, and that there was no hidden art critic within them waiting to savage their efforts.

There were many pros and cons to the Creative Tasks. The pros were a joy: the students were interested in the assignments, doing the readings, and were very appreciative of having part of their mark entirely under their own control. From my perspective, the tasks were wonderful to "mark," as all I had to do was enjoy them; it made the marking of eighty-seven final research papers less tedious.

The cons were more troubling. The most obvious question is whether they were actually learning anything about Buddhism, or were the tasks simply "fluff"? Could that 10 percent have been better spent somewhere else? The ultimate value of the exercise was hard to judge. As expected, a few students put in a token effort and probably got little of value in return. Most, however, seemed to learn from the tasks, and put in an amount of effort that often surprised me. This brought up the concern that they were spending too much time on the tasks. Were they neglecting the other 90 percent of their mark in order to concentrate on the 10 percent?

I don't know.

What I hope is that they learned something, and that they had a bit of fun while doing it. My desire is that they not only retain an interest in and a respect for Buddhism, but that they nourish this little flame of creativity and carry it with them into other courses and into their lives, and no longer believe that they can't or shouldn't be creative.[1]

Appendix A: Caribini, the Bodhisattva of Tropical Vacations

Appendix B: The Bodhisattva of Bureaucracy

Appendix C: Pamprin, the Bodhisattva of Water Retention

THE GODDESS PAMPRIN : THE BODHISATTVA OF
WATER RETENTION. NOTE THE SWOLLEN JOINTS, BELLY, AND
BOOBS. THIS BENEVOLENT BODHISATTVA BRINGS CHOCOLATE AND TAMPON

Notes

[1] My thanks to all the members of the University of Alberta's Religion 240 "Introduction to Buddhism" (Sept.–Dec. 1998) for their enthusiasm, and for their generous contribution of tasks for this paper. Thanks also to Professor Sonja Arntzen, who started this whole business in the first place.

The Peripatetic Class: Buddhist Traditions and Myths of Pedagogy

E. H. Rick Jarow

This paper has its roots in a classroom incident that took place during an introductory course on Buddhist Traditions. I had been working through a standard introductory curriculum: the life of the Buddha, the Four Noble Truths, the twelve-fold chain of interdependent origination, and so forth, when after class, a student from Thailand came to me in tears. She had a Buddha-image around her neck, a talisman that she had been wearing since childhood, and she could not reconcile the god "Buddha" she grew up with, with the "Buddhism" being taught in "Religion 152."

This incident typifies one aspect of a greater issue; that of "disembodied pedagogy." It is not that our information is wrong, or that our intentions are pernicious in any way; it is just that most of the scholastic traditions inherited from Descartes, and from humanistic disciplines trying to prove themselves by aping the natural sciences, do not favor embodiment. Mind is to be developed and sharpened, a reasonably healthy body is needed to carry the mind on its way, but the two shall rarely if ever meet. Schools known for their athletic departments are generally not the same ones known for their English or Religion departments. Students learn about religious traditions in ways that favor detached observation over engagement, textual study over fieldwork and practicum, universals over particulars, and sitting over movement, to name but a few areas of body/mind separation. These areas are amplified by a tradition of academic study in religion that must uphold non-engagement as a prerequisite for serious scholarship.

This may have much to do with the subject itself; with the fact that religious fervor has more often than not been characterized as the antithesis of reasonableness and critical acumen (and not without good reason at times). Nevertheless, when the pendulum swings full-blown in the direction of disembodied objectivity, entire areas of religious experience are rendered invisible or insignificant. The subject (i.e., the Buddha) tends to be gazed upon, with the researcher taking on the role of an educated tourist, camera in hand, going into a temple. Those of us who have actually gone to temples know that such an approach is considered to be fundamentally rude at best, and is not at all appreciated by people who live and worship in particular sacral environments. But, in most contemporary institutions of higher learning, there is an "experiential line" between practice and study that is considered dangerous to cross.

The teaching of Buddhist traditions may itself be inherently problematic in this regard: after all, the historical Buddha is said to have balked at the idea of teaching. How do you teach what lies beyond all conditions? Buddhist teaching traditions came up with many ingenious solutions to this question, many of them revolving around the concept of *upāya* or "skillful means" adapted to particular circumstances. But academics are not partisans, and indeed teaching from a partisan position is not critically responsible. Ronald Grimes and his associates at the Ritual Studies Laboratory identified the partisan position as "whoring" of an academic discourse in service of ideology and thus suspicious of both criticism and dialogue. To counter this, we are cautioned to avoid the pitfall of evaluating the truth-claims of various religious traditions. We feel secure with an extrinsic approach to our subject: one can discuss the history of the Buddhist tradition, its various doctrines, central ideas, and practices.

But does this position lead to a full engagement with the subject of study? Does it help one understand what it may mean to practice or believe? It certainly can help, but it can also move over into Grimes's other category of avoidance; the posture of the impartial observer, said to be one of "voyeurism," the non-involved gaze that may theorize without risk of contact. What I am wondering about here are strategies of pedagogy that can negotiate through these polar positions and provide us with possibilities of a more comprehensive engagement with the subjects of our study.

Discussions of pedagogy in the college classroom generally focus on content and on various methods of presenting content. As long as we remain uniquely in this paradigm, however, the unbridgeable gulf between objectivity and engagement may also remain with us. Content-focus, as the all-in-all of an instructional scenario, only touches certain aspects of experience, usually verbal/analytic ones. This is particularly problematic in the teaching of Buddhist traditions, since so much of the "material" is dependent upon psycho-physical awareness: how one sits, breathes, and moves. Is there any possibility of introducing more embodied dimensions into the classroom experience that do not cross the lines of intellectual integrity?

The resonant issues run widely here: not just in terms of academic versus popular culture or objectivity versus engagement, but with regard to questions about the functions of scholarship, pedagogy, and liberal education itself. What do we in the "humanities" do when we teach? Do we engage in a pure intellectual enterprise free from other repercussions? Do we "make knowledge," the oxymoron that emphasizes the social assumptions underlying "pure research"? Do we inspire one another to experience life in a more profound and meaningful way? Another way to express the depth of this issue is to simply ask, Who do we serve? Frank Reynolds invokes "democracy" in his discussion of the current state of Buddhist studies; Monier-Williams, the British scholar who compiled the massive Sanskrit-English dictionary found on the desk of every graduate student who studies Indian religions, invoked the Queen of England and her glorious mission of converting heathen peoples.

On one level, there are our conscious intentions in teaching Buddhist traditions: to inform, compare, inculcate critical thought, and so forth. For the question, Who does one serve? presupposes people, institutions, and powers, to whom we direct our research and pedagogical agendas. On another level, however, there may be an entire slew of less than conscious presuppositions that inform our teaching methods. I am referring specifically to the deep myths, the underlying archetypal constructs that inform the scholastic endeavor.

Myths and legends, of course, are rarely invoked when considering pedagogical discourse, even in the so-called humanities. Perhaps this is because recent theoretical practice is dedicated to "demythologizing." For many have suffered from skewed applications of myths, be they ones of "manifest destiny" or "a thousand years of glorious rule." And yet, incidents such as the one that occurred in my classroom, in which a person's own myth is shattered by the unbridgeable gulf between historical scholarly discourse and human experience, leads one to ask what constructs animate our practice, not only socially but psychologically? This is where I would like to focus our attention. Let us ask, Who are the forces now being served in the academy? How do they mesh with the academic study and teaching of religion? And where, in particular, might the study and teaching of Buddhist traditions fit into the mix?

A Head without a Body

The archetype of "the thinker" (versus "Man thinking," as Emerson articulated it in his essay, "The American Scholar") presupposes the primacy of content, information, and analysis. The body is a secondary inconvenience that needs to be ensconced in a row of chairs. In a classroom of rows, there is literally no interfacing, and there is an implicit architectonic hierarchy as students sit facing an all-knowing teacher/text. Moreover, the repeated goal of methodological "rigor" (derived from the natural sciences) tends to minimize anecdotal evidence as well as the suggestive power of myth and metaphor. "Rigor" translates into "hard evidence"—the "male-hardness" of rigorous data; true potency found in technological application and theoretical standardization—whereas the impotent softness of anecdote, suggestion, and non-conclusive multiplicity produces no exterior technology. We encourage hard-headed thinking, a bodiless vision of Buddhism (the "ism" already tips one off to this) that tends to devalue embodied forms of religious life: ritual, meditation, social interaction, and non-liturgical lifestyle.

The Individual and Social Body

Another assumption that underlies much contemporary study and pedagogy is that of the primacy of the individual. The lone quest of the Buddha, for example, is given much more attention and glory than the intricacies of the *sangha*. And even discussions of the *sangha* are often undertaken under the assumption of a separated "individual monastic tradition," as if it arose in a vacuum. The society that produced and supported monastic ways of living is often given passing mention at best. We learn and teach that Buddhism grew out of India, but the process of that growth, the way in which Buddhist practitioners managed to feed, clothe, and shelter themselves, is relatively unexplored.

In a similar vein, the writing and study of texts is often thought of as an individual enterprise. Much of the literature that is taught in classes on Buddhist traditions, for example, is discussed as an individual achievement, when they were in fact produced, and are still largely transmitted, through communities. But the communal process is rarely given its due. Pedagogy that fosters the constructs of individual ego-boundaries and uniquely personal processes would be considered to be a "patriarchal phenomenon" by feminist critics, and—no matter what terminology you prefer to use—the construct of the "individual" does seem to be deeply set in the prevailing demeanor of research and pedagogy. How ironic in face of a tradition that eschews the idea of a separate self. Whole areas of possibility are lost in this scenario, and one can only wonder how this particular bias has swayed our visions of Buddhist traditions.

Modalities of Intelligence and Learning

The construct of the classroom is taken for granted, usually thought of as a given. So-called "innovative" ways of teaching often turn to media—slides, movies, or computers—without challenging the underlying configurations present in pedagogical situations. All well and good innovations perhaps, but all in forgetfulness of a tradition that was born outside of a classroom, that lived and breathed in a natural environment. The Buddha, it is said, answered the final challenge of

Māra by tapping the ground, but we teach with literally no ground, no reference to the natural world. The Cartesian figure seated alone, heroically isolated in a self-created thought experiment, is only one of many possible learning modalities. Is thinking the only human function worthy of academic discourse? And is the thinking function the natural, detached province of the academy, or does it serve other agendas such as the economic interests of technological productivity?

These are greater questions than cannot be addressed here, although addressed they should be. For present purposes, I want to briefly invoke Howard Gardner's work at the Harvard School of Education on multiple intelligences. For the last twenty years, Gardner and his colleagues have been arguing that a comprehensive education needs to acknowledge a broad spectrum of intelligence: verbal/linguistic, mathematical/logical, spatial, kinesthetic, musical, and interpersonal, to name but a few. To date, humanistic education (and hence the way Buddhist traditions are studied and taught) focuses almost overwhelmingly on the verbal and mathematical modes. One can only imagine the rich veins that would be discovered through the employment of intuitive methods to learn about meditation, spatial viewpoints to learn about *maṇḍalas*, musical awareness to enter more deeply into the practice of chanting, and interpersonal perspectives to further explore the Buddhist ideal of compassion. From the Buddha to Mozart to Einstein and on down, significant research is inspired by something beyond one's known boundaries, and this sense is shared by the humanist, artist, and scientist. To entertain new modalities of knowing is to accept a greater sense of one's personhood, to be able to relate more freely, that is less fixedly, with the rhetoric of one's discipline and its attendant archetypal forces. The Buddha worn around the neck may not mirror the discourse of the historical Buddha, but it may provide its own perspective, its own sustenance, and a grace that needs to be listened to.

The Peripatetic Possibility

In response to the above situations, I configured a series of pedagogical experiments here referred to as the "peripatetic possibility." In doing so, I was inspired by the likes of Aristotle, Gandhi, and, the historical Buddha: for it is said that Aristotle walked with his students, that Gandhi walked five miles a day, and that, after achieving his enlightenment sitting under the Bodhi tree, the Buddha walked (hence the mythological origin for *kinhin* or "walking meditation"). I was also moved by the story of a doctor acquaintance of mine, who was asked by the residents of an Native American reservation "Can you dance?" meaning "Why should I accept your medicine if you are unable to dance for five days without food like our medicine people?" The doctor, wisely, did not try to dance in such a manner, but he did take the challenge seriously, and perhaps so should we in our encounters with "the other."

Thus, I began the "peripatetic experiments" that I have performed in the classroom over the last two years; focusing not just on content but on the architectonics of pedagogy. These particular classes were held out of doors, in a moving, fluid environment. Students were asked to pay attention to what they heard and felt as well as to what they saw. Interestingly enough, we found that the walking class complemented the text-based classroom, with embodied experiences becoming automatic mnemonic devices that brought home a number of concepts that had previously been difficult to grasp. The following description details parts of our "classroom-stroll" through the Vassar College campus, and ways in which we engaged the terrain and the environment to deepen our understanding and experience of Buddhist traditions.

We begin our journey by walking through the Vassar farm, and immediately the issue of violence/non-violence comes to the fore. How would a Buddhist feel about stepping on ants, about the inevitable loss of life that occurs in the agricultural endeavor (this thread often leads to a discussion of the Jain tradition whose growth was somewhat concurrent with the Buddhist *sangha*, and how they handled the issue of harming other living beings). The farm is a perfect backdrop for the story of the historical Buddha cautioning a farmer not to plow up a snake, and subsequent reports that the Nāga or serpentine-kingdom favored the Buddha from that moment on. The entire issue of Buddhism and environmentalism rises to the surface:

what was the relationship to nature in the time of the Buddha? Does Buddhism, with its views of interdependency, lend itself to an environmental ethic, or are we transposing our own concerns onto the past? Finally, the "truth of impermanence" is brought to our attention with the Buddhist parable of the mustard seed: the Buddha asking a woman, who complained about the death of her child, to collect a mustard seed from every house that had not experienced death.

We pass the stream-fed lake on campus and discuss the example of "the frog in the well" that we recently heard and saw in a film featuring monks from Sri Lanka. Just as the frog in the well cannot begin to imagine the boundaries of the ocean, so too the conditioned being cannot begin to conceptualize the unconditioned state of *nirvāṇa*. The caterpillar, moving from leaf to leaf, becomes a model for transmigration, with the metamorphosis from caterpillar to butterfly engendering a discussion of "who transmigrates from body to body" in Buddhist thinking. The rushing stream next to the pond brings the class's attention to issues of temporality and the insubstantiality of a separate self. Where does the stream begin and the lake end? Was Heraclitus a Buddhist of sorts?

In Spring, we are given the *darśan* of the cherry trees on Vassar's front lawn, whose blossoms open under the clear sky. Instead of just discussing the Japanese aesthetic of beauty in the face of death, and its transformation into various forms of Buddhist understanding and practice, we see it embodied before us. Moreover, we see it as we are walking, not sitting. Students speak to each other. The teacher and the text pale before the panorama of nature. There is no need to sit, study, and memorize concepts here; for they are being coded into the body.

Later on, we pass Vassar's rather large and imposing chapel. High up on the face of the stone chapel is a circular rose stained-glass window. Could this be considered a *maṇḍala*? Are *maṇḍalas* universal as Jung contended or are they culturally relative constructs? How does the twelve-petaled circular window of the Vassar chapel compare with the *kālacakra* visualization that we recently studied?

The library, the next large building on our walk, becomes a jumping off point to discuss canonicity and the translation of Buddhist texts, particularly in China. What determines the authoritative texts of a tradition? How was the Pāli Canon transmitted? Who decides what volumes are to be reproduced, published, and included in the various collections of works that an "educated person" should read? Who paid for the recent renovation of the library? Could the Bodhisattva appear as a librarian, as a builder of buildings? If the Bodhisattva would come to campus now, what form might she take according to the application of skillful means?

As we pass the Junior Year Abroad Office, the discussion deepens. Is the Zen practiced by the Vassar Zen group congruent with Zen Buddhism practiced in Japan? Is the entire college set-up correspondent with an ancient monastery in any way? This thread often opens into a discussion of how Buddhist traditions adapted to whatever environment they found themselves in. We pass the Baldwin Medical Center and note the metaphor of the Buddha as physician. And we end our walk by the Main Building on campus, where the name of Matthew Vassar is inscribed, leading to a discussion of the "Founder" of the college, his "original intentions" and what the college has now become, all in terms of the Mahāyāna *trikāya* theory (the teaching as the *Dharma-kāya*, the construct of the campus as the *saṃbhoga-kāya*, and the historical founder as the *nirmāṇa-kāya*). Finally, after taking this long walk through campus, students are asked if they were aware of their feet touching the ground during the walk (mindfulness), what they noticed, and if walking through the campus in this way changed habitual experiences of the terrain.

These "experiments" were clearly effective, with the great majority of students expressing appreciation for the experiential component of the course, and even amazement at the way that the teachings seemed to come alive in a new light. Some offered suggestions for further peripatetic possibilities in the future, others discussed their initial resistances to a different kind of class and how they worked through them. At the end of the semester, this class was frequently mentioned in teaching evaluations as the "clincher" that led to a deepened engagement with Buddhist traditions and with the entire learning process itself.

Now all of this is admittedly problematic in an age in which the disembodiment of the learning experience is taken as a given. But the academy needs to find a way to address the parts of the person that exist outside of the head; to offer ways of understanding that involve the panorama of human faculties, ways that do not subtly reinforce the divisions between the observers and the observed. Our teaching is charged to engage more than verbal intelligence, to consider the visions of nature, of silence, of space between and around thought. We may not be able to "dance" while fasting for five days, but we can begin to consider a fuller range of religious experience and expression, we can soften the boundaries between subject and object, mind and body, and in doing so honor the depth and breadth of the subjects that we are privileged to teach.

References

Gardner, Howard. 1983. *Frames of Mind: The Theory of Multiple Intelligences*. New York: Basic Books.

Grimes, Ronald. 1982. *Beginnings in Ritual Studies*. Washington, DC: University Press of America.

Buddha Body,
Buddha Mind

Buddhism and the Teaching of Jūdō

David Waterhouse

I shall begin by outlining something about my involvement with Buddhism and teaching about it in university courses.[1] My curiosity was first roused when I was a teenager, through reading Ananda Coomaraswamy's *Buddha and the Gospel of Buddhism*, which I discovered in my grandfather's library and which was after all not such a bad introduction to the subject. From there I progressed rapidly to D. T. Suzuki, Eugen Herrigel and Alan Watts;[2] and my interests in Asia shifted steadily eastwards. Eventually, through twin interests in Zen and in jūdō,[3] I came to Japanese studies. However, before then I had made some formal study of both ancient Greek philosophy and modern analytic philosophy; and by the time I started learning to read Japanese my primary goal was to see how problems discussed by modern Western philosophers would look if you thought of them in terms of a non-Indo-European language. I was not then and am not now a Buddhist believer in any sense: I cannot accept the idea of rebirth, and I am sceptical that Awakening, even if the individual thinks it has taken place, has any other-worldly, magical significance.

Nevertheless, I have been influenced in various ways by Buddhist values; and, having spent four formative years at an English boys' boarding school, feel quite at home when I visit a Buddhist monastery. More to the point, I retain strong intellectual and historical interests in Buddhism, and am especially drawn to the long history of Buddhism's cultural contributions across Asia: in visual art, in music and in other arts of performance, including the so-called martial arts. I am also interested in making cultural comparisons with Europe, if I deem them to be appropriate and illuminating. For thirty years I have been teaching undergraduate and graduate courses on Buddhist arts

or on Buddhism itself; and since 1990 have taught a third-year undergraduate course entitled "Jūdō in Japanese Culture." This course
attempts to bridge the gap between theory and practice which is ines-
capable in most academic instruction, and to give the students a
glimpse of the possibilities for acquiring knowledge non-verbally,
through use of the body. I describe the course in more detail below.

Jūdō and Buddhism

As one who teaches about Buddhism and not only teaches about jūdō
but also how to do it, I have been asked to discuss the teaching of
jūdō in relation to Buddhism. This presents me with a dilemma, since
Buddhism does not enter very much into the way that I teach jūdō, or
even what I teach about it. Moreover, it is my considered opinion
that Buddhism has had little influence on jūdō—whether on its history and development, or on the way in which it is taught and practised worldwide. Jūdōka, unlike practitioners of some other martial
paths, tend not to discuss religious matters at all; nor do they tend to
religiosity as individuals. Rather, the philosophical and religious implications of jūdō are left to emerge implicitly out of jūdō practice. I
can say this with some confidence, having been involved in jūdō for a
long time, and having had the privilege of meeting and training under
very senior people in the jūdō community, both in Japan and elsewhere. Nevertheless, there are connections between jūdō and East
Asian religions, especially Taoism and Shinto; and, if one looks hard
enough, Buddhist elements too can be detected. Perhaps Buddhist
morals can even be drawn from my course on jūdō. So, in addressing
the topic of this paper, I need to be only moderately creative.

Jūdō was the brainchild of a remarkable man, Kanō Jigorō (1860–
1938). Kanō's father was born into a very old and distinguished
Shinto family, with the surname Shōgenji. They were tutelary priests
for hundreds of years at Hie Taisha, the great Shinto shrine which
guards Hieizan, headquarters of the Tendai school of Japanese Buddhism. When Oda Nobunaga burned down the monasteries on Mt.
Hiei, he also destroyed Hie Taisha; and Kanō's ancestors were responsible for rebuilding the shrine. The present buildings, dating
from the early seventeenth century, rank as National Treasures, and

are indeed impressive. The setting of the shrine, in a thickly wooded dell between Mt. Hiei and Lake Biwa, with small mountain streams channelled between and around the various structures, adds greatly to its atmosphere.

Those who know Japanese will realize that the unusual surname Shōgenji is Buddhist. In fact, it is the name of a small monastery erected near Hie Taisha at the birthplace of Saichō (767–822) founder of the Tendai school. However, Kanō Jigorō's father, and his uncle, were both adopted as young men into the Kanō family in Mikage, a small town then just outside Kōbe but now swallowed up by it. Mikage was the traditional center of the *sake* industry, and the Kanō were proprietors of the oldest brewery in Japan, makers of the Kiku Masamune brand. The Kiku Masamune firm is still owned by the Kanō family; and I can testify that they make excellent *sake*.

Kanō Jigorō's father chose not to go into the family business; but, after his wife died, brought his son to Tokyo. There the young man received most of his education, and became one of the very first graduates of Tokyo University. He studied both traditional subjects, including classical Chinese and calligraphy, and English language and political thought. He became a fluent writer and speaker of English, even keeping his private diaries in English, rather than Japanese, and he was influenced in his thinking by such writers as Herbert Spencer, Samuel Smiles and John Stuart Mill.

It is tempting to write at length about Kanō Jigorō, whose life and achievements were quite extraordinary and who imprinted the jūdō movement with his strong personality. (Just as a religion tends to bear the mark of its founder's personality, so too do several of the Asian martial arts or martial paths which have developed in the past hundred years.) However, it is necessary here to abridge the story, so I shall merely pick out some highlights. Somewhat against his father's wishes, Kanō Jigorō took up jūjutsu, the old Japanese system of unarmed combat, and studied it successively in two of the traditional lineages, Tenjin Shin'yō-ryū and Kitō-ryū. In 1882, while still a graduate student at Tokyo University, he founded his own institution, the Kōdōkan. The first classes took place at his lodgings, a room in the precincts of Eishōji, a small Buddhist monastery in the Ueno district

of Tokyo; but the Kōdōkan was to move and expand many times. Today it occupies a purpose-built seven-story structure containing not
only several practice halls but also a museum, library and archive,
dormitories, offices and study rooms, and a restaurant and shop. It is
perhaps worth mentioning that the Japanese word for a practice hall,
whether for jūdō or for various other kinds of training, is *dōjō*, a Buddhist term which translates Sanskrit *bodhimaṇḍa*, referring to a site for
obtaining Awakening.

One distinguished Western practitioner of jūdō, Trevor Leggett,
also happens to be very knowledgeable about Zen and about yoga.
He has written books on all three topics, as well as essays and books
on a host of other things.[4] When I lived in London, I had the privilege of training at the Renshūden, the jūdō club which he founded,
and of being thrown by him with his favorite *ōguruma*.[5] He is still active as an author and charismatic public speaker, although now in
frail health and almost totally blind. I believe he has not practiced
jūdō since the later 1960s. In recent years I have had the pleasure of
renewing acquaintance with him and of quizzing him a little about
jūdō history. I have to say, though, that Trevor Leggett is unique in
his combination of interests. Whether in Japan or elsewhere, it is rare
to find a jūdō teacher who is drawn to any religion, except jūdō itself;
and, as I have indicated, in jūdō the religious message, whatever it is,
is largely left to speak for itself. You could exclaim that this goes to
show how Zen-like it really is, but I no longer interpret it that way
myself. John Goodger, under the influence of Trevor Leggett, was led
to treat jūdō as a species of gnosticism.[6] A less extreme interpretation
along the same lines would be to regard it as exemplifying what in
some circles is coming to be called "implicit religion."[7] In any case,
Trevor Leggett's influence on the development of British jūdō has
been considerable, and is widely acknowledged among jūdōka.[8]

In one of his books, Leggett has discussed informally the terms
mushin, isshin and *zanshin*.[9] At first sight, these difficult words constitute a trio, and any of them is to be encountered from time to time
in martial arts discussion; but inquiry reveals that they have diverse,
separate origins. The first two are Buddhist; the last, however, is peculiar to martial arts. *Mushin* (Ch. *wuxin*), "no mind," translates in the

first instance Sanskrit *acitta*; but it was given new interpretations in the Ch'an/Zen tradition—in Japan most notably by Takuan Sōhō (1573–1645), in his *Fudōchi shinmyōroku*, written for the swordsman Yagyū Munemori (1571–1646). *Mushin* thus came to connote action which was unimpeded by the conscious self: like the egoless archery of the Master who taught Eugen Herrigel, or the effortless tennis shots executed by Timothy Gallwey's "Self Two."[10] The notion of *mushin* is hard to grasp, and harder still to realize in practice. *Isshin*, "one mind" or "single-mindedness," renders Sanskrit *ekāgra-citta*; it is a less subtle concept, but has technical interpretations in some schools of Buddhist thought (especially T'ien-t'ai/Tendai). It refers to the state of mind of one who pursues a goal whole-heartedly and earnestly, not allowing any deflection. This is all very well for purposes of training, but in a combat situation it can lead to defeat, because one may overlook attacks from behind or even from the side. Hence *zanshin*, "left-over mind": the wariness or alertness which should be cultivated by the hunter or the warrior, and whose importance is emphasized in several traditional texts on martial arts.

In some of the Asian martial arts and ways there is more overt Buddhist influence than there is in jūdō. I have little doubt that the Indian sage Bodhidharma existed, and that he found his way to China in the sixth century, although there is no evidence to connect him directly with the practice of martial arts at the Shaolin Monastery. The latter was a late addition to the body of legends about him. Even so, it is possible to trace the history of Buddhist influence on martial arts all the way from India to Japan; and the history of Buddhism, like that of other world religions, has always been closely linked with both political policy and "the continuation of policy by other means," as Clausewitz characterized war.[11] The Buddhist connection is strongest in swordsmanship and certain other traditional martial arts, and, in Japan at least, comprises Tendai, Shingon and other elements as much as Zen.[12] There are, for example, swords with Tantric inscriptions on them.[13] One thinks also of Benkei and the warrior monks (*sōhei*) of Tendai and Hossō monasteries;[14] of the quasi-martial traditions of the mountain ascetics (*yamabushi*); of Takeda Shingen and other military leaders who took ordination; or of warriors such as

Jion and Miyamoto Musashi, who embarked on personal quests (*musha shugyō*), like medieval European knights.

The various systems of jūjutsu preceded jūdō, and were above all systems of unarmed combat. The oldest surviving system, Takenouchi-ryū, goes back to the sixteenth century.[15] There was a proliferation of other lineages in the later eighteenth and early nineteenth centuries.[16] Some of these show a degree of Buddhist influence, so far as one can tell from imperfect and often cryptic records of their techniques and philosophy preserved in their "transmitted writings" (*densho*). Besides Takenouchi-ryū, several others have continued into modern times, or have been revived during the past thirty years. In a number of cases, however, Shinto has to be regarded as a stronger influence than Buddhism.

When jūdō came along in the Meiji period, it developed along largely secular lines, and the founder imposed his own order on it, purging from it many of the oddities and excrescences to be found in jūjutsu. Much of the terminology of jūdō is due to him, and it is far more organized and scientific in spirit than that of jūjutsu. He and his associates devised or modified many of the techniques of throwing and grappling, and they also created several special *kata* for jūdō (though in training the primary emphasis was, and still is, placed on unscripted *randori*).

Kanō did retain two *kata* virtually unchanged from the two lineages of jūjutsu in which he had trained; and today these *kata* are regarded as the most spiritual, or at least the most profound, of the seven *kata* of present-day Kōdōkan jūdō. One of them, known in jūdō circles as Koshiki no kata, is taken from Kitō-ryū. It consists of twenty-one throws: fourteen *omote* (grouped in pairs, and performed almost with the slowness of Nō drama); and seven *ura* (re-capitulating the first fourteen, and performed in rapid succession).[17] The other *kata*, known as Itsutsu no kata, "Kata of Five," is usually credited to Kanō himself; but it is actually the supreme *kata* of Tenjin Shin'yō-ryū, as re-interpreted by Kanō. However, he never managed to work out an interpretation which completely satisfied him. It would take us too far afield to discuss here the meaning of this *kata*, whose movements embody cosmic symbolism, but it is worth drawing attention to the fivefold grouping of techniques, which is found also in four other *kata* of Kōdōkan jūdō. In Itsutsu no kata it may originally have referred in some way to the Five Agents (or Processes: Jp. *gogyō*; Ch. *wuxing*) or to the Five Great [Elements] (Jp. *godai*) of Shingon Buddhism.

Despite the secular atmosphere of most *dōjō*, even in Japan, it is common for them to have a *jōseki* (literally, "seating place for superiors") or *kamiza* (literally, "seat for the gods") against one wall. This may simply take the form of a photograph of the founder, but it will sometimes include a shelf or an alcove, with an inspiring piece of calligraphy or even some Shinto paraphernalia. At the beginning and end of a practice, respect will usually be paid to this, as well as to the instructors, with a seated bow. Further, in many clubs, including those outside Japan, there will commonly be a short period of *mokusō* (literally, "silent contemplation"). It is easy to assume that this is a form of meditation, but the term is not to be found in Buddhist dictionaries. Even if it is quasi-religious, it is possible to treat *mokusō* simply as a useful opportunity for the student to collect his or her thoughts, and to focus on the practice of jūdō. As such, it is of practical psychological value for its own sake. In conformity with the principle of *zanshin*, it is recommended that the student keep his eyes open.

Jūdō has preserved or developed other little rituals of etiquette, particularly with regard to competition. There is an elaborate set of rules for the latter, both in the interests of safety and to ensure a fair result. At the beginning and end of a competition bout, or of a session of free practice (*randori*), it is customary for the participants to bow to each other. However, as the aim is to throw or otherwise vanquish one's partner, this is little more than common courtesy, the Japanese equivalent of shaking hands (or making the gesture of *namaste*), and it would be wrong to read a religious meaning into it.

Jūdō in Japanese Culture

Since September 1990 I have been offering every year, through the Department of East Asian Studies at the University of Toronto a third-year half-course entitled "Jūdō in Japanese Culture." Students taking this course receive academic credit, and 85 percent of the marks are earmarked for written work; but it is a requirement that they also undergo practical training in jūdō. No prior experience of jūdō is necessary, but I have sometimes had students with considerable first-hand knowledge of jūdō or of another East Asian martial system. The course lasts for thirteen weeks, and entails two hours of lectures and two hours of practical work per week. The course has proved extremely popular, and for many years I have had to limit enrollment (currently to thirty-five students). Even with these numbers (and two paid teaching assistants in the *dōjō*), it can be hard to supervise the class and to ensure that they all receive a measure of individual coaching in jūdō movements. Considerations of safety, and the size of the *dōjō*, are also limiting factors. Historically, the class has attracted more or less equal numbers of both sexes. I like the class to be as international as possible in its composition, since jūdō was designed for people the world over; but it is hard to realize this ideal, and probably impossible to legislate it. In most years I have tried to select the students by means of a ballot form in which they are asked various questions about their prior knowledge or experience of jūdō, Japan, the arts, and so on, as well as about their current academic program. Of necessity I give preference to students taking a specialized program in Japanese studies, but on principle I try to reach out to other sectors of the university, including the sciences.

The course is intended as an introduction to Japanese culture through jūdō. The current lecture syllabus is appended to this paper; and the course is usually followed in the Spring Term by a companion course entitled "Art and Religious Experience in Japan." The latter is more conventional in structure, and the jūdō course is not a prerequisite for it, but many of the same students do sign up for it. In most cases I do not know what the long-term effects of either course have been, but it has pleased me that a number of students have been motivated to continue with their jūdō training, or have gone to live and work for a period in Japan. Years later, several have continued to keep in touch with me, either from Japan or on their return to Canada.

In the classroom, as well as lecturing, I find it useful to show video documentaries or slides, to illustrate jūdō and its history, some other Japanese martial system, or other aspects of Japanese culture. By now, I have a large personal collection of material to select from. For their essays (a shorter one and a longer one), the students are asked to choose from a list of topics which varies from year to year, and ranges over many aspects of Japanese culture other than jūdō. However, at the end of the course they are also asked to write 300 words entitled "Impressions of Jūdō." This is not an opportunity for them to tell me what they think about the course, or to offer false compliments in the hope of getting a higher mark, but for me to learn what they think about jūdō, as a result of taking the course.

I retain these pieces, and have files covering all years of the course since its inception. They make interesting reading. In general, it is clear that students find the practical component of the course an attractive challenge. First of all, it is a novel experience for them to wear the white jūdō uniform, and to follow the ritual of lining up along the mat, sitting in formal kneeling position (*seiza*), performing a kneeling bow, and undergoing a short period (perhaps one minute) of *mokusō*. Jūdō is a contact sport, and for some it is also a novel, or rather forgotten, experience to touch and be touched by another person. For the majority it is certainly a novel experience to be thrown onto the floor, and to feel the power of jūdō armlocks and strangles.

The practice begins with a series of warm-up exercises, to get the heart and lungs working and to stretch and strengthen muscles and tendons over the whole body. These exercises are selected from a large repertoire, and may include some which are based on jūdō movement. The purpose is not only to prepare the body and mind for actual jūdō practice, but also to minimize the risk of injury and strain. Even so students often tell me, or write, that they have suffered from aching muscles and minor bruises as a result of the classes.

The preliminary exercises each week conclude with practice in executing breakfalls (*ukemi*), of which several kinds are used in jūdō. The most difficult of these for students to master is a forward rolling breakfall (*zenpō kaiten*). Learning to fall without hurting oneself is not only a useful skill for any one to acquire, but also has its psychological aspects.[18] The students gradually come to realize that there is no shame in being thrown in jūdō practice; and it can be a satisfying or even thrilling experience, when one is thrown expertly and lands correctly.

The syllabus of techniques taught in the course varies slightly from year to year. As a specimen, I have appended that from the Fall 1999 course. Readers with experience of jūdō will see that it is fuller than the usual introductory course at a club; but I pitch it at university level and, through the lectures as well as the practical work, seek to give the students an intellectual overview of jūdō—even if they cannot yet execute the techniques fluently. The course hand-out includes a comprehensive listing of the sixty-seven throwing technique names, and twenty-nine grappling technique names, currently approved by the Kōdōkan for *randori*; as well as tables of *kata* and other information. In common with most jūdō instructors, I use Japanese terminology, which, as I tell them, is the international language of jūdō, in the same way as French is the international language of fencing and ballet, English of air traffic controllers, and so on.

By the end of the course, the students have experienced a selection from each of the major groups of throws, and have been introduced to all the standard immobilization techniques (*osaekomi-waza*), as well as to basic constriction techniques (*shimewaza*) applied to the neck, and joint locks (*kansetsuwaza*) applied to the elbow. Even more than the throwing techniques, *shimewaza* and *kansetsuwaza* are potentially dangerous, and would not be included in a children's introductory course, but I think it is quite proper to show them to university students, so long as one prefaces the demonstration with a few words of caution.

As with the breakfalls, possession of this knowledge has its psychological aspects; the controlled practice of jūdō does seem to be beneficial to the psyche, and there is no intrinsic reason to suppose that it promotes violent behaviour. Populist writers on martial arts and ways frequently make strong claims for them, and one has to discount both hyperbole and mysticism. Moreover, purportedly scientific studies often turn out on careful examination to have been poorly designed. As for jūdō, it must be admitted that little of consequence has been written, except concerning its physiological effects.[19] In practice, much will depend on the individual teacher, pupil and club. My own experience of jūdō, over many years and in several countries, has left me with firm convictions as to its value for body, mind and spirit. Long-term physical injuries occasionally result from its practice, but I have never encountered anyone who became mentally warped as a result of jūdō. On the contrary, it is designed to promote a stronger sense of social as well as bodily and personal awareness.[20] The competitive ethic of jūdō does seem to bring out the ego of some practitioners; but this is less likely to reveal itself on the mat (where the etiquette of the *dōjō* and the agreed contest rules prevail), than sometimes in the councils of jūdō organizations.

The immediate inspiration for my own jūdō course was one which has been offered for many years at the University of Chicago by Professor Donald Levine, on the theme "Conflict Theory and Aikido."[21] Professor Levine has argued eloquently in favour of the value of martial arts in a liberal education (in the North American sense of that term);[22] and his example has been followed at one or two other U.S. universities. In Japan, the practice of martial paths has been part of school or university curricula since the later nineteenth century, when first jūdō and then kendō were officially adopted by the Ministry of Education. Since the 1950s such martial activities as karate, Shōrinji kenpō, aikidō and kyūdō have also been available at many universities; and there has been a significant revival of interest in other, older systems. It is even possible to study martial paths full time at certain universities, notably at the International Budo University (Kokusai Budō Daigaku), founded in 1984 by Dr. Matsumae Shigeyoshi.[23]

As I have indicated, my approach to teaching jūdō is almost entirely secular, and therefore neither explicitly nor even covertly Buddhist. However, it could be regarded as embodying Buddhist principles. For example, it incorporates my view of knowledge as comprising mostly non-verbal cognition: information from the senses does not have to be reducible to, or reduced to, words in order to count as knowledge.[24] Similarly, the experience of works of art, whether visual (paintings, sculpture, decorative arts, architecture) or performative (music, dance, theater), counts as a form of knowledge, or rather as many forms of knowledge, on many levels of the psyche. Beyond this, the experience of performing oneself, as opposed to watching someone else performing, counts as knowledge. The understanding one has of a performance art from the inside, as a performer, is definitely not the same as the appreciation of a watcher or listener. My interest in performing music, and in performing jūdō, as well as in teaching others to do so, all spring partly from this. I therefore find relevant the Tantric Buddhist techniques of imaging, where one first visualizes a supernatural being from the pantheon, and then imagines oneself as that being. However, I do not find it helpful to practice meditation as such, and am not personally interested in such grand religious goals as Awakening. To me, life is full of little secrets; perhaps the only Big Secret (one which is quite well kept) is that there is no big secret.

Another implicit Buddhist principle in my approach to jūdō is my conviction, originally inspired by Moshe Feldenkrais, that it inculcates a better awareness of the body, and so promotes a greater sense of union between mind and body; or, if you wish, between mind, body and spirit. In the course I spend time early in the term surveying theories of mind and body, East and West; though in recent years I have laid less emphasis on philosophical theories of mind and body, and more on actual techniques for improving mind-body coordination, including those of Feldenkrais and Alexander. I also discuss methods of describing and analyzing body movement, such as those of Rudolf Laban, and I try to survey the history of physical and martial education in East and West, and of attitudes towards the body. In this connection Kūkai's famous theory of *sokushin jōbutsu*, "becoming a Buddha in this very body," seems especially relevant, and I discuss briefly with the class a few other aspects of Shingon theory. Jūdō is not for everyone, because it does not offer instant solutions, and because it makes considerable physical demands, but anyone can do it up to a point, regardless of age, sex or build. Obviously it is impossible for those with major physical disabilities, such as paralysis, but those with mild disabilities, such as blindness, can practice it usefully. The doctrine of *sokushin jōbutsu*, taken over and re-interpreted by Shingon from T'ien-t'ai/Tendai Buddhism,[25] is flexible enough to serve as a motto for non-Buddhists and jūdōka as well.

By Way of Conclusion

I suspect that the best case for jūdō (or indeed for other martial paths, martial arts and martial sports) can be made from the standpoint of educational philosophy. The earliest Western thinker to advocate martial education was Plato, and its psychological, social and moral benefits are, naturally enough, emphasized by medieval writers on knighthood and chivalry. The theme was taken up anew by Renaissance writers on education. For Pietro Paulo Vergerio (1349–1419) Sparta was the model; in his *De Ingenuis Moribus* (c. 1404), he insisted: "It is of the greatest importance that boys should be trained from childhood in feats of courage and endurance."[26] In *De Librerorum Educatione* a similar chord was struck by Aeneas Sylvius Piccolomini (1405–64), later to become Pope Pius II: "Every youth destined to exalted position should...be trained in military exercises."[27] These ideas were echoed in England by such writers as Sir Thomas Elyot (1490?–1546) in *The Boke Named the Governour* (1531), which recommends wrestling and other physical exercises; and by John Milton (1608–74), in his *Tractate on Education* (1644), which recommends sword drill for school pupils, as "the likeliest means to make them grow large and tall, and to inspire them with a gallant and fearless courage, which being tempered with seasonable lectures and precepts to them of true fortitude and patience, will turn into a native and heroic valor, and make them hate the cowardice of doing wrong. They must be also practised in all the locks and gripes of wrestling...."[28] In more recent times William James (1842–1910), an avowed anti-militarist, nevertheless recommended that "We must make new energies and hardihoods continue the manliness to which the military mind so faithfully clings. Martial virtues must be the enduring cement...."[29]

Such views are in accord with the long tradition of Japanese thought concerning *butoku*, "martial virtue"; a tradition which continued into the late nineteenth century and beyond. The Dai Nippon Butokukai, "Great Japan Martial Virtue Society," was founded in

April 1895 in Kyoto, and in 1899 it erected a special hall, the Butokuden, for the performance of martial arts. The inspiration for this was the Butokuden set up in 819 within the Imperial Palace, for similar purposes. Regional branches of the Butokukai were established; its magazines, *Butokushi* and *Butoku*, urged the revival and inculcation of martial virtues; the Butokuden (which survives today at the heart of the Kyoto City Budo Center) was regularly used for jūdō and other tournaments; and, by 1930 total membership of the Society was estimated at 2,192,000. It was dissolved in 1945. In hindsight it is easy to criticize some of its expressed aims, but the patriotic language in which they are couched can readily be matched by the Western sources cited above, including William James. The term *butoku* (Ch. *wude*) may be traced to the last centuries B.C.E.,[30] and throughout Chinese and Japanese history it is regularly contrasted with *buntoku* (Ch. *wende*), "civil virtue." As such, it has no Buddhist associations;[31] but, as we have seen, the history of martial arts is constantly intertwined with that of Buddhism.

Kanō Jigorō had a universalistic vision of jūdō as something which was suitable for all humankind, and which could help to bring people together in greater harmony with one another. I am not sure that he was influenced by Buddhist doctrines of salvation for all, but his vision is certainly consonant with them. I share his hope that jūdō can play its part in reducing world tension, and have certainly seen how jūdō can unite in a common pursuit people from all over the world. In later life Kanō formulated two mottoes for jūdō, *Seiryoku zen'yō* and *Jita kyōei*. He himself translated the former into English as "Maximum-Efficiency with Minimum Effort," but it might be rendered more literally as "Effective Use of Mind and Body." He translated the latter as "Mutual Welfare and Benefit," but it might be rendered more literally as "Togetherness and Well-being for Oneself and Others." Again, the source may not be Buddhist, but up to a point the sentiments can be construed as Buddhist. In the founder's mind, the two mottoes were linked: personal well-being was to be attained partly through bringing about greater well-being in society.

In a paper published some years ago I likened the role of the coach in jūdō to that of a bodhisattva.[32] This was said half in jest, but up to a point the analogy will stand. From a logical point of view, reasoning by analogy (Skt. *upamāna*; Jp. *hiyu*) is invalid; but it was recognized in the Nyāya and other schools of Indian philosophy as a source of valid knowledge.[33] In daily life we are guided by analogy (in the form of metaphors, symbols and signs) more often than we realize or care to admit.[34] The human brain likes to use images more than words, and the human spirit is fired by imagined goals more often than by reason. One of my philosophy teachers, the late Professor R. B. Braithwaite, professed to be a Christian but did not believe in God. He argued that Christian beliefs did not have to be true to be useful, or to motivate one; any more than inspiring characters in a novel had to exist in reality to inspire and enhance one's own life.[35] An imaginary Japanese schoolboy, in a story whose author and title I have now forgotten, launched me on a long quest into jūdō and Japanese culture. In jūdō practice and in other endeavours, I therefore give myself license to invoke metaphors, if they will serve the purpose at hand—whether from Shingon or from Zen or from anywhere else.

APPENDIX: COURSE SYLLABI

(1) The syllabus of lectures, the *dōjō* syllabus, and the essay assignments for my half-course "Jūdō in Japanese Culture" have varied from year to year (I rarely repeat an essay topic.) Those listed here are from the Fall 1999 term.

(a) Syllabus of lectures

1. Introduction to the course, and overview of jūdō
2. Theoretical orientations: mind, body and language in relation to Japan
3. Survey of Japanese arts: education and artistic training in Japan
4. Outline history of budō and bujutsu: martial traditions in Japan
5. Budō, religion and philosophy in Japan
6. Outline history of jūjutsu and the early jūdō movement; life and career of Kanō Jigorō
7. Jūdō in Japan and elsewhere since World War II
8. History and classification of jūdō techniques
9. Outline history of European martial arts and physical education
10. Outline history of martial traditions in East Asia (except Japan)
11. Historical overview of Buddhism, with special reference to Japan
12. The Shinto religion in Japanese history
13. Other intellectual and religious currents in Japan: Confucianism, Western thought, new religions

(b) Dōjō syllabus (important technical terms in italics)

1. dōjō etiquette; jūdōgi and how to wear it; ukemi (rear and side); *ippon-seoinage*; *kesagatame*
2. ukemi (side, rolling); *ōgoshi*; *ippon-seoinage*; *katagatame*; escapes from *kesagatame* and *katagatame*
3. ukemi (side, rolling); *ōuchigari*; ōuchigaeshi (for reference); *kuzure-kesagatame*; escapes from *kuzure-kesagatame* and *kesagatame*
4. ukemi (side, rolling); *tai-otoshi*; *kami-shihōgatame*; basic kansetsuwaza (*udegarami, udehishigi-udegatame, udehishigi-jūjigatame*)
5. ukemi (rear, rolling); review of techniques (4 nagewaza, 4 osaekomiwaza, 3 kansetsuwaza); *yokoshihōgatame*; basic shimewaza from rear (*hadakajime, okuri-erijime*)
6. ukemi (rolling); uchikomi practice (*ippon-seoinage*; *ōuchigari*); *de ashiharai*; tsubamegaeshi, okuri-ashiharai & haraitsurikomiashi (for reference); *yokoshihōgatame* (basic style, munegatame & kuzure-yokoshihōgatame styles); *okuri-erijime* (review); *katahajimr*
7. ukemi (rolling; straight forward); *haraigoshi*; ōsoto-otoshi & ōsotoguruma (for reference); randori (in newaza); *namijūjijime, katajūjijime, gyakujūjijime* (demonstration only)
8. ukemi (side; rolling; straight forward); *ōsotogari*; *namijūjijime, katajūjijime, gyakujūjijime*; *kuzure-yokoshihōgatame* (two styles); attacks from supine position

9. ukemi (rolling; straight forward); more attacks from supine position (inc. kansetsuwaza & shimewaza); *tateshihōgatame* (two styles); randori (in tachi waza, throw for throw)
10. ukemi (rolling); review of nagewaza techniques
11. ukemi (rear; rolling); *kouchigari* (two styles); newaza attacks from between legs
12. ukemi (rolling); newaza practice; *tomoenage*; yoko-tomoenage (for reference); introduction to *kata*: *uki-otoshi* (Nage no kata); *hidari-eri-dori* (Kōdōkan goshin jutsu)
13. GRADING TEST

(c) Essay assignments

1st essay (750 words). ONE of the following:

1. Give a historical and technical sketch of any Japanese combat system **except** jūdō.
2. Write a short account of **one** of the following traditional Japanese arts, with particular reference to its history: men's **or** women's hair-dressing; carpentry; bridge-building; massage; umbrellas.
3. Political aspects of the life and work of **one** of the following figures: Yamagata Aritomo; Richard Sorge; Ogyū Sorai; Nichiren; Will Adams.

2nd essay (2000 words). ONE of the following:

1. Japanese parlor games
2. The upbringing of children in Tokugawa Japan
3. The training of actors in traditional Japanese theatre
4. Japanese mirrors and their cultural significance
5. Ship-building in Japan
6. Japanese military music
7. *Kimono* styles and patterns
8. Japanese visitors to Europe **or** Chinese visitors to Japan, before 1941

ALSO (300 words):

Impressions of Jūdō

(2) The lecture syllabus for my companion half-course "Art and Religious Experience in Japan" has also varied slightly from year to year. That listed here, for purposes of comparison, is from the Spring 2000 term.

1. Approaches to religious art, and to Buddhist art in particular
2. Early Japanese Buddhism and Buddhist art
3. The same continued
4. Tantric Buddhism and Buddhist art in Japan
5. The same continued
6. Shugendō: mountain worship and the *yamabushi*
7. Buddhist cosmology, the Pure Land and Pure Land Buddhist art in Japan
8. Taoism and the arts of divination in Japan
9. Zen Buddhism and the arts
10. Shinto history, ritual and art

11. Early Christian missions in Japan and Namban art
12. Intellectual currents and the arts in Tokugawa Japan
13. Religious and artistic movements since 1868

Notes

[1] The nature of the topic has obliged me to be more personal than is normal in an academic paper. I ask the reader's indulgence for this.

[2] For effective antidotes to each of these, see respectively: Sharf 1995; Scholem 1961; Furlong 1986. They are nevertheless interesting and stimulating authors in their own right, and I am not conscious of suffering long-term harm from having read them. An earlier and less benign influence on my intellectual development as a teenager was the writings of Paul Brunton, for whom see likewise Masson 1993.

[3] I first became aware of jūdō, or rather jūjutsu, from reading an English boarding school story for boys, and from E. J. Harrison's *The Art of Ju-Jitsu* (London: W. Foulsham & Co., Limited, n.d.). The latter, which ran into several editions, is illustrated with charming line drawings by H. Shepheard, and I recall trying to visualize the techniques from these and from Harrison's descriptions. In the present essay, I spell the word jūdō with pedantic macrons on both vowels, even though in ordinary parlance these are omitted. Similarly, the word jūjutsu is usually written without its macron, and (reflecting everyday Japanese pronunciation) often spelled *jujitsu* or even *jiujitsu*.

[4] Among his many publications may be mentioned particularly *A First Zen Reader* (1960); *The Tiger's Cave: Translations of Japanese Zen Texts* (1964; re-published as *A Second Zen Reader*); *Championship Judo: Tai-Otoshi and O-Uchi-Gari Attacks* (1964, with K. Watanabe); *The Chapter of the Self* (1978); *Zen and the Ways* (1978); *Encounters in Yoga and Zen: Meetings of Cloth and Stone* (1982); *Kata Judo* (1982, with J. Kano; originally published in 1963 as three separate volumes); *The Warrior Koans: Early Zen in Japan* (1985); *Fingers and Moons: Zen Stories and Incidents* (1988); *The Complete Commentary by Śaṇkara on the Yoga Sūtras: A Full Translation of the Newly Discovered Text* (1990); *Three Ages of Zen: Samurai, Feudal, and Modern* (1993); *Lotus Lake, Dragon Pool: Musings in Yoga and Zen* (1994); *The Dragon Mask and Other Judo Stories in the Zen Tradition* (1995); *The Spirit of Budo: Old Traditions for Present-Day Life* (1998). Mr. Leggett has his own Web site (www.leggett.co.uk/welcome.htm), which lists and describes available books by him, together with extracts from them. It also provides biographical information about the author, and includes a monthly teaching point, training story, and question and answer of the month.

[5] One student friend of mine noticed that, whatever technique his partner tried, Leggett-sensei would execute the same technique in return. Having the opportunity of practicing with him, and being unaware of his speciality, my friend therefore attempted ōguruma, the most exotic technique he could think of—and was promptly thrown with it himself.

[6] Goodger 1982. The article does not mention Leggett by name, but clearly alludes to him.

[7] Cf. *Implicit Religion* (Leeds: Maney Publishing), the recently launched Journal of the Centre for the Study of Implicit Religion and Contemporary Spirituality.

[8] John Goodger's doctoral thesis and that of his brother Brian Goodger, both of which are cited in his article, contain much further information about the history of British jūdō. A very detailed history of British jūdō and of the Budokwai (the leading jūdō club in England) is being prepared by Richard Bowen. I am obliged to all three gentlemen for their publications, and for other advice about British jūdō. For further insights I am indebted to two former British Olympic jūdōka, Tony Sweeney and Syd Hoare, who have both continued to be very active as jūdō teachers in England.

[9] Leggett 1978, 22–25, 136–37.

[10] See Gallwey 1975. Gallwey has written or co-authored several other books on the same lines, covering not only tennis but other sports and even music performance.

[11] Clausewitz 1976, 87. For an illuminating historical study of Buddhist attitudes to war, see Demiéville 1957, 347–85.

[12] For some further information and references, see Waterhouse 1996, esp. 27–37.

[13] See, for example, Draeger 1976-78, lecture 4, p. 4.

[14] See Renondeau 1957.

[15] For the history of Takenouchi-ryū, see Shimada 1971; Takenouchi-ryū 1979; Takenouchi 1993. I am indebted to my former student Michael McCarthy for assistance in obtaining materials on Takenouchi-ryū.

[16] For information about these lineages, see above all Watatani and Yamada 1978.

[17] The paired terms *omote* ("front; outward, exoteric") and *ura* ("rear; inward; esoteric") are found in many contexts in Japanese culture, and have a slightly religious flavor.

[18] I have been greatly influenced in my thinking about these matters by the early writings of Moshe Feldenkrais, who was a pioneer of jūdō in France, and whose later method for enhancing body awareness partly derives from his training in jūdō. See, for example, Feldenkrais 1949, 84f.; 1952, 19–21. The following extract will have to suffice: "The fear of falling, or more correctly, the reaction to falling, can be observed immediately after birth.... [B]y teaching the art of falling properly, we further the person's maturity towards a more adult independence of the gravitational force" (1952, 20).

[19] Two convenient surveys with further references are Maliszewski 1992, esp. 64; and Pieter 1994, esp. 32–35. Published research on the psychological effects of martial arts mostly relates to karate and kindred arts. Since 1958 the Kōdōkan has published eight volumes of scientific papers, which focus on the physiological effects of jūdō practice. These volumes, in Japanese with English summaries, are entitled *Kōdōkan Jūdō Kagaku Kenkyūkai Kiyō/ Bulletin of the Association for the Scientific Studies on Judo, Kodokan*. Some of the findings are summarized in Matsumoto 1975. It is to be hoped that further research will be undertaken also on the lines proposed by Feldenkrais, whose early works are out of print and little known today.

[20] Again, cf. Feldenkrais: "The essential aim of Judo is to teach, help and forward adult maturity, which is an ideal state rarely reached, where a person is capable of dealing with

the immediate present task before him without being hindered by earlier formed habits of thought or attitude" (1952, xii–xiii).

[21] I am indebted to Professor Levine for supplying me with a set of his course materials, and for his encouragement over the years.

[22] Levine 1984; 1990, 173–87. Aikidō, like jūdō, has its roots in jūjutsu; but, except in the Tomiki style, generally disavows competition. This distinguishes it sharply from jūdō.

[23] The late Dr. Matsumae, a notable patron of both jūdō and education, was also President of Tokai University (Tōkai Daigaku), the Nippon Budōkan, and the International Judo Federation.

[24] I therefore disagree sharply with A. J. Ayer's definition of knowledge: "I conclude...that the necessary and sufficient conditions for knowing that something is the case are first that what one is said to know be true, secondly that one be sure of it, and thirdly that one should have the right to be sure" (1956, 35).

[25] Groner 1989.

[26] Quoted in Woodward 1905, 96.

[27] Woodward 1905, 137.

[28] Milton 1872, III: 475.

[29] James 1912, 287.

[30] Morohashi Tetsuji (1955-60) cites the *Guoyu* (*Jin*, chapter 9) and the *Shiji* (*Qin Shihuang ji* chapter).

[31] However, the concept of *toku/de* is found in Buddhist (and Taoist) contexts, in various special applications. For example, *tokuhon* (Ch. *deben*) is "the source of virtue" (identified often as Amitābha); and *tokuden* (Ch. *detian*), "field of virtue," refers to an Arhat or Buddha.

[32] Waterhouse 1982, 168–78.

[33] Nakamura Hajime 1981, 1120(2), *s.v. hiyu*; Grimes 1996, 329, *s.v. upamāna*.

[34] See Lakoff and Johnson, 1980, *passim*; also Johnson 1987.

[35] See Braithwaite 1955.

Bibliography

Ayer, A. J. 1956. *The Problem of Knowledge*. Hammondsworth, U.K.: Penguin.

Braithwaite, R. B. 1955. *An Empiricist's View of the Nature of Religious Belief*. Cambridge: Cambridge University Press.

Clausewitz, Carl von. 1976. *On War*. Translated by Michael Howard and Peter Paret. Princeton: Princeton University Press.

Demiéville, Paul. 1957. "Le Bouddhisme et la Guerre." In *Mélanges publiés par l'Institut des Hautes Études Chinoises I*, 347–85.

Draeger, Donn F. 1976–78. *The Draeger Lectures at the University of Hawaii*. Typescript transcript.

Feldenkrais, Moshe. 1949. *Body and Mature Behaviour: A Study of Anxiety, Sex, Gravitation and Learning*. London: Routledge & Kegan Paul.

———. 1952. *Higher Judo: Ground Work (Katame-waza)*. London and New York: Frederick Warne & Co.

Furlong, Monica. 1986. *Zen Effects: The Life of Alan Watts*. Boston: Houghton Mifflin Company.

Gallwey, W. Timothy. 1975. *The Inner Game of Tennis*. London: Jonathan Cape.

Goodger, John. 1982. "Judo Players as a Gnostic Sect." *Religion* 12: 333–44.

Grimes, John. 1996. *A Concise Dictionary of Indian Philosophy: Sanskrit Terms Defined in English*. Albany: State University of New York Press.

Groner, Paul. 1989. "The *Lotus Sutra* and Saichō's Interpretaion of the Realization of Buddhahood with This Very Body." In *The Lotus Sutra in Japanese Culture*, edited by George J. Tanabe Jr. and Willa Jane Tanabe, 53–74. Honolulu: University of Hawaii Press.

James, William. 1912. "The Moral Equivalent of War." In *Memories and Studies*. London: Longmans, Green, and Co.

Johnson, Mark. 1987. *The Body in the Mind: The Bodily Basis of Meaning, Imagination, and Reason*. Chicago and London: University of Chicago Press.

Lakoff, George, and Mark Johnson. 1980. *Metaphors We Live By*. Chicago and London: University of Chicago Press.

Leggett, Trevor. 1978. *Zen and the Ways*. London: Routledge & Kegan Paul.

Levine, Donald N. 1984. "The Liberal Arts and the Martial Arts." *Liberal Education* 70 (3).

———. 1990. "Martial Arts as a Resource for Liberal Education: The Case of Aikidō." In *Japanese Martial Arts and American Sports: Cross-Cultural Perspectives on Means to Personal Growth*, edited by M. Kiyota and H. Kinoshita, 173–87. Tokyo: Nihon University.

Maliszewski, Michael. 1992. "Meditative-Religious Traditions of Fighting Arts and Martial Ways." *Journal of Asian Martial Arts* 1 (3): 1–104

Masson, Jeffrey Moussaieff. 1993. *My Father's Guru: A Journey through Spirituality and Disillusion*. Reading, MA: Addison-Wesley.

Matsumoto Yoshizō. 1975. *Jūdō no kōchingu*. Tokyo: Taishūkan Shoten.

Milton, John. 1872. *The Prose Works of John Milton*. London: Bell and Daldy.

Morohashi Tetsuji. 1955-60. *Dai Kan-Wa Jiten*. 13 vols. Tokyo: Tsishūkan Shoten.

Nakamura Hajime. 1981. *Bukkyōgo daijiten*. 1-vol. edition. Tokyo: Tokyo Shoseki.

Pieter, Willy. 1994. "Research in Martial Sports." *Journal of Asian Martial Arts*. 3 (2): 10–47

Renondeau, G. 1957. "Histoire des moines guerriers du Japon." *Mélanges publiés par l'Institut des Hautes Études Chinoises I*. Pp. 159–341.

Sharf, Robert H. 1995. "The Zen of Japanese Nationalism." In *Curators of the Buddha. The Study of Buddhism under Colonialism*, edited by Donald S. Lopez. Chicago: University of Chicago Press. Pp. 107–60

Scholem, Gershom. 1961. "Zen-Nazism?" Letter to *Encounter* 89.

Shimada Shūsei. 1971. *(Higo denrai no bujutsu) Takenouchi santō-ryū jūjutsu*. Kumamoto: Seichōsha.

Takenouchi-ryū Hensan Iinkai, ed. 1979. (*Nihon bujutsu no genryū*) *Takenouchi-ryū*. Tokyo: Nichibō Shuppansha.

Takenouchi Tōichirō, ed. 1993. (*Shinden no bujutsu*) *Takenouchi-ryū*. Book and Video. Tokyo: Gakushū Kenkyūsha.

Watatani Kiyoshi and Yamada Tadashi. 1978. (*Zōho daikaitei*) *Bugei ryūha daijiten*. Tokyo: Tokyo Kopī Shuppanbu.

Waterhouse, David. 1982. "Kanō Jigorō and the Beginnings of the Judo Movement." In *Proceedings, 5th Canadian Symposium on the History of Sport and Physical Education*, edited by Bruce Kidd, 168–78. Toronto: School of Physical and Health Education, University of Toronto. Reprinted in *Judo Ontario's Newsletter* 8, 1 (March/April 1983): 14–16, and 8, 2 (May/June 1983): 15–17; and separately, as a pamphlet, by Judo Ontario.

———. 1996. "Notes on the Kuji." In *Religion in Japan: Arrows to Heaven and Earth*, edited by P. F. Kornicki and I. J. McMullen, 1–38. Cambridge: Cambridge University Press.

Woodward, W. H. 1905. *Vittorino da Feltre and Other Humanist Educators*. Cambridge: Cambridge University Press.

Introducing Buddhism in a Course on Postmodernism

Susan Mattis

In the academy today there is an ongoing debate over whether it is more important to ground students in an understanding of the Western cultural tradition or to expose them to the thought and culture of a multiplicity of traditions. The views of a faculty and administration on this issue are usually embodied in the way a school's required core curriculum is designed. In spite of the widespread recognition of the importance of preparing students to live in a world of diverse peoples, many schools have maintained their traditional emphasis on the study of Western culture, placing priority on examination of the worldview most likely to have shaped the students' own thinking. This is not the place to enter into the debate on this difficult issue; I bring it up merely to call attention to the fact that many people teach in colleges and universities where there is little institutional support for teaching undergraduates, other than those majoring in certain select fields, about different cultures and their religious and philosophical teachings. With this in mind, I think it is useful to consider ways of introducing students to Buddhism in courses designed to focus on aspects of the Western intellectual tradition. This can be done legitimately only if the presentation of Buddhism can be integrated with the themes and concepts of the rest of the course. In this paper I will present a strategy for introducing the teachings of the Madhyamaka school of Buddhism in an undergraduate course on postmodern thought and culture.

In the course on postmodernism which I teach, the semester begins with Nietzsche, who, though not chronologically a postmodern, is certainly one of the most important progenitors of the movement and still is one of the most eloquent exponents of its fundamental ideas. Reading Nietzsche introduces the students to several ideas which will facilitate their understanding of Buddhist concepts introduced later in the semester. In *The Will to Power* Nietzsche declares that the notion of "things that have a constitution in themselves" is a "dogmatic idea with which one must break absolutely."[1] He proceeds with several striking arguments to demonstrate that the idea of a thing freed from all relationships is a logical absurdity; rephrasing this in Buddhist terminology, his arguments show that it is impossible for an entity to possess self-essence (*svabhāva*), that every existence is a relative existence.[2]

Using a variety of types of arguments and examples, Nietzsche also demonstrates that our conceptualizing mind creates an interpretation of the world that has no objective ground. He argues that all notions of enduring, self-identical "things" are constructs imposed on an ever-changing flux of experience, and he directs his most compelling arguments against the notion of a unitary, enduring self.[3] He also demonstrates that concepts such as "causality," which are essential to our comprehension of the world, are falsifications we impose on the world,[4] and he calls attention to the arbitrariness of conceptual demarcations of experience into elements such as "will" and "thought."[5] Frequently he takes antithetical concepts such as "freedom" and "determinism" and proves that both members of the duality are absurdities, illustrating that none of the possible ways of conceiving the world grasps an objective truth.[6] Exploring the sources of these concepts and our implicit belief in their objectivity, Nietzsche points to our linguistic habits. For instance, he suggests that one reason for our inability to conceive the world without the concepts of the underlying self or substance is the subject-predicate structure of our language.[7] He also suggests that our conceptual interpretation of the world, which allows us to manage and manipulate things, ultimately serves the interests of the will to power.[8]

If every belief, every act of considering something true, is necessarily an interpretation, a falsification, it also holds that there are no objective values and no ultimate purpose or aim for our existence. In

The Will to Power Nietzsche defines the position he holds, that there is no "truth," and that the world of becoming has no ultimate aim, as "nihilism."[9] Nietzsche recognizes that this way of thinking can lead to a devaluation of life, to the sense that our existence, having no purpose, has no value, and that our world, having no truth, has no significance. But he insists that what he calls nihilism is a "divine way of thinking" and that those who truly devalue life are those who, unable to accept the conditions of life as they are, seek a truth and a ground for the meaning of existence outside of this world of appearance. Nietzsche sees in the longing for truth only the impotence of a soul that cannot posit its own values and create an interpretation or vision of the world as it wills the world to be. Nietzsche urges us to give a resounding "yes" to the world of impermanence, relativity and interpretation.[10]

Nietzsche's epistemology (for lack of a better word) is remarkably similar to that of Nāgārjuna and his followers in the Madhyamaka school of Buddhism. The Madhyamaka tradition also denies the existence of any truth, characterizing all our conceptualizations as conventional constructs, lacking any objective ground. But while Nietzsche makes a compelling case for the Buddhist repudiation of truth claims, he does not defend his position by focusing on the nature of language as a system of relatively constructed concepts. In the Western tradition, this line of reasoning, which parallels that of the Madhyamaka Buddhists, is initiated by the thinking of the founder of structuralism, the linguist Ferdinand de Saussure. Although in a class on postmodernism Saussure is studied primarily to provide a basis for the study of the post-structuralists, he is particularly important in reference to approaching Buddhism, for it is not what is unique to the post-structuralists so much as the principles they carry forward from structuralism which most closely approximate Buddhist concepts.

In his *Course in General Linguistics*, Saussure explains that the meaning of a word is wholly a function of its difference from other words in the language system. The elements of language are not "positive terms" possessing a definite identity or meaning of their own; rather, what gives each linguistic term its significance is the differences between it and the other elements of the language system.[11] With this conception of meaning, Saussure repudiates the traditional belief that the meaning of a concept lies in its reference to an object. Instead, he proposes that meaning originates within the linguistic system, as a function of the structure of relations among the elements of language. It follows that it is not the perceptual or intellectual intuition of objects which determines how we will form concepts, but how our concepts divide up the world which determines how "objects" will be intuited. Our language and its "differences" are matters of convention, and what we call "reality" or "truth" is a construct of this conventionally established linguistic system.

Derrida initiates post-structuralist thought by suggesting that the language system is not a fixed, finite structure of relations in which each language element has a definite place and therefore a definite meaning but rather an unbounded matrix of constantly shifting relations. Rethinking language in this way, Derrida observes that since the linguistic system is an endless shifting "play" of differences, meaning is indefinitely "deferred"—it can never fully come to presence.[12]

Although it is difficult to relate Derrida's post-structuralist ideas about the "deferral" and "undecidability" of meaning to the Madhyamaka tradition, he does introduce some considerations that offer intriguing parallels to Buddhist thought. Because every element in the language system is defined through its difference from other elements, Derrida suggests that each holds in itself the "trace" of those meanings from which it differs, including the traces of prior associations and the anticipated effects of future configurations.[13] The significance of this is particularly evident in the case of binary oppositions, such as subject/object, essence/accident, eternal/temporal, presence/absence, male/female. The idea of the trace suggests that although we think of each member of these dichotomies as standing on its own, independent of the other, the opposing terms are in fact interpenetrating and inseparable. For instance, we can only understand the meaning of the "subject" if we distinguish it from and relate it to the "object." Rather than being a reality separate from the object, the subject is determined and defined by the object; in Derrida's image, the subject is "contaminated" by the object. Since, from the point of view of structuralism and post-structuralism, reality is always mediated by language, the relativity and mutual contamination which holds for concepts is true of the things conceived, of reality itself. Derrida's vision of the absence of separate identity and interpenetration of all cognized beings approximates the most radical Buddhist visions of empty, relative existence.

Derrida also provides an introduction to Buddhist ways of thinking with his critique of "logocentrism." Logocentrism is the belief that there is a fundamental principle which exists independently and is the foundation for everything else. Heidegger pointed out that all of Western philosophy (and religion) has posited or at least sought to discover this foundational principle. If, however, the being or meaning of anything is a function of its "difference" from other elements in the linguistic system, there can be no self-identical, independent origin.[14] Derrida suggests that the epistemological error of logocentrism has definite social and political consequences. The search for a foundation or point of origin gives rise to hierarchical binary thinking in which one member of an opposition, such as male/female or mind/body, is posited as the foundation or origin and the other as a dependent or derivative being.[15] The value placed on what is conceived as the origin or associated with the origin and the corresponding devaluation of the derivative element, which is generally seen as a deterioration or fall from the origin, results in the marginalization or repression of the derivative element. The practices of "deconstruction" reverse these hierarchies by demonstrating that the supposedly independent concepts are derivative of the dependent concepts.[16] The objective is not to establish a new hierarchy but to reveal the complete interdependence of the opposing concepts; the impossibility of positing either one as self-sufficient origin. Derrida's linkage of undesirable ethical and political behavior with the illusion of self-existent realities supplies a helpful bridge to the Buddhist understanding of the ethical and soteriological significance of epistemological views.

After the students have studied Nietzsche, Saussure, Derrida and other postmodern thinkers, I introduce Buddhism as a religious and philosophical tradition which, like postmodern thought, is grounded in a consideration of the role of language and conceptuality in constructing our experience. To acquaint the students with the basic concepts of Buddhist thought, I briefly explain the early Buddhist analysis of composite things and persons into their simplest, constituent elements, the *dharmas*. The students read the famous passage in the *Milindapañha* in which the monk Nāgasena and the king's chariot are analyzed into their constituent parts. This passage effectively expounds the Buddhist view that enduring, composite objects and persons are merely "designated" existents, the product of conceptualizing acts which impose an artificial unity on aggregates of discrete mental events and elementary sensed qualities. It is helpful at this juncture to remind the students that Nietzsche also argued that all notions of enduring things or persons are an interpretation imposed on the flux of phenomena by our conceptual acts and to ask them to compare Nietzsche's arguments against the notion of an underlying self or substance with the dialectical arguments of Nāgasena.

With this background provided, the epistemology of the Madhyamaka school can be introduced by explaining that in the Madhyamaka tradition the idea of the linguistic-conceptual construction of our world is taken one step further. While the early Buddhist teachings make a distinction between composite objects which are conceptually constructed and *dharmas* which are held to be simple, directly intuited elements of experience, the Mādhyamikas maintain that there are no entities that can be cognized apart from conceptual activity. Further, the Mādhyamikas emphasize that all concepts are relative constructs, that is, that their meaning is a function of their relation to other concepts. Students who have been introduced to structuralist and post-structuralist thought can quickly be led to understand the implications of this position. They should be able to see that this entails that meaning originates within the linguistic system itself, not in reference to a directly intuited object, and that lacking an objective basis, our concepts and their relations to one another are established through socio-linguistic convention. Having seen similar reasoning by Saussure and Derrida, the students should have little difficulty understanding the Mādhyamikas' conclusion that all cognized beings are merely "conventionally" existent.

When the students have understood the Madhyamaka views on the relativity of concepts, it is a simple matter to explain the use of the term "emptiness" (*śūnyatā*) to express the ultimate truth of our world. It follows from the relativity of concepts that no cognized being possesses any nature or characteristic in itself. As Saussure insists with his declaration that the units of language are not "positive terms" but obtain their identity by their "differences" from other terms, so the Mādhyamikas insist that all cognized beings are "empty" of any self-existent nature or characteristic and possess only relative being. Further, for both the structuralists and post-structuralists and the Mādhyamikas, the relativity of concepts entails that what is conceptually cognized lacks or is "empty" of an objective ground and is merely conventionally existent. For both the postmoderns and the Madhyamaka Buddhists the relativity of concepts entails "emptiness" in the two-fold sense of the absence of a self-existent nature or characteristic and the absence of an objective ground of cognition.

Students often misinterpret the Madhyamaka epistemological claim that nothing known exists apart from the groundless, merely conventional constructions of consciousness as an ontological claim about the nature of phenomenal existents. The Madhyamaka position is mistaken for a kind of idealism asserting that the things of ordinary cognition are merely "fabrications" of a solipsistic consciousness. A student who has read Nietzsche and Derrida, however, will be inoculated against this error. In the work of both authors, any statements about the way things are, including any of their own statements about reality as an "interpretation" or groundless "construct" of our concepts, must be understood as interpretations, as relative constructs, and not as positive assertions about the nature of anything. Like Nāgārjuna, Nietzsche uses logic to destroy the ontological claims of his opponent but denies that he is asserting the validity of the logic he uses.[17] Nietzsche also maintains, like Nāgārjuna, that the refutation of one position does not entail the assertion of its antithesis, a fact he demonstrates repeatedly by refuting both sides of antithetical ontological positions. Thus, having studied the postmoderns, the students should readily understand that to deny that our cognitions have objective referents is not to assert that all reality is subjective or can be reduced to consciousness. For Nietzsche and Derrida, as for Nāgārjuna, the refutation of the objective existence of what we cognize leaves us only with the realization that we cannot make any ontological claims at all.

In addition to facilitating a grasp of the Madhyamaka doctrines, familiarity with postmodern thought provides a context in terms of which the students can reflect on the existential and soteriological import of this teaching. Students encountering the Madhyamaka exposition of emptiness frequently believe that this way of thinking entails that nothing in our ordinary experience has any value or significance. The Buddhist tradition's promise that one who realizes emptiness will attain "liberation" appears to confirm this view. If this liberation is understood as a liberation from all attachments to our existence in this world which ultimately brings to an end the cycle of rebirth, it appears that the Buddhist expects the realization of the relativity and ultimate groundlessness of our cognitions to result in a pervasive indifference to the objects of cognition. Nietzsche condemns such aspirations to detachment from this world as "nihilistic" devaluations of life; from his viewpoint, the Buddhist caveat that this world is significant because we attain ultimate freedom through realizing its emptiness and through our acts of compassion within it would do nothing to subvert the fundamental message, that the real value of this world is in transcending it. Although Nietzsche's negative assessment of all such soteriological goals may be disputed, it is a fact that few students will embrace either in principle or in practice the goal of achieving complete detachment from this world. If Buddhism and the teaching of emptiness are to mean anything to them at all, it is important to direct their attention to more nuanced conceptions of the liberation to be attained upon the realization of emptiness.

To overcome the tendency of the students to see emptiness, and therefore Buddhism, as a viewpoint that devalues life, it is helpful to point out that few Western postmodern thinkers feel that their views deprive the world of significance or value. The highly political nature of the thought of Derrida and most other post-structuralist thinkers makes it clear that these thinkers do not associate their epistemological views with detachment from this world, and Nietzsche, as mentioned earlier, explicitly rejects the suggestion that the arbitrariness of our interpretations of things need make them any less important to us. Once the students are persuaded that the realization of the ultimate groundlessness of all cognition is not intrinsically equivalent to an understanding of all things of this world as without meaning or value, they can be encouraged to reflect on other views regarding the significance of a realization of emptiness for life.

Within the Mahāyāna tradition there are suggestions that the liberation achieved upon realization of emptiness need not be conceived as a categorical detachment from the whole of phenomenal existence. Such alternative conceptions of liberation entail specific claims about the soteriological and ethical function of a realization of emptiness. As the students are introduced to these views of liberation, critical reflection on the Buddhist claims about the significance of emptiness can be stimulated by juxtaposing the Buddhist beliefs with those of the Western postmodern thinkers who appear to either reinforce or reject them. According to one Mahāyāna view of liberation, the realization of emptiness leads not to detachment from the groundless, relatively cognized entities of phenomenal existence but to detachment only from the illusion of objectively existent entities defined by their own independently existing natures or essences. The realization that nothing exists independent of its relations to everything else, it is suggested, overcomes the exclusive attachment to the self by revealing the inseparability of the self from all others. The result is not indifference to the whole of phenomenal existence but rather a compassion that extends to all beings without discrimination.

Reflecting on the Western thinkers they have studied, the students find both some support for this suggestion and an explicit repudiation of it. On the one hand, Nietzsche has no expectation that realization of the relativity or interdependence of all things will lead to universal compassion; indeed he unites the most trenchant critiques of the reality of the "self" with a glorification of self-assertion. On the other hand, Derrida's suggestion that logocentric thinking, which fails to realize the complete interdependence of all dualities, leads to repressive hierarchical systems lends some support to the Buddhist correlation of the realization of emptiness with more desirable ethical behavior. Another Buddhist view of liberation which can be interrogated by comparison with postmodern thought suggests that a realization of emptiness will bring about the dissolution of dogmatic attachments to any view or value. It is held that the freedom from attachment that accompanies a realization of the groundlessness of all views leads to an expansion of awareness and to the elimination of all the negative emotions that arise with the need to assert and defend one's views. Again, a serious challenge to the Buddhist's optimistic projections is presented by Nietzsche, who assumes that one who has realized the groundlessness of all views and values will seize their radical freedom and arbitrarily assert their own values. In contrast, the post-structuralists' expectation that the deconstruction of traditional hierarchies can function as a political tool to help bring marginalized and repressed voices to the center appears to confirm the Buddhist sense that those who understand that relatively of all views will be more open, inclusive people.

Tracing the source of human evil to false conceptions of the self and things and dogmatic views, Buddhists suggest that the refutation of all truth claims will eliminate these evils. Although not expecting such a sweeping reform of human character, post-structuralists also hold that a realization of the relativity and groundlessness of all views will mitigate some of humanity's most destructive tendencies. Nietzsche, on the other hand, sees in the refutation of all truth claims only the elimination of all grounds for ethical values and the freedom to live "beyond good and evil." The differing positions of the Western thinkers compel students to reflect critically on the ethical, spiritual and social implications of the Buddhist teaching of emptiness and to question whether it is the realization of emptiness per se, or the realization of emptiness within the context of a religious tradition that cannot be entirely grounded in this philosophical view, which could be responsible for the kinds of liberation attested to in the Buddhist tradition. Simultaneously, the Buddhist development of the soteriological dimensions of the realization of emptiness can help the students to understand more clearly the case for the positive ethical and existential implications of post-structuralism and the political dimensions of post-structuralist thought. Most importantly, the juxtaposition of the two traditions compels the students to appropriate each in a more critical manner, in what is perhaps a more Buddhist manner, with an awareness of the provisionality of all views.

Notes

[1] Nietzsche 1968, 302 (Bk. 3, #559).

[2] Nietzsche 1968, 300–307 (Bk. 3, #553–69). Note particularly aphorism #567, in which the argument leads to a vision of reality remarkably like that of Indra's Net of the Hua-yen tradition.

[3] For critiques of the "subject" see Nietzsche 1968, 267–72 (Bk. 3, #481–92); 1989, 23–24 (Bk. 1, #16, #17). For general critiques of all notions of enduring, self-identical "things," see Nietzsche 1968, 301 (Bk. 3, #556), 306–7 (Bk. 3, #569), 313–14 (Bk. 3, #583), 330 (Bk. 3, #616, #617); 1974, 171–72 (Bk. 3, #111).

[4] Nietzsche 1974, 171–72 (Bk. 3, #112) and 1989, 30–31 (Bk. 1, #22).

[5] For arguments against causality, see Nietzsche 1989, 25–26 (Bk. 1, #19); 1968, 263–65 (Bk. 3, #477, #478) and 295–97 (Bk. 3, #551).

[6] For arguments against both freedom and determinism, see Nietzsche 1989, 28–30 (Bk. 1, #21).

[7] Nietzsche 1989, 24 (Bk. 1, #17).

[8] Nietzsche 1968, 330–31 (Bk. 3, #616, #617).

[9] Nietzsche 1968, 14–15 (Bk. 1, #15).

[10] Nietzsche 1968, 9–15 (Bk. 1, #2–#16) and 316–19 (Bk. 3, #585).

[11] Saussure 1966, 120–22.

[12] Derrida distinguishes his view of the linguistic system from Saussure's in "Différance" (Derrida 1982, 3–27).

[13] See Derrida (1982, 12–13) for a discussion of the "trace."

[14] For a definition and critique of "logocentrism" see Derrida 1976, 6–26.

[15] Derrida 1977, 236.

[16] Derrida 1981, 41.

[17] A sustained critique of logic can be found in Nietzsche 1968, 276–86.

References

Derrida, Jacques. 1976. *Of Grammatology*. Translated by Gayatri Spivak. Baltimore: Johns Hopkins University Press.

———. 1977. "Limited, Inc." In *Glyph, 2*. Baltimore: Johns Hopkins University Press.

————. 1981. *Positions*. Chicago: University of Chicago Press.

————. 1982. "Différance." In *Margins of Philosophy*, translated by Alan Bass. Chicago: University of Chicago Press.

Nietzsche, Friedrich. 1968. *The Will to Power*. Translated by Walter Kaufmann and R. J. Hollingdale. New York: Vintage Books.

————. 1974. The *Gay Science*. Translated by Walter Kaufmann. New York: Vintage Books.

————. 1989. *Beyond Good and Evil*. Translated by Walter Kaufmann. New York: Vintage Books.

Saussure, Ferdinand de. 1966. *Course in General Linguistics*. Translated by Wade Baskin. New York: McGraw Hill.

Zen in the Classroom

Zen and the Art of Not Teaching Zen and the Arts: An Autopsy

Ronald L. Grimes

One reason I avoid workshops and seminars on teaching is that they are so regularly prescriptive. My view, informed by a commitment to ethnographic field work, is that you haven't earned the right to prescribe until you have adequately described, and that adequate description arises from attending to actual performances in local places at specific times. For twenty-odd years I have taught a course called "Zen Meditation, Zen Art." When I first proposed it, darts arrived from several directions. A colleague at another university assured me that I was less than qualified to teach it, my several years of Zen practice notwithstanding. My Japanese was non-existent; so was Sanskrit. Chinese we didn't talk about. And I was no buddhologist. What did I think I was doing?

I said I was not teaching classical Buddhism on the basis of classical or canonical Buddhist texts. I explained that the bulk of the course was on Zen and its acculturation in North America. I poked back by asking how qualified he was to teach the last leg of Buddhism's historical journey, the one that culminates in contemporary North America—my field, not his. I asked: Would we require a course on Christianity in North America to begin with Jesus and the New Testament? There are roots courses, I said, but there are also fruits courses; one was not better or worse than the other, just different. My colleague was unmoved by my quips even though he knew I meant what I said.

Then there were members of the university's arts and science council, who, never having seen a course description involving any kind of Buddhism, read it with a mixture of bewilderment and be-musement. The first question was tossed out by a testy professor of English: "Why isn't this course being offered at the community col-lege, where they teach bricklaying and underwater basket weaving and god knows what else? Surely, the so-called arts in this course descrip-tion, can you believe it, flower arranging and martial arts? These have no proper place in an arts and science curriculum of a modern West-ern university." Fortunately, a Japanese-sword-collecting colleague from our school of business and economics (quarters from which I did not expect support) sparred my colleague from English and won straight-away. So my only entry into that fray was to remind another inquirer that, no, I had not been hired to teach "theology and litera-ture" but "religion and the arts in North America" and that "the arts" were variously construed in different cultures and that, no, I did not think a course on Milton's Paradise Lost and Christianity would be a better alternative; the English department, thank you, was doing that.

Students would like the course offering whether colleagues did or not. It was the mid-1970s, and Zen still had an exotic appeal; it rang mystical, if not true. So the first time I taught "Zen Meditation, Zen Art" it flew. The students said so, and I knew it. By the second and third times around, I realized that it was the most revision-free course I had ever taught. Students arrived in droves eager for enlightenment, more than willing to practice *zazen* on the floor, chant *sūtras*, and visit Zen centers in Toronto. Though they left unenlightened, they had a sense for the practice and its cultural ramifications. The only com-plaint was that the course was not more experiential. Why not *zazen* in the Ritual Studies Lab twice a week, tea ceremonies, a makeshift *sesshin*, and encounters with a few visiting Zen masters? Some years I relented and offered *zazen* outside class.

A few students from that era, especially those who sat, stay in contact some twenty-five years later. One is now a Buddhist priest; others have spent time in Zen centers and monasteries. Testimonies arrived, unbidden, extolling the course's life-changing, life-enhancing qualities. I did not set out to make converts, only to convey or evoke the sense of Zen. I believed—and still believe—that if students do not sense a subject, they will not understand it. Education is of the senses as well as of the emotions and the brain.

After those initial, successful years there was an interlude created by several converging forces: the need to teach other courses, sabbatical, my own struggles in a Zen teacher training program, and the availability of part-time faculty with impressive credentials. For a decade or so I did not teach the course even though I sometimes wanted to. Then came the academic year 1999–2000. Once again I was scheduled to teach the Zen course. Fondly remembering the early days of the course, I anticipated it. But when students stopped by to sign up for the course—it had a waiting list—I found myself tipping backward rather than looking forward. The students talked about Zen in a tone that struck me as different, not what I remembered. They were mildly curious, hoping to be entertained. They were not looking for masters or expecting to be enlightened.

By mid-term it was evident to both my teaching assistant, Barry Stephenson, and me that something was not taking, that we were failing to cultivate a sense for Zen among the students. So we resorted to more dramatic means. We arranged a debate. Students were to come to class in the persona of some Zen figure. They didn't have to dress up, but they were to maintain the demeanor, attitude, and speech of a Zen student or Zen master they had read about. In an attempt to have them encounter Zen as embodied in named and located persons rather than as a set of generic ideas and practices, the course had introduced them to half a dozen practitioners whom they now got to "be."

Barry and I provoked debate among the virtual Zen masters and students in class. If we couldn't inspire them, then we'd tease them into crawling into someone else's skin. Two Zen teachers, themselves the spiritual offspring of a common master, were pressed to take up their differences in public. An entrepreneurial teacher was confronted with students who thought he had lost touch with the point of the practice. Marginalized and exploited female Zen students confronted marginalizing, cavorting American male teachers. Even though students playing the roles had absorbed few of the details of the lives they were representing, once they loosened up, they did enter into the spirit of *dharma* horsing around (however unlike *dharma* combat it may have been.)

Later in the course we tried another performance strategy. When it became all too obvious that the students didn't understand *kōans*, that, in fact, they were not even intrigued by them, we resorted to acting out. Barry became the Zen master and I, his student. He got to slap me publicly, and, coached by our rubrics and texts, we stood on desk tops, acting the fool in search of the oxlike self. But the best we could do was titillate a lethargic, slightly amused audience; they marveled that we would make such a desperate spectacle of ourselves. A key component of the course is the final "Zen and the art of" project. The number of "Zen and the art of" books is large. Many of the books are junk, but they reflect North American ways of selectively adapting and distorting historic Zen. A major aim of the class is to attend to the values that determine patterns of adaptation and modes of distortion. And the populist artsiness of the American "Zen and the art of" industry is a good example for study. My aim in having students study this motif is partly to incubate their creativity and partly to inculcate a healthy iconoclasm. Doing so successfully requires a delicate balancing act.

I had remained foolishly hopeful right up to the very end, even though the course was one of the flattest I had taught in thirty years. But the "Zen and the art of" projects set me back. With each new paper I was faced with my own failure to teach even the most basic ideas, attitudes, and practices that I had set out to teach in the Zen course. The students wrote as if they had not taken it. Students were allowed to write on an Asian art traditionally associated with Zen—*haiku*, tea, Noh, *sumi*, and so on—or on a Western art such as photography, sculpture, literature, poetry, or dance, provided they first conducted research on a traditional Asian form. If students chose to pursue a project on a Western art, they were to read about Zen's relation to the traditional arts of Asia, particularly Japan, as well as study some of the enormous "Zen and the art of" literature now flooding the North American market. Then they were to ask, for instance, What would it mean to engage in photography as an extension of practice, as if it were a Zen art? Photographers were advised to look at the Zen Mountain Web site for examples.

In addition to discussing ways a specific art and a distinctive religious tradition interact, students were invited to submit their own art and to describe the process, for instance, of shooting and developing. In the "old days" of the Zen course students had begged to be allowed to experiment and practice with Zen and art. But this time the requirement was met with incredulity and indifference, with only an occasional flash of interest.

The papers written about Asian arts inevitably emphasized form, content, or technique, and they stuck closely to the scholarly texts they had read; largely they summarized sources. Those written on Euro-American arts emphasized spontaneity and personal expression. Despite repeated lectures and discussions on the Western acculturation of Zen, students inevitably settled on flow or spontaneity as the Zen quality and then wrote entire papers showing how their photographs, shot five years ago, surprisingly exhibited this very quality. One student opened a project this way:

> Chuang-Tzu once said, "flow with whatever may happen and let your mind be free. Stay centered by accepting whatever you are doing. This is the ultimate." To me, this is the essence of Zen and the art of photography. When one can concentrate on the pictures they are taking and be free from all the surrounding distractions, not only will they be happy with the results, but they have captured the Zen way. Although there are multiple ways to do this, I think the three most important are being flexible and spontaneous, being "in the moment" of where you are, and being personal with your work instead of detaching yourself from it.

This student not only assumes Zen art has an essence and cites a Taoist to illustrate a Zen Buddhist attitude but talks as if happiness with results is the obvious aim of Zen. In this view, the proper Zen way to achieve that goal is to tune out the surroundings (even though course readings and lectures repeatedly emphasized that Zen meditation was not about tuning out distractions or quelling thoughts). The writer, by no means a poor one, emphasizes flexibility and spontaneity despite the fact that *zazen*, the most basic of Zen Buddhist practices, is so heavily structured that expressions of spontaneity usually violate its decorum. The student's paper identifies "the Zen of" an art with its expression of the personal, despite the fact that Zen monks shave their heads, dress alike, obey their teachers, and otherwise comport themselves in ways designed to quell the ego rather than enhance the personality. In short, the writer of this paper sees only similarities between the style of her photography and the style of Zen. To me, the differences were blatant. When the Western way of photographing is laid alongside either Zen practice or Zen-influenced Asian arts, I have to work to find continuities. We had repeatedly talked about the ritual grounding of Zen, about learning by imitation, about formality, and about structure. Never mind, Zen is spontaneity, presence to the moment.

The student told about having been forced in a high school photography class to shoot a roll of film a week for twenty weeks. The subject matter was the schoolyard itself. She experienced the assignment as boring but nevertheless included some stunning old photographs along with this comment, "All of these pictures are pictures that I may not have taken had I not been forced to adapt to my surroundings; however I was pleased with the results." So even though she knows that there was a rigid structure and that it, in part, was responsible for her photographic success, Zen was still about flexibility, spontaneity, and self-expression. What did the assignment teach her? She quotes Lao Tzu, not a Buddhist: "Softness triumphs over hardness." I wrote in her margin: "Zen photography is not merely about spontaneity. If you hadn't had the rule that forced you, you wouldn't have discovered the scenes you shot. The story you tell here is not only about adaptability and flexibility, as you seem to believe, but also about a strict form: Shoot a roll a week on and of the school grounds. The story is not about the triumph of softness over hardness, but about the integration of softness (be flexible) and hardness (follow the rules). Right?"

This student was one of the better ones in the course. I cite her paper as an example not because it was among the worst but because it was among the most articulate. Like the others in class, she had heard me say that Zen is not identical with spontaneity, or even with presence, and certainly not with personality enhancement—that's what North Americans want to find in Zen.

But saying is not teaching.

I was struck by how doggedly and systematically students were able to tune out what they had learned—rather, what I imagined they had learned. However I squeezed the balloon of their brains, they returned stubbornly to the shape they originally had. Some force greater than I, "the culture," was responsible. Even though many students equated "the Zen" or "the art" of something with spontaneity, they neither noticed nor articulated the contradiction involved in submitting paintings or photographs done several years ago. Old photos and high school art work were pulled out of drawers. Many of the projects implied the title: "Zen and the art of retrospective interpretation of old works of art as if they were executed under the influence of Zen practice." It had not occurred to me that an "art of" project would elicit such desperate or lackadaisical methods, so I had not written into the course requirements "You cannot hand in old art work" any more than I had specified, "You may not hand in papers from last year's courses." I had assumed that a new course meant new work. I had assumed too that the heavy Zen emphasis on attending to the present would elicit present-oriented experimentation and research. I expected student to pay concentrated attention to the details, fluctuations, and foibles of the creative process. I was dead wrong.

I had hoped that students would raise and explore difficult questions and struggle out loud with some of the perpetual quotation marks that plague courses on contemporary North American Zen:

Would a "Zen photographer" sensibility search out "natural" rather than industrial content?

Is a black and white photograph "more Zen" than a color photo?

Does "the Zen of" something consist of its content? Its style? The attitude with which it is done? The manner of its performance?

Should a "Zen photo" look "more Japanese" than "American?"

Does photography become a "Zen art" when preceded or followed by meditation?

Is "the Zen" of an art dependent upon how it is interpreted (rather than how it is executed)?

Is an edited or touched up photo by definition a "non-Zen" photo? (After all, you can't erase or edit the tracks of an ink brush.)

Wrestling with such questions in lectures did not guarantee that they would be considered in projects. Why not? Why was I so unsuccessful at eliciting paradox, play, irony, iconoclasm, and the other processes that had made the course work so well in years past? I have considered obvious ways of accounting for the failure of the 1999-2000 version of RE298: I am getting old and stale; this was a remarkably stupid bunch; the failure was a mere fluke and things will improve next time around; Tibetan Buddhism is now in and Zen, out. But in the end I have concluded that the most decisive factor is the cultural milieu, the culture of learning at university and the larger culture surrounding it. It is not merely that Zen no longer has the exotic appeal that, say Tibetan Buddhism has, it is also that students fret over rather than long for creativity and experimentation in the classroom. They are desperate to be given explicit rules and directions, preferably coupled with marks that can be achieved by following them. They are disoriented, even threatened by paradox, silence, simplicity, playfulness, and the other "virtues" that made Zen and student life seem so obviously connected in the 1970s and 1980s.

In short, the milieu makes "audience reception" of this course content much more difficult than it was a quarter of a century ago. The social stream in which we all swim is not the stream that once was. We professors talk about religious traditions and religious studies topics as if they are eternal verities that a good teacher can teach anytime, anywhere. In actuality, certain traditions and practices make better, or at least easier, sense in one time or one place than in another. Teaching about Zen now is different and, for me, more difficult, than it was two decades ago because the motivating predispositions have evaporated. Even though it may well be deluded to enter a Buddhism course looking for enlightenment or for a master, that is at least a motivation. It is easier by far to redirect a motivation than to create one.

But the story I tell is not entirely dreary. Near the end of the course, two students working jointly on Zen and the art of tea asked if they might supplement their paper on traditional tea ceremonies with one performed for, and with, the class. Of course, I said. In years past I had been flooded with initiatives like this, so I was grateful for this glimmer of hope.

On the evening of the class, the two young women came by my office at 6:15 to set up for a 7:00 class. I took the lateness of arrival, the harried looks on their faces, and the presence of a boom box as bad signs. Barry accompanied them to the room they were preparing as their tea hut. At a quarter to seven, when I arrived and figured out they were using beer cups, plastic flowers, and paper cut-out stepping stones leading down the hall to our tea hut, I wanted to go home and pull weeds in the back yard. If I had sensed even the slightest tinge of irony in their demeanor, I would have danced a jig. Would I be the chief guest, they queried. Yes, of course, but what is my job? I asked, ever the educator. I should enter first, they said, and wash my hands so the other guests could see how it was supposed to be done. And I should leave last.

What music is on your CD player, I queried. It was some soupy, dreamy, astonishingly inappropriate piece. I suggested: Silence would be quite fine. No, they said, we want music. Well, okay, if you want music, I said, how about something a bit more in keeping with the spirit of the ceremony? Sure, they said. I hurried away and returned with Tony Scott's "Music for Zen Meditation," only slightly more appropriate. When improvising, improvise. I didn't know whether to laugh or cry during the demonstration/ceremony. So, of course, I did neither. The ethos was that of a grade four Shakespeare play or a Christmas pageant. We were awkward, self-conscious, and nothing showed much sensitivity to the tea ceremony or suggested that educated choices had been made on the basis of serious reading. I was not expecting a replication, only something "in the spirit of" Zen. We sat uncomfortably on the hard tile floor having tiptoed across the treacherous white cardboard stepping stones, which, not having been taped down, slipped this way and that across the hall floor.

Not until the hot tea began to burn my hand through the plastic beer mug did I settle down into my belly and notice that several other participants were doing likewise. For ten minutes perhaps we sat sipping hot tea and watching our self-consciousness fade. For a few moments even the spilling of tea and the shifting of untrained, weary bones became part of the event. A few "guests" drifted off into boredom; a few were embarrassed; but most began to inhabit the cluttered, sterile place and actually taste the tea.

We returned back across the bridge of cardboard stones to our regular class room. Expecting criticism or indifference, I opened with a preface calculated to protect the two students: "I appreciate your courage in taking on such a difficult topic. I am also delighted to have had time in the midst of end-of-term madness to sit and sip tea that warms the hands and belly. So let me ask your classmates: 'If you were to perform a Canadianized tea ceremony, what would you do that is the same or different from what your two classmates have just done?'" I was hoping to elicit gentle critique and some comparison of Japanese tea and Canadian tea (or even Canadian beer).

The first response came quickly and energetically from a student who had regularly been critical of the class. "This is the highlight of the course," she exclaimed. "Now, for the first time, I get it," she said. I believed her. The outpouring from other students echoed her sentiment. The enthusiasm and sense of recognition were so pervasive that I felt free to joke about the beer cups, the music that almost got played, the cardboard slipping stones, the plastic flowers, and the jammed up desks that had surrounded us like a stack of ghostly bones in an elephants' graveyard.

The truth is that I would have been embarrassed had the ceremony been witnessed by any of my finely tuned, linguistically well-educated colleagues who teach university courses in Buddhism. It would not have measured up to their expectations or mine, and it would have been loud testimony that I had failed to teach Zen or the art of anything. The ceremony lacked simplicity. It lacked precision. It lacked silence. And it lacked attentiveness. Never mind the fine points of gesture and posture, its tone and tenor were off.

But something worked despite all that. The beer-cup tea ceremony became the high point of the course. I remind myself that the rite was not of my doing and it transpired despite my resistance and self-consciousness. It succeeded despite me, despite the course, despite the two students, even despite itself. Ritualizing, it seems, works even when it fails.

Writing Religion

This story is not quite over. Running simultaneously with RE298 was RE400, "Writing Religion," a required course for Religious Studies honors students in their last year. As fate would have it, the course had only a dozen students, which meant it could be held in the Ritual Studies Lab, which, as karma would have it, is outfitted with just that many *zafus* and *zabutons*. "Ah," I said to someone, "writing close to the floor: good for the ass, the bones, and the soul." The course is partly a reward and partly remedial. It is a reward for those who, in their last days at university, have finally learned enough to wish they could write well. It is remedial for those who not only don't, but also don't care if they don't. Half the class consists of "creative" writing on religious themes; the other half is analytical. The first half is soft, nurturing, and vaguely Buddhist; it aims at producing a story or personal essay. The second half is hard-edged, secular, editorial, and critical; it aims to produce an article for a scholarly journal. Each student's writing goes through multiple drafts and multiple readers.

Except for having chosen Natalie Goldberg's *Writing Down the Bones* as one of the books for the first half, everything else "Buddhist" about the course came about by accident or improvisation. One afternoon a student complained about writing trash, so we did some deliberate trash writing and needed a god to whom we might offer such stuff. I remembered there was a sleepy-eyed, tilted-to-one-side Mexican Buddha in the closet; he would do. So out came a bowl, the Buddha, and a bell with which to mark the moment for feeding trash to the Hungry Buddha of Bad Writing. Had there been a Goddess of Bad Writing in the closet, we'd have used her.

Then the obvious dawned: Why not offer Buddha some good writing too? Then Christian and "other" students were invited to bring Christian and "other" gods for our improvised writing altar. We would not play favorites here. The advantage of Lord Buddha, I teased, is that he is indifferent to judgments of good and bad. Isn't he? Almost by accident "Writing Religion" became as much about religion as it was about writing. Why learn only about the craft of writing religion? Why not also play along the edges of a religion too? Write Christian. Write Hindu. What does it mean to write not only using this or that technique but to write in, or at the edge, of this or that religious practice? Education by indirection.

Indirectly, the writing course became more of a Zen course than the Zen course was. We sat. We drank tea. We wrote. We shared what we wrote. We trashed what we wrote. We treasured what we wrote. We offered Buddha the fruits of our writing. When celebrating, we blew bubbles over his dozing head. When disappointed, we burned or shredded.

The writing course was not a proper Buddhism course, but it kept becoming one by indirection and happenstance. Since this was a workshop, not a lecture course, aphorisms and *teisho*-like utterances popped out on their own accord. And the space of Ritual Studies Lab had its own mind about such matters, since it has been the scene of several decades of ritual experiment and critique. It, we noticed, seemed to be asking for aphorisms to be posted on the door, painted on the wall, and written in green ink on writers' hands so they would not be forgotten: "Show. Don't tell." This is the standard advice of creative writing teachers. Uttered repeatedly atop round cushions and punctuated by bell ringing and incense burning, the attitude is absorbed from underneath the writerly consciousness. While we debated the placement of commas and jerked misplaced modifiers into line, we also cultivated writing attitudes. Excerpted rightly, writing about writing can easily be made to echo sentiments we North Americans have learned to associate with Zen:

Writing is not...an art but breathing. – Anaïs Nin

The ideal view for daily writing, hour on hour, is the blank brick wall of a cold storage warehouse. Failing this, a stretch of sky will do, cloudless if possible. – Edna Ferber

Only the hand that erases can write the true thing. – Meister Eckhart

Every time I sit at my desk, I look at my dictionary, a Webster's Second Unabridged with nine million words in it, and think: All the words I need are in there; they're just in the wrong order. – Fran Lebowitz

We must write where we stand; wherever we do stand, there is life...
– John Updike

If you wish to be a writer, write. – Epictetus

One reason religions are so poorly understood is that they are so flatly and unevocatively described. One reason they are woodenly described is that we were never taught how to attend carefully and fully to words. Both as students and as teachers we spew them, rushing from term paper to term paper, then article to article. We don't sit with them. Writing in the Lab, we sat with words, sometimes even a word.

When I inquired how many people revised papers submitted for courses, one student raised her hand. For everyone else, revision, editing, and searching for just the right word were foreign activities. So "Writing Religion" became a course about attending, dwelling, pausing, and taking time with words. Words are treasures, we said, yet eminently deletable. Every word is special, even sacred, you could say. Even so, every word is subject to deletion. What we learned about writing in RE400 was not much different from what Zen teachers say about an inhalation or exhalation.

Natalie Goldberg's *Writing Down the Bones* is not only a Zen book, it is a period piece and cultural artifact. The stench of popular psychology, Western aestheticism, and the American workshop circuit are all over it. It not only stinks of Zen but of American Zen. Americanized Zen writing is different, very different from Japanese calligraphy, not just in form or content but in fundamental sensibility. But Guatemalan Christianity differs radically from Roman Christianity, and African Caribbean religions differ remarkably from Ashanti religion. So how much does it matter whether the Buddhism taught is North American rather than Japanese or Korean, whether it arrives indirectly in a writing course or directly in a Zen course? They all reek, and they should; that is the nature of acculturation.

Is writing under Goldberg's tutelage "Zen" writing? Or merely American writing? Or turn-of-the-millennium writing? The answer to the question does not matter much. For the purposes of the course what mattered was that students learn to care about writing and then develop a writerly rhythm: attend, discard, treasure; attend, discard, treasure; attend fully, then discard. Have no attachment to a word, phrase, paragraph, or paper; yet write something you treasure passionately. Just remember: Treasuring has a life-span. Today's treasure will become tomorrow's discard.

In the Ritual Studies Lab and with Goldberg's assistance we ritualized the act of writing. In other versions of the course, the aim had been the production of a work of verbal art or scholarship. In this version, the aim was to perform the act of writing in a ritualized manner. It just so happened that the ritual idiom was indebted to Zen Buddhism.

At the beginning of the course I hung a blank scroll on the wall. This is how Ritual Studies Lab courses always begin. I invited students to sign it using traditional Japanese ink and brush. I gave no mini-lecture on calligraphy. "In your own good time," I said, "please sign the scroll, thereby formally entering the course. Write: 'I am a writer,' then sign your name below that." Most participants sat still. I had deliberately made the task of signing in too heavy. Eventually, I made the task less onerous: "You may mean whatever you wish by those words: 'I aspire to be a writer.' I am hot stuff because I am published. I am a student, therefore I write papers, therefore I am, by definition, a writer." Whatever students meant, they had to discover or invent it in the act of putting brush to scroll. Their first act required them to attend to a signature and to do so with an uncharacteristic intensity. The advice, "Every word in a story or article is like your name signed at the bottom of a check," is not much different from the advice, "Let every breath be your last" or "To sit is to die."

When the writing course was over, I felt it a success. When the Zen course ended the same week I felt it a failure. Where I had intended to teach Zen I had not. Where I had not intended to teach

Zen I had. In authoring this autopsy it occurs to me that perhaps I taught neither Zen nor writing but only Pauline theology: That which I would do, I have not done, and that which I would not do, I have done. I teach Buddhism and I teach writing in unorthodox ways, but not because I think either is special. The arguments for "experiencing" Zen are no stronger than those for experiencing, say, Anishnabe or Muslim religion.

The line between teaching and practice is fine, never easy to walk, but always worth trying. If I were teaching Christianity, I'd likely have students singing hymns in class. Pressed to defend the practice, I say something like this: Such subjunctive experiences, however complex and dangerous, are a necessary part of the process of participant observation, an ethnographic method that, in my view, is not for the field only but also for the classroom. I do not claim that everyone should teach every course in Buddhism in this way, only that an embodied, "participatory" pedagogy is a valid form of teaching and learning and that it is not a propagandistic move to make converts.

The quotation marks around "experiencing" and "participatory" are necessary. They signal the crucial as-if. The as-if does not render the experience and participation unreal, but it does put them in brackets, suggesting that the reality of the Zen and the writing that I teach is peculiar, even fictive. But fiction has real consequences.

Liberal Education and the Teaching of Buddhism

Victor Sōgen Hori

For many years, Frank Reynolds has been writing both about the teaching of Buddhism in the modern university and, in a wider context, about the crisis in liberal education in general. In an article "Introducing Buddhism," Reynolds identifies four problems internal to the pedagogy of teaching Buddhism in the university classroom. He cautions us against transmitting an overly simplistic picture of what Buddhism "really is," against depicting the history of Buddhism as either a one-directional degeneration from its originally pure form or a one-directional unfolding of its true essence into its modern form, against overly romanticizing Buddhism in a way that caters to disaffected Western intellectuals, and against emphasizing its "other-worldly" aspects while ignoring the social, political and economic forms in which Buddhism has actually appeared.[1] Teachers of university and college courses in Buddhism everywhere will wince with guilt at hearing Reynolds expose so clearly this list of the unexamined assumptions we so often impose on our subject matter.

In "Reconstructing Liberal Education: A Religious Studies Perspective" and "Teaching Buddhism in the Postmodern University: Understanding, Critique, Evaluation," his keynote address at the Teaching Buddhism Conference, Reynolds turns his wide-angle lens onto the troubling plight of liberal education in general. To break up the rigid idea that liberal education is the study of some fixed core of Western values, Reynolds pans across the spread of history to show us that the notion of liberal education itself has evolved and changed. In its early form, which Reynolds calls "Renaissance humanism," only the intellectual and cultural elite had access to liberal education. It constituted an initiation process for those who, by being born into the upper echelons of bourgeois society, were destined to be the leaders of the social world of their times. Although students were exposed to the new Enlightenment notion of Reason, nevertheless the major part of the curriculum was devoted to a study of classical texts in Greek, Latin and Hebrew. Through the study of these texts in which they encountered discussions of the training of the mind and the instilling of virtue, it was thought that the students themselves would become trained in mind and instilled with virtue, as befit those meant to assume leadership in society.[2]

This Renaissance notion of liberal education held sway until the end of the nineteenth century, when social and intellectual changes forced liberal education to evolve into a second stage. With this second stage, which Reynolds calls "modernist" liberal education, in the social realm, education got extended to new kinds of people (like women) and in intellectual content, the study of Reason thoroughly overran the study of classical texts. The empire of Reason pushed its boundaries past the physical world to include the human world through the newly emerging social sciences. In response to this expansion, classical studies, which hitherto had known no boundaries, shrank back into an enclave called "the humanities." At the same time, where the voices in Renaissance liberal education more or less supported the religious, social and economic institutions of Western bourgeois society, the voices in modernist liberal education (e.g., Marxist, Freudian, militant secularist, and more recently feminist) were often harshly critical. What Renaissance liberal education took as obvious truth, the modernist saw increasingly as false consciousness.[3]

Although the ideals of modernist liberal education still determine the curricula of many fine liberal arts programs across the continent today, its basic assumptions are starting to visibly disintegrate. We are thus now entering a postmodern period where the very idea of liberal education is being challenged on many fronts. Globalism has brought the West face to face with the "other" of Asia and Africa, starkly revealing the cultural chauvinism of much liberal education.

The most corrosive postmodern change, however, has been the spread of deep skepticism against the Enlightenment notion of Reason itself. Reason was supposed to be a prejudice-free means for transcending divisive religious conflict; it was supposed to be the critical instrument for exposing the false consciousness of our traditional institutions and for making visible the objective truth. But in the postmodern period, even Reason itself is said to be a humanly constructed thing; even objective truth itself is said to be historically, socially, culturally and politically determined.[4]

Reynolds notes that in Renaissance liberal education, the "liberal" in liberal education referred to the "free men" whose background and education fitted them to inherit and transmit the religious and cultural values of the West. In modernist liberal education, it came to refer to the freedom which a critical education provided in exposing the unexamined religious and cultural prejudices of inherited tradition.[5] But what meaning, if any, does "liberal" have in the postmodern period? Reynolds does not directly discuss this question. In the postmodern period, is there still some real sense in which to become educated is to become free, or has "liberal education" become the latest oxymoron?

Institutional Practices and Autonomy

Reynolds's historical survey focuses primarily on the intellectual content of the curriculum of the university where there is now great confusion as to what to teach and why it ought to be taught. While such a historical survey is essential for any discussion of modern education, nevertheless, by focusing on intellectual content, it does not take into account the actual institutional practices through which the university teaches. Reynolds's discussion focuses, as it were, on the *sūtra* and *śastra* of liberal education and neglects the *vinaya* of liberal education. When I speak of the practices of the university, I am referring to the actions and policies of the numerous individual teachers and instructors, administrative and curricular officers, committees, departments, student advisors, and other parts of the educational and administrative machinery of the university which sets admission, program and degree requirements; which runs the student advising offices, disciplinary boards, offices for students with disabilities, ombudsperson; and which manages residences, athletic teams, students activities, publications, and so forth. These people and offices all set policy and make many individual decisions guided by highly politicized notions of equality, freedom and education. We are all familiar with the vocabulary of these ideas, vocabulary which labels some injustice and its remedy: "discrimination" and "equal access," "systemic racism" and "affirmative opportunity," "powerlessness" and "empowerment," "sexual harassment" and "respect," and so on. The watchwords dealing with education include such things as "student rights," "empowerment of the student," and "student centered learning."

In this paper, I will use the phrase "autonomy of the student" to cover this loose set of usages. Any attempt to define this loose notion of autonomy would trigger highly charged disagreements, but its cash value can be seen in new institutional apparatus like student participation in university decision-making bodies, a student charter of rights, student ombudsmen, judicial councils, and new regulations such as our local rule that the professor cannot change a course syllabus in mid-term without the consent of the class. Everyone more or less agrees that while they are in the university, rather than the university telling students what to study, the students should be "empowered" to make their own decisions. Everyone more or less agrees that the mission of the university is to provide students with the knowledge and skills necessary to function as an autonomous member of the wider society without need for dependence on others. While, as Reynolds shows, intellectual disagreement reigns in philosophical discussions of liberal education, in institutional terms, it is widely agreed that liberal education is education which both respects and enhances the autonomy of the student. If "liberal education" can be defined in institutional terms, this is the definition.

It is not obvious to me that unreflective agreement on the notion of autonomy is any better than the self-conscious disagreement on the nature of liberal education.

For those who may think that "autonomy" is a meaningless plati-
tude without concrete application, one need only recall the ambiance
of the university one or two generations ago when universities still
defined liberal education as that which promoted loyalty to America
and automatically assumed that part of their task was to instill a
proper morality in their students. When I was a university student in
the mid-'60s, we bridled under the university's assumption *in loco parentis* of authority over students. Legally the university was the representative of the parents in matters of student discipline. On this legal
ground, the university enforced gender segregation in the dormitories, forbade drinking, imposed noise rules, and in general assumed
authority, when necessary, for telling students how to run their lives.
This prim façade never did contain the restless energy of youth bent
on experimenting with alcohol, ideas, sex, and freedom from parents
and authority. But *in loco parentis* made it clear that the university as
an institution was daddy and the students were children.

By the end of the '60s, however, youth around the world were in
full and open revolt against such presumptuous authority not only in
universities but in large institutions in general. The revolt was fed by
the social turmoil caused by the war in Vietnam, which showed con-
cretely that the government, the military and big industry lived in its
own ideological world, pursued its own agenda and responded only
under extreme pressure to popular criticism. It was fueled by the civil
rights movements in the United States which reminded the American
public conscience that it had failed to bring an end to systematic ra-
cial discrimination. In the wake of popular protest, many large institutions which had a culture of hierarchy and authority were forced to
redefine their working procedures around new watchwords: openness,
equality, dignity, truthfulness, autonomy. In hospitals, for example,
no longer was the doctor accepted as an all-knowing paternal figure
with the authority to make decisions for the patient; no longer was
the patient a child-like dependent who could be kept deliberately
ignorant of the nature of his or her medical condition. In the new
patient empowerment movement, the patient demanded to be
treated with dignity and respect, to be told the truth about his or her
own medical condition. At the same time, patients criticized the in-

creasing dehumanization of hospital treatment, a product of increasing technological mechanization and ever-creeping bureaucratization. Even so rigidly hierarchical an organization as the military was put on the defensive by events such as the congressional investigation which showed that American forces had committed an atrocity at My Lai in Vietnam, and it too reviewed its hazing procedures, its cover-ups of sexual harassment, its institutionalized abuse of authority, its treatment of gays.

Reformers in education started at the kindergarten level and worked up in criticizing traditional classroom practices. Rote learning, testing, streaming, the teacher's authority in the classroom, corporal punishment, were all criticized for deadening the student's innate creativity or vilified as barely disguised social indoctrination. Students would enthusiastically teach themselves, it was said, if only their creative instincts were released. New schools with romantic names like Rivendell were devoted to de-institutionalizing education so that spontaneity could thrive. Education was no longer thought to be training in the culture and civilization of the great tradition; it was supposed to be the release of one's original nature, the nurturing of spontaneity, a return to naturalness, play. In universities and colleges, students reacted against the social hierarchy which glorified the professor and demeaned the student, against the bureaucratic and mechanized university system which told students what to study and reduced student identity to a number. After the Age of Aquarius swept through the university, students and professors called each other by their first names, they all wore jeans and sandals, the university created an increasing number of degree and program options so students could have freedom of choice, and grades got inflated so that few failed or even did badly. The idea that the university's mission was to inspire loyalty and instill morality now came to seem quaint and in response the university abandoned its old stance of benevolent paternalism and paid lip service to a new ideal, the student as autonomous agent.

It is worthwhile remembering how deeply conservative these social protests were. Despite the fact that the popular revolts of the '60s and early '70s attacked traditional mainstream institutions like government, universities, big business and the military, nevertheless they attacked in the name of the rights of the individual, one of the oldest rocks upon which American democracy stands. The contemporary emphasis in the university on the individual person as an autonomous agent similarly sounds liberal but is essentially very conservative. It reiterates the deeply held American belief that the state, the institution, and society in general must refrain from compromising the rights of minorities and individuals. This ambiguity between what is liberal and what is conservative should remind us of one of the lessons of history: ideologically speaking, sometimes very little separates the social critics of society and the mainstream institutions they attack.

Before I move on to the topic of classroom practices, I would first like to mention the effect of institutional procedures outside the classroom. Students learn social virtues or vices as much from the actual institutional practices of the university outside the classroom as from the texts they study in their courses. Let us get away from the romantic notion, still current, that simply studying a text about virtue teaches a student to be virtuous (my alma mater, Stanford University, used to publish testimonials from people who said they had developed a strong sense of ethics from their humanities courses at Stanford). Whatever the content of liberal education, the university's institutional procedures teach an ethics of "me first." In a large class where grades are distributed on a bell curve, students know that a limited percentage of the class gets an A grade. Grading on a bell curve immediately tells a student that he or she is in competition with all the other students in the class, that for one student to get an A grade, some other student must get a B grade or less. Students thus have little motivation to cooperate with other students in joint teaching and learning unless the professor structures the grading to deliberately encourage cooperation between students. In a large class with several teaching assistants, students immediately compare grades to learn which teaching assistant is the easy grader and some students will maneuver themselves into the easy grader's group. It is common knowledge among students that when they cannot meet a deadline, they need only obtain a medical statement from a doctor or a letter from a parent pleading a "family emergency" in order to get an extension. Teachers know that the medical excuse or the parent's letter is often a charade but students also know that their teachers have no option but to connive with them and accept the excuse. When the final grades are announced, students unhappy with their grade can appeal the grade. In some universities, the appeal machinery does not even inform the professor that the student is appealing a grade and allows no chance for the professor to defend his grade in the appeal process. In class, the students are reading about Plato's philosopher-king or about the career of the compassionate bodhisattva but outside class, the university is giving students onsite training in how to maneuver in the institution and inculcating an ethics of "me first."

I once had a student who at the end of the term had high grades in all her assignments for the course except for one which was a zero. When I called her and asked if she had submitted an assignment, she told me that at the time of the assignment, she had broken up with a long-term boyfriend and had been in no emotional state to write a paper. She knew that she would get a zero for failing to submit a paper but she said, "That's my responsibility and I will take the zero." I am not saying that students are inherently deceptive. But this student stands out in my memory because for every such student who says to herself, "No excuses," there are ten who will manufacture an excuse, and they will do so because the university's procedures encourage them to do so.

Alternative Perspectives

Instead of performing a top-down analysis of what autonomy means in the classroom, for the sake of economy, let me proceed bottom-up by describing my teaching strategies. Like every teacher in a college or university, I have devised my own set of teaching strategies for standard classroom problems of how to motivate students who expect to be spoon-fed, how to get students to participate in class discussion, how to get students past their own invisible cultural assumptions, and so on. I think of these teaching strategies as experiments to be redesigned year by year, course by course. My experiments merit no more interest than any other teacher's except for the fact that I try to implement some of the cultural lessons I learned in Japan while living in the Buddhist monastery. Some people will think that no Japanese institution can have any lessons to offer the modern Western classroom. The Japanese educational system is often depicted as a stultifying institution whose real function is to condition young people into becoming passive adults in Japanese society and the Zen Buddhist monastery is depicted as an even more totalitarian institution designed to stamp out the individual self under the guise of bringing the monks to awakening. In previous articles,[6] I have tried to explain the teaching and learning practices of the Rinzai Zen monastery which I believe are misunderstood. My classroom experiments fly in the face of political correctness. They seem to be the opposite of liberal education, but I claim they teach the students to be free.

Question and Answer

Of the many teaching techniques available to a teacher in a classroom, one-on-one dialogue with an individual student is one of the most powerful. In question and answer, I expect the student to be an active participant, not a passive receptacle. Another way to say this is that I refuse to be the spoon for students wanting to be fed. When students ask questions of fact, I will give a straightforward answer. But when students ask questions of interpretation or meaning, I often do not answer but instead turn the question or statement back to the student and try to engage the student in dialogue.

"Isn't Zen a kind of individualism?"

"Confucian ritual is primarily a means by which people in power control others."

"The constant chanting of the name of Amida Buddha is a magical practice."

"The members of New Religions are emotionally weak people in search of a substitute family."

And so on.

I believe that many such student questions cannot be given a neat and simple answer because the questions proceed from wrong assumptions invisible to the student doing the asking, or from rather vague concepts which the student should clarify for himself or herself. So instead of answering, I ask the student to examine his or her own question. When successful, we engage in an extended conversation in which the student recognizes for himself the assumption he is bringing into the question, in which the student identifies for herself the knot that needs more careful analysis. With upper-level students, this kind of conversation works well. Inevitably in lower-level classes, there will be some students whose faces will be cross with frustration: "Just tell me the answer."

In addition, I also believe that part of education involves practice in good expression and articulation. A student may think he or she understands a point well but yet not be able to articulate it so that others understand. Or, in explaining themselves students often lose their point and go off on a tangent. I have seen teachers in this situation take the inarticulate comments of a student, rephrase them into something intelligible and ask "Is this what you mean?" I refuse to do this. Instead I ask "What's your point?" and put the responsibility for making sense back onto the student.

In general, I am following Confucius.

The Master said, "Only one who bursts with eagerness do I instruct; only one who bubbles with excitement do I enlighten. If I hold up one corner and a man cannot come back to me with the other three, I do not continue the lesson."[7]

Although the teacher has greater knowledge and experience, essentially the learning process is student-driven, not teacher-driven. The teacher's task is to motivate the student to take the initiative, to be the responsible party.

In this question and answer session, I feel it is important to carry on the dialogue in such a way that the students do not feel they are being played with or manipulated. Our local campus teaching and learning center likes to "model" a small group discussion technique which can be extremely manipulative. The teacher poses a question to the class and then asks the class to break up into small groups to discuss the question. After ten minutes of discussion, the teacher asks each group's representative to report out. The teacher listens to the group representative and then sums up each group's point with a word or two which is then written on the blackboard. After all groups have reported out, the blackboard has a list of words from which the teacher can give a short lecture giving a complete answer to the original question. Rather than the teacher giving the answer to the students from on high, this small group technique is designed to elicit the answer to the question from the students themselves. This technique, familiar to most teachers, can be the instrument of manipulation. Even before the class begins, some teachers have a list of the important points to be written on the blackboard; for them, the small group discussion is only a charade to give the appearance of "listening to the voices of students." Even though the students may have expressed quite different opinions, the teacher, by substituting words which supposedly sum up the student's point, deftly inserts the keywords for the already prepared lecture. Sooner or later, where there is such dishonesty, students will become aware they are being toyed with and will justly resent such manipulative question and answer sessions.

Honesty is always an issue. I think it a disservice to make the standard non-committal comment when a student makes a mistaken or irrelevant remark, "Well, yes, that's very interesting." Out of an exaggerated fear of hurting the feelings of the student, many a teacher today fails to say clearly that the student's statement was mistaken or irrelevant. Students want to know if what they said was on target or off, and it is the responsibility of the teacher to say so without vagueness or ambiguity.

One-on-one dialogue with a student, conducted even within a class of many students, serves many useful pedagogical functions. It directly involves the student so that the student is no longer passive. It lets the teacher directly gauge the student's comprehension and ability to articulate. It allows each student to shine for a moment performing in front of the class. But most of all, in the one-on-one dialogue, the teacher pays attention directly to the individual student and says "I am speaking to you." More important than trying to teach some subject matter is making a human connection with the student. When a teacher is asked, "What do you teach?" the answer should always be, "I teach students."

Rote Repetition and Memorization

In question and answer, I sometimes ask students to "regurgitate"; to repeat a point both in its original wording and then in their own words. Rote learning is currently out of style. When people hear the words "rote repetition," they are apt to think of the brute force memorization of medieval poetry which they had to endure in high school. Critics say that where rote repetition is practiced, a teacher mindlessly reads yellowed lecture notes, the students mindlessly copy them down, and knowledge merely gets transmitted from the teacher's notes to the students' notes without passing through the minds of either ("mindless to mindless transmission"). Despite such criticism, I believe that memorization definitely has a place in academic learning. One cannot do arithmetic in one's head unless one has first memorized the times-tables, nor can one speak another language unless one has first memorized the vocabulary. I believe it valuable that students be able to "regurgitate" and repeat a point in their own words, for such repetition is a sign of beginning understanding. More generally, rote learning is a form of learning by imitation, and learning by imitation is the most primitive and perhaps the most powerful form of learning for humans and animals. Building upon their genetically determined potential, baby animals learn their basic repertoire of behavior by imitating their parents; animals raised by humans even try to imitate their human parents (a phenomenon called "imprinting"). Like it or not, children imitate their parents and students imitate their teachers. Of course, mere repetition is not yet genuine understanding, but the problem is the "mere" part, not the "repetition" part.

Memorized facts and theories are pointless unless those facts and theories are mobilized to do something. Intellectual understanding is not merely a matter of recording a fact or theory as if the human mind were a cassette tape player. Intellectual understanding is an exercise of intellectual skills. Just as any tool like a crescent wrench or a tennis racket is useless unless one has developed the skills to use them properly, so also facts and theories are totally inert until one has developed the skills to use them in understanding, explanation, argument, analysis, interpretation, and criticism. All skills are at first practiced intentionally and deliberately. They are repeated and repeated until they become second nature. Once acquired, the exercise of the skill—like the ability to ride a bicycle—becomes invisible to the practitioner. The stereotypical idea that asking students to repeat and repeat inhibits creativity is to me quite wrong-headed. Mere repetition for the sake of repetition is pointless but only through repetitive practice does it become second nature to understand well, analyze well, and criticize well.

Furthermore, rote memorization, repetition and imitation are the stepping stones to insight. In another paper I have argued that one gets insight into a *kōan* through repetition.[8] But much more ordinary forms of insight also presuppose rote memorization and learning through repetition. When presented by an equation:

$$\frac{21 \times 45}{7 \times 9} = ?$$

most people can easily calculate the answer as 15. This is because they can just see that in the numerator, 21 can be divided by 7 leaving 3, that 45 can be divided by 9 leaving 5, and 3 times 5 is 15. The insight is to be able to "just see" that 21 is 7 times 3 and "just see" that 45 is 9 times 5. One is able to "just see" because once, long ago, one memorized the times table, repeating over and over again "7 times 3 is 21" and "9 times 5 is 45." But to a person who has not memorized these basic equations of arithmetic, the ability to "just see" that the answer is 15 seems like a supernormal gift, like having perfect pitch. If you have memorized a few basic algebra equations and can recognize the squares of 25 and 13, you can "just see" that,

$$\frac{625 - 169}{25 - 13}$$

is equal to 38. If you cannot, you are liable to think that the ability to "just see" this must be a genetic endowment you lack. Rote learning is the very basis of insight.

"The sage on the stage is now the guide at your side."

These days, teachers are much more aware of the use and misuse of the power of the professor in the classroom. In response to the increasing politicization of the classroom combined with the present ritual informality of campus culture (remember when male students wore white shirts and ties to class, no women wore "slacks," and professors addressed their students as Mr. and Miss?), partly in an attempt to be politically correct, some teachers try to erase hierarchy in the classroom. They sit with the students in an egalitarian circle of chairs, ask democratically to be called by first name and "facilitate" rather than lead discussion. The rationale is that the all-too-imposing authority of the old-style professor encouraged merely imitative rote learning, and such imitation discourages students from developing their own individual selves. But as I have said, learning by imitation is one of the most primitive and basic of forms of learning and it cannot be simply wished away by political correctness or abolished by fiat.

If there is no sage authority to imitate, students will imitate the new "guide at your side" style of egalitarian teacher. When students learn by imitation, they are not merely learning new facts and theories; they are learning who to be, what kind of person to be. Because they learn who to be by imitating a person, like it or not, every teacher is a potential role model for students. And when students imitate, they imitate not merely the part of the professor they know in the classroom, but the whole professor as they imagine him or her to be outside the classroom. Many teachers will be uncomfortable with this conclusion. Some teachers, aware of their own shortcomings, will declare emphatically they do not want to be the object of imitation. Rather than encourage students to copy-cat their teachers, we think it part of liberal education to encourage students to "be your own self" rather than encourage an unhealthy adulation of authority. But such imitation does not hinder genuine learning, I believe. On the contrary, the student develops his or her own authentic self by successively imitating, trying on, living in, acting out, different personas. In large enrollment classrooms where there is little contact between professor and student, students are unlikely to imitate the professor. But there is definitely imitation of the teacher in mid-size classrooms. At the graduate level, I recall a female professor, known for combining a distinguished teaching and publication record with a strong sense of social responsibility, whose graduate students were remarkably like her—female, intellectually bright and endowed with a strong sense of social responsibility. Because a teacher is a figure of authority, both in the intellectual and the institutional sense, a teacher makes a specially strong impression on students. One has no choice over being a role model, only over how to be a good one.

Mutual Polishing

The teacher has authority in the classroom by virtue of greater study, greater experience, age and institutional position. Yet imposing one's authority is not politically correct. What to do?

I have been experimenting with various kinds of group learning all based around what I call "mutual polishing." "Mutual polishing" is my translation for *sessa takuma*, the Japanese pronunciation for a term taken originally from Chinese literature. Literally "chipping, filing, polishing, rubbing," the term describes the long process required to produce a gem and symbolizes the long detailed training of a sage. The term in Japanese culture now has also acquired a social meaning. In the image of "mutual polishing," a pile of rough rocks is placed in a stone basin and stirred around. Through mutual friction, the rocks gradually knock the chips off each other; over time, the rocks polish each other to reveal the individual pattern that lies underneath the exterior surface.

Rather than try to direct the class by imposing authority top-down, I try to organize group work so that students are motivated by peer pressure which they experience as coming from their fellow students. When they see other students coming to class prepared, engaging knowledgeably in discussion, showing original insight, then they too work harder to attain the same level of competence (at least, that's my theory). Class discussion can become quite disorderly as I am willing to give the students much latitude. The disorder and excitement, I feel, positively motivates the students who come to form and share high expectations of the group and of themselves. Nevertheless I can still retain the position of natural authority as the person in the classroom with both the greatest understanding of the subject matter and with institutional responsibility for running the class. Neither sage on the stage nor guide at the side, I am the hand that cradles the rocks in the stone basin, so to speak.

Group work itself helps to break down the idea that students are in competition with each other. Rather than emphasizing the autonomy and independence of the student, group work shows students that cooperation makes for a more exciting and obviously intellectually beneficial class. The teacher can also use the opportunity for teaching group skills. In an application of "using a thorn to dig out a thorn," I take the group discussion hog aside and tell him (it is usually a male) that he is endowed with extra gifts (fluent speech, loud voice, quick wit) which make him a natural discussion leader and that therefore it is his special responsibility as discussion leader to make sure that all members of the group are encouraged to express themselves.

I have tried many kinds of group activities. Some discussion groups exist just for the duration of the class. Others exist for the duration of the semester as the students must complete a project together (see the *renku* project below). In one of my more successful experiments, the class was divided into three groups A, B, C, of four students each; the students remained in the same group throughout the term. Six texts were studied, two weeks for each text. On Tuesdays, I would lecture. On the first Thursday of each two-week period, students spent the first half of the class in discussion with their group and in the second half with the entire class. On the second Thursday of each period, they had a Presentation Day modeled on an academic conference. Two members of the Presenter Group for the day each prepared and circulated in advance an Issues paper. Two members of the Response Group for the day wrote Response papers. The third group provided the Chairperson for the panel, wrote a book report of the text under study and gave evaluations of the panel. The entire exercise was supposed to emphasize professional standards of documentation, rigor of argument, clarity of oral presentation, and good manners.

This experiment was very successful. Presentation Day was always the climax of each two-week section. The students ran the entire class. The Thursday panels were very good; often I thought that I had heard less interesting panels at national conferences. The level of discussion was always extremely high and everyone participated enthusiastically. In this class, students not only taught and learned from each other, they also, through their written evaluations of each other, contributed to grading. The students liked Thursday so much they proposed to extend the Thursday class to two hours (from 4 to 6 P.M.) because they did not wish to end discussion at 5:30. In return for this extension, they asked that I shorten my Tuesday lecture class to end at 5 P.M. I agreed.

In the current climate of political correctness, it is not part of liberal education to emphasize authority and hierarchy. One would think that Buddhist monastic models, shaped in Asian cultures which emphasize authority and hierarchy, could not be successfully imported into a Western classroom. But one must remember that in Asian cultures, hierarchy is imbedded in a group. A monk in a monastery spends only a few minutes a day with the teacher where they play out their hierarchical roles of master and disciple, and the rest of the day in the company of other monks where he is either older brother or younger brother to every other monk. The vertical relation between master and disciple is mediated by the horizontal relations which the monk has with other monks. The master delegates as much authority as possible to the body of monks, and the senior monks in turn pass on responsibility to junior monks (scholars of Japanese business management have studied this practice in Japanese companies under the name of *ringi-sei*). These days, the word "authority" immediately connotes "abuse of..." but in a Buddhist monastery, despite the nominal supreme authority of the master, the monks themselves run the monastery (again this is similar to Japanese business practices, for example, as in the Toyota automobile production system where the workers themselves design their own work routines). Within the body of monks, every monk shares in some measure of the delegated authority, learning from senior monks and teaching junior monks. Buddhist organizations in the West which have imported the master-disciple relationship without importing the group structure of delegated and shared authority have fallen ill with the American disease of abuse of authority and subjected Buddhist teachers to the American ritual of impeaching the president.

In the classroom, the professor has both intellectual and institutional authority; nothing can change this although some people deemphasize it by doing things such as sitting in circles with the class. But while ritual acts like sitting in a circle with the students make a political statement, they have no obvious educational impact because the teacher's authority for teaching and learning is not delegated to the students. Nothing changes in the vertical hierarchy of authority unless the students form a real group which receives authority and shares it horizontally. To retain authority, the teacher needs to give it away.

Cultural Perspective: Insider and Outsider

When we study another culture, we first approach it as an object. But another culture is a lived world which other people occupy and through which they experience things, people, time, space, an entire universe. One can read novels and poetry which evoke the feel of that other culture, but to subject those narrative works to intellectual study "analyzes them to death" so that they are no longer imaginary worlds which one can enter. Is there a way of getting students to inhabit another culture while yet maintaining intellectually rigorous standards?

I have borrowed a classroom exercise from Professor Dennis Lishka of the University of Wisconsin at Eau Claire with quite good results. On the first day of the course, students in my Mahāyāna Buddhism course are all given a sheet of paper with sixteen lines of a Chinese poem written in Chinese characters. Each line has sixteen characters divided into four verses. Instead of the usual term paper, the students' task is to translate the Chinese poem into English and then write a commentary. I supply a customized dictionary (first compiled by Dennis Lishka) keyed to the characters in the poem (character one in the dictionary is character one in the poem, character two in the dictionary is character two in the poem, et cetera). Several lectures, at spaced out intervals, are devoted to the rules of Chinese poetry, the nature of Chinese characters, parallelism and contrasting images, and so on. The students write two preliminary drafts and one final translation with commentary, each spaced a month apart. The poem itself is basically Buddhist in tone with lots of Taoist vocabulary and imagery thrown in. During the regular lectures in the course, the students are learning Nāgārjuna, Madhyamaka, Consciousness-Only, Seng Chao and learning to spot Chinese Taoist vocabulary used to express Indian Buddhist concepts. By the end of the course, they have the philosophical concepts required to translate the Chinese poem and to write the commentary.

This project had excellent results on both counts: it was an intellectually rigorous exercise and it got the students to think and understand to some degree from the perspective of a cultural insider. The students learned first-hand the difficulties of reading a primary text and attempting to translate it into English. They faced all the questions that professional scholars face in translation: Is this character used as a noun or a verb here? Is the verb active or passive? Does this negation word negate just the next character or the entire rest of the sentence that follows? Are these two characters used individually or as a compound? Does this translation fit the context? In the commentary to the translation, the students had to justify the choices they made. As each draft progressed, the students worked themselves more and more into the world of a Mahāyāna poet. The first drafts, submitted at an early stage in the course, were very much a reflection of their own Western religious and philosophical ideas which they imposed upon their text. As they learned more and more about Chinese religious and philosophical ideas, they were increasingly able to understand the Chinese text in its own terms, increasingly able to understand the imagery in its own terms.

In my Japanese Religions course, the students must all compose a *renku*, "linked verse," as the term assignment. The *renku* (Ch. *lien chü*) is one of a great variety of intellectual games played originally among the scholarly elite in China and members of the imperial court in Japan and which spread subsequently into the population at large. In simple "capping phrase" games, one person gives the first verse from a poetic couplet, and the second person is required to give the matching or "capping phrase." Of course, this game presupposes that both players have memorized a huge corpus of verse. In more complicated games, one person composes a first verse and the second person is required to compose the capping phrase according to fixed rules of composition. Variants of these games spread into popular culture and became used in drinking games, state diplomacy, romantic courting, rites of passage and religious ritual. In *renku* a group of poets composes a poem together, each contributing a verse; the verses are alternately triplets or couplets formed according to set rules. The challenge of the *renku* is that each pair of verses, a triplet composed by one person and a couplet composed by another person (or vice versa), taken together must form a thematic whole poem of five lines called a *tanka*. Each single verse however appears in two different pairs, once with the preceding verse and once with the succeeding verse where it usually has a quite different meaning.

In my Japanese Religions course, I divided the class into three-person groups and asked each group to compose a 36-verse poem by the end of term. The *renku* project had two pedagogical goals: (1) Writing from the inside: I hoped that students would learn to think and write not as a scholar trained in Western academic disciplines looking from the outside at the writings of Japanese people, but as a Japanese person writing from inside a world of aesthetic feeling. In particular, I hoped the students would learn the "haiku" use of language, i.e., the use of language to "present" the object, the moment, the emotion as it is in itself and not "represent" it through imposed metaphors, philosophical interpretation and personal points of view. (2) Mutual polishing: I also hoped students would learn "mutual polishing" group behaviour, helping each other to learn through mutual criticism and support.

This project was less successful than the translation project in the Chinese Religions course. At the end of the term, very few could explain in theory how language might be used to just "present" an experience, as opposed to "representing" it. In addition, they avoided engaging in "mutual polishing." I had hoped that in these *renku* groups, students would engage in responsible criticism of each other. This did not happen. Although they knew the rules of *renku* composition (one person, one verse), in all groups on the first draft, the students instinctively moved into composition by committee, all three people arguing about, and jointly composing, each and every line. No one was willing, at first, to allow any one person total authority over an entire verse, especially since all members of each group got the same grade for the *renku*. Not surprising, much of the first drafts was "lowest common denominator" verse. On later drafts, instead of mutual polishing, many groups engaged in mutual flattery. In only one group did the members engage in mutual criticism.

Free From and Free In

The teaching strategies described above are meant to give students autonomy, but both the means and the final goal of this way of teaching are quite differently conceived from what we associate with liberal education. Both the intellectual justifications offered for liberal education, as surveyed by Frank Reynolds, and the day-to-day institutional practices of the university pay lip service to the notion of an autonomous agent empowered to make its own decisions without outside interference. But in what factual sense could human beings ever be autonomous in this way? The oft-rehearsed arguments against individualism can be used again here. It is quite mistaken to think that humans are basically individuals who secondarily come together to form groups, like atoms coming together to form molecules (this similarity between individualism as a social theory and the physical theory of atomic structure is no coincidence). Despite the relentless ideological insistence on individualism in North American culture, nothing can change the fact that human nature is fundamentally not individual but social. Human beings are social animals, cannot survive unless nurtured in families, and possess language and culture only because they (we) live in groups. Human beings considered in isolation are animals; only in groups are we human. Not only that, human beings are intimately related to the physical and biological environment. Hot and cold, darkness and light, wind and rain, noise and silence, cold epidemics and flus, pesticides and AIDS, clean tap water and sealed food packs, all directly influence human mood, bodily health and felt experience. Individual human beings live every moment in a dense web of constantly changing physical and social relations. The circle of the environment visible in the lamplight around an individual self is quite limited. In this limited circle, it is possible to think that one's own individual decisions are the essential determining factors in charting a passage through life. Here the language of autonomy seems to make sense. But beyond the limited circumference of the self, each person is charting a life passage through a great heaving sea of constantly changing social and physical relations, a teeming sea of many human and non-human others which creates and limits the possibilities of action.

What does autonomy mean here? When university officers and university policy documents speak of respecting and enhancing the autonomy of the student, they encourage us to think of human beings as self-sufficient entities (as *dharmas*), independent in their relation to others, removed from the great web of physical and human relations. They encourage us to think that life is a "me first" competition in which the greater knowledge and skills acquired at a university will give a single person an advantage over others. If liberal education is education which gives us freedom, if freedom or autonomy is conceived as a "me first" independence from the people and things around us, then from the point of view which recognizes the fundamental inter-relatedness of self and environment, such liberal education aims at a goal neither factually possible nor desirable.

There is no such thing as freedom *from* the social and physical world; there is only more or less freedom *in* the social and physical world. I find the following image useful in explaining the difference between "free from" and "free in." When human beings developed understanding of gravity and understood that gravity kept them on the ground, they also started to imagine that if they could get beyond the pull of gravity, they would be free to fly like the birds. For a long time, it was not possible to get beyond the pull of gravity, but now we have rocket technology which can lift human beings out of the earth's gravitational field, and what do we find? Out beyond the pull of gravity, humans are not free to fly like the birds. Humans float helplessly in space, barely able to move around. Rather than being free, they are out of control. Human beings are free to move around only within gravity. Rather than depriving us of freedom, it is gravity itself which gives humans freedom of movement. Similarly, our interdependence on the people and things around us is not what prevents us from being free and autonomous but what gives us freedom and autonomy in the first place.

Despite fantasies that one might get *free from* gravity and fly like Superman, all people of necessity learn at an early age to be *free in* gravity. Gravity simultaneously allows human beings control over their movements and puts limits upon those movements. Babies learn to walk balanced so as not to fall. They learn not to jump from too high, not to walk on narrow edges. When older, they learn how to ride a bicycle, not to drive around sharp curbs at too high a speed, not to walk on ice without a cane. Some professionals in martial arts learn how to take thundering breakfalls without injury, some dancers learn how to leap in midair as if floating, some athletes learn how to run, leap, skate, ski, swim very very fast. All these are different kinds of freedom within gravity.

Similarly, despite the rhetoric of independence and autonomy, of necessity students in fact learn how imbedded they are in the great web of social and physical relations by sharing rooms and apartments, cooking and eating together, talking long into the night, falling in and out of love, even sometimes by studying together. They (we) change and grow every day. They (we) are nodes in the even greater web of causality, constantly actualizing the intellectual, emotional, athletic and artistic potential which they (we) received from parents and constantly reflecting the intellectual, emotional, athletic and artistic stimuli in the environment. Students develop and become free not by learning how to be independent of the physical and social world around them, but by learning through being inextricably related to it.

The university through its rhetoric and its institutional practices promotes an ethic of "me first" and a chimerical ideal of autonomy where we are encouraged to think of the self as independent from its social and physical surroundings. It is time to redefine liberal education starting from different assumptions.

Notes

[1] Reynolds 1991, 71–73.
[2] Reynolds 1990, 6–7.
[3] Reynolds 1990, 8–9.
[4] Reynolds 1990, 10–11.
[5] Reynolds 1990, 9.
[6] Hori 1994, 1999.
[7] Waley, 1938, 8.
[8] Hori 1994.

References

Hori, Victor Sōgen. 1994. "Teaching and Learning in the Rinzai Zen Monastery." *Journal of Japanese Studies* 20 (1): 5–35.

———. 1998. "Japanese Zen in America: Americanizing the Face in the Mirror." In *The Faces of Buddhism in America*, edited by Charles S. Prebish and Kenneth K. Tanaka. Berkeley: University of California Press.

Reynolds, Frank E. 1990. "Reconstructing Liberal Education: A Religious Studies Perspective." In *Beyond the Classics: Essays in Religious Studies and Liberal Education*, edited by Frank E. Reynolds and Sheryl L. Burkhalter. Atlanta: Scholars Press.

———. 1991. "Introducing Buddhism." In *Teaching the Introductory Course in Religious Studies*, edited by Mark Juergensmeyer. Atlanta: Scholars Press.

Waley, Arthur, trans. 1938. *The Analects of Confucius*. London: Allen and Unwin.

The Wheel Comes
to the Web

Teaching Buddhism by Distance Education: Traditional and Web-based Approaches

Mavis L. Fenn

The purpose of this paper is to inform instructors of Buddhism about recent developments in course delivery systems for distance education.[1] A recent Web search of university distance education offerings in Canada and some selected sites in the United States and Europe reveals that there are few religious studies courses offered through distance education.[2] Further, to date there is only one distance education course in Buddhism available in Canada. This course was offered by Russel Legge at St. Paul's United College for many years. I recently inherited it and am in the process of converting it to a CD-ROM Web-based course.

Given that there are so few offerings in Buddhist Studies through distance education, the whole point of this paper might seem moot. However, I believe there is good reason for those in Buddhist Studies to become informed about teaching by distance education and, in particular, about the use of technology in that teaching. Budget slashing and funding cuts have affected faculties of humanities much more than faculties of business or science. Across Canada and the United States, several departments of religion have folded or have been molded into departments of convenience.[3] The use of sessionals (who receive few, if any, benefits) is increasing, and retiring professors are not being replaced. At the same time, rising tuition and declining incomes mean that more students, both the adult learners traditionally associated with distance education and younger, campus-based students, are looking for ways to continue working while pursuing a degree.[4] Enrollment in distance education courses is increasing and will, in my opinion, continue to grow. The primary reason given by distance education students for choosing Web-based courses is convenience.[5] The convenience demanded by students, along with the rhetoric to which we have been subjected for many years—globalization, the need to be competitive, and the importance that information technology will have in this new marketplace—are causing administrators looking for an edge in enrolling both campus-based and distance education students to invest a great deal of money in technology and to encourage (in some cases, perhaps, to force) faculty to develop Web-based courses.[6]

The seemingly natural response to this information would be to launch a whole slate of distance education courses in Buddhism, most of which would be Web-based, as a means of ensuring that Buddhist Studies continue. That seems unlikely for a variety of reasons. First, given that there is only one distance education course in Buddhism offered in Canada, it is clear that instructors are either uninterested in distance education per se, or have concerns about it. I would speculate that areas of concern might be (among others) the quality of materials, the quality of students, pedagogical concerns, course overload, and lack of administrative interest or support.[7] Second, most scholars I have spoken with consider themselves unequipped for using any kind of technology with the possible exception of e-mail.[8] Third, many people in the academy have philosophical and ideological objections to the use of technology in education. They see its use as part of a capitalist conspiracy on the part of universities, software producers, and businesses that will result in the value colonization of the Third World, the commodification of education, the destruction of the education profession, and other unpalatable consequences.[9]

While some of the concerns listed above appear somewhat "over the top," there are good reasons to proceed slowly, if at all, in this area. I cannot hope to provide an exhaustive discussion of all the factors to be considered, as I am not an expert in technology, education, or philosophy. However, my recent readings in the field should provide a broad overview of what is involved, enhanced by my perspective on these matters as a professor who is interested both in teaching Buddhism and in distance education, and who is currently in the process of developing a Web-based course.

To date, there are few analytic studies of Web-based courses other than those that focus on the technology itself.[10] What I was looking for was material that dealt with the narrow issues of concern to instructors: accessibility, instructor time-commitment, quality control, and pedagogical value. A great deal of the available information is anecdotal and produced by those who are clearly for the use of technology in education. Interestingly, there is little material that focuses on the learner's perspective. Indeed, gathering information on the learner's perspective is difficult, since surveys are usually taken toward the end of a course and studies indicate that politeness and perhaps the relief of completing a course tend to produce results that are insufficiently analytical. My resources were drawn from a variety of publications dealing with education and technology (many of which were, understandably, available on the Web), personal experience, and informal conversations and e-mail with a variety of faculty members (those who were interested and involved, those who were staunchly against the development of online courses, and those who were indifferent). Most sources agree that the use of technology in education represents a revolution, one that has not proceeded at the pace many predicted, but a revolution nonetheless. Like all revolutions, it brings in its wake both promise and problems.[11]

Concerning accessibility, most often mentioned is that Web-based courses can provide equality of educational opportunity for people who are disabled, who live in rural or remote areas, or who live in Third World countries. Web-based education also opens the doors to a global academic community presaged by those virtual universities that are now taking shape.[12] There are several constituencies, however, which are excluded. I have had at least two prison inmates in my distance education classes, neither of whom had access to a computer (or a typewriter for that matter). Also excluded are those who are sight- or hearing-impaired.[13] The largest category of exclusions is the poor. While one might argue that the cost of courses has always affected the poor, the cost of a computer with Internet access,

CD-ROM, and so on, is a considerable additional expense. Not an exclusion factor per se, computer access can be problematic for campus-based students who either have a computer component to their campus classes or who are trying to take additional courses through distance education.[14] Students who do not have access to a computer off campus must often stand in line for long periods or use the computer facilities during off hours, often late at night after a long day of classes when they are mentally fatigued. Because the initial costs of purchasing technology and providing training for staff and faculty can be quite high, providing a course in dual format—traditional and Web-based—may not be an option for many institutions.

Some scholars are also concerned about "value-colonization." Most of the providers of Web-based education are Western universities whose premises and approaches may not be suitable for other countries or cultures. Further, there is the concern that, as with the building of large dams in many countries to provide hydro-electric power for a small elite, valuable state resources that could be used to provide a basic education for a large populace might be diverted to providing computer access to a small elite. This concern is not, however, one that is specific to Web-based education.

There is one thing upon which all individuals working in the field of education via technology agree: it is faculty labor intensive. Even if faculty are up to date and comfortable with technology (studies indicate the vast majority are not), and even where the university provides a fully trained staff to assist the instructor, it requires more time to launch a course online. Further, few universities provide faculty incentives such as credit towards tenure or promotion, leave time, or financial rewards to develop Web-based courses.[15] Once an online course is launched, it also requires more time to monitor student discussions, answer e-mails, and assist with technical problems (students tend to contact the instructor first about technological problems even when expert technical help is listed). As students have increased expectations regarding access to the instructor, instructors of Web-based courses can find themselves feeling overwhelmed. David Noble, a historian of technology, points to other dangers. He argues that once instructors become engaged in the production process, they become prone to the problems that have plagued production workers in other industries: increased scrutiny, extension of working time and intensification of work and, most distressing of all, redundancy. As evidence he provides the example of York University where untenured faculty have been required to put their courses into a technological format and then have been rehired at less money to teach the automated courses. Concerns about administration pressure to technologize courses led to a faculty strike for a contract that ensured that no course could be converted without faculty agreement.[16]

Giving up the classroom is the number one resistance to Web-based courses. Removal of the classroom threatens both instructor and student with a loss of identity. Because the traditional system is professor-oriented, instruction tends to be fairly passive—we impart information, they write it down and regurgitate it to us periodically on exams. While many instructors are unhappy with this arrangement, any radical change threatens the core of our identity as teachers. As Jaffe states, "faculty identity as a professor, as an expert, as a source of knowledge and information, is heavily shaped and reinforced through the role of classroom instructor and the face-to-face interactions that make up the classroom teaching arrangements."[17] Further, as asynchronous learning tends to be learner-focused rather than instructor-focused, instructors face a measure of loss of control. Professor-student identity is clearly not the sole reason for opposition to asynchronous learning, but we do a disservice to all parties in the debate if we do not acknowledge our vested interest in the current system, both practical—loss of jobs; and sociological/psychological— potential loss of identity.

Faculty concerns, however, are about much more than redundancy. There are pedagogical concerns as well. We have a long tradition that understands higher education to be about much more than "the facts" or performance levels. Higher education is about teaching critical thinking skills, which requires instructors who have read extensively and who are prepared to make extensive comments on students' work and provide guidance. That requires small classes and reasonable work loads, something many professors do not currently have.[18] Given that all studies, either for or against information technology in education, agree that technologically-based courses are faculty labor intensive, instructors are wise to question the push on the part of many administrators to rush into widespread conversion of courses, especially when "no form of distance education or any other widely applicable educational use of information technology has yet proved so much more effective and/or less expensive than 'traditional' forms of teaching and learning as to become a complete replacement for them."[19] High technology is not synonymous with high quality.

Distance education and high technology are not, however, synonymous with poor quality either. The view that distance education and information technology are illegitimate means of education has been remarkably resistant to change despite studies indicating that distance education students do as well as campus-based students, and studies that indicate that information technology is as effective as other forms of learning—indeed, some kinds of learning seem to be improved.[20] This attachment to the classroom appears to be shared by many students, and some studies indicate that students taking Web-based courses tend to feel the need for more feedback, clarification, deadlines, and benchmarks than their in-class colleagues. Many of these concerns are related to the absence of physical cues that are present in face-to-face interactions.[21]

Other studies, however, show more positive results. Some students feel more comfortable asking questions because of the anonymity of e-mail and they appreciate the fact that they can take more time to formulate their answers. Most courses using information technology appear to be learner-centered and competency-based.[22] Pedagogically, I see this as a plus because students can proceed at their own pace, and performance-based minimum standards ensure that students should emerge from the course with a basic grasp of all materials. It also makes students more active in their own learning experience, a corrective to what many professors refer to as the "dead class."

In terms of Buddhist Studies, I am able to provide education students with the opportunity to further their research or personal interest by using a series of links to various Buddhist resources on the Web. Thus, a student interested in Buddhism and vegetarianism can search the *Journal of Buddhist Ethics* for articles by Buddhist scholars on the subject and read popular journals like *Shambhala Sun* to see what North American Buddhist practitioners believe about the subject. I could never hope in a classroom to provide the breadth of resources to my students that they have available on the Web, both primary and secondary sources.[23] Further, by examining these resources in light of their course material, they gain experience in weighing and assessing the variety of materials to which they have been exposed— an application of critical thought. Anecdotal evidence from e-mail discussions I have had with students in the past indicates that they frequently ask profound or provocative questions that they might be reluctant to ask in class. Students in online discussion groups have commented that they benefit from hearing the views of a wide variety of people as well as the instructor.[24] The downside is that monitoring such discussions to make certain students are on track or not misinformed, and giving e-mail messages the attention they require, can be a time-consuming process.

Quality control was the final issue I examined, and it is a major one. Technological problems with Internet access, e-mail, discussion group software, and so on, is rated as a major frustration by both faculty and students. More disturbing are the serious concerns raised by David Noble concerning the "commodification of education." Because of the high cost of technology, upgrading, training, and so forth, universities search for partnership financing with business interests which see education as a market for their technology and software. Universities seek to gain intellectual property rights to the Web-based courses produced, not only to employ what Noble refers to as "less-skilled, and hence cheaper" instructors for those courses, but to sell them to other universities. Universities are also becoming the site of the production of courseware. For example, the University of British Colombia is the producer and marketer of Web-CT, now a major player in the market.[25] Noble expresses concern that the content of education in the future will be shaped by profit rather than pedagogical motives. In this regard, he refers to UCLA's Extension Division agreement with the Home Education Network, whose founder's background lies in cable television and public relations.[26] Noble also notes that the corporatization or capitalization of education also raises privacy issues. Universities in Canada have been provided with Virtual U software in return for providing data to the providers on its use. Students must release ownership and control of their online activities, and these activities are monitored and archived for the use of the company.[27]

While cost was not a factor I set out to examine, it frequently presented itself as a concern. The optimistic view was that the high capital costs of implementing information technology in education would, in the long term, prove to be no more expensive than other modes of delivery and might even be a revenue producer. The pessimistic view was that the higher cost which produces no better results at the moment will force out other modes of educational delivery in distance education and will result in a further restriction of access and, if David Noble is correct, produce an education that bears more resemblance to entertainment than edification.[28]

What are we to make of all this? The problems should not be minimized. Value colonization, the commodification of education, instructor "downsizing" and overload, are real concerns. But, they are also concerns that are not specific to the use of information technology. They are another indication of the malignant relationship between university administrations and their faculty caused by a complex of factors that fall outside the scope of this paper. Such problems should not be laid exclusively at the door of information technology. Recent statements by the administration of UCLA that they will not convert any course without instructor permission, combined with the success of the resistance at York and the growing opposition across Canadian universities to government attempts to commercialize research and gain intellectual property rights over research funded through grants, indicate that there is an opportunity to influence the speed and direction that development takes.[29]

Financial and practical considerations are also problematic. If instructors are to be encouraged to use the new technology, they have to be provided with adequate training and incentives. Faculty who are interested in developing Web-based courses should be rewarded with credit towards tenure and promotion. To date, universities have been, for the most part, unwilling to do so. Some universities have tried to offset the costs of new technology by charging extra student fees for its use. This strategy provides evidence against their claim that students are clamoring for technological courses.[30] Small colleges face the threat of losing their share of the distance education market to larger institutions if the use of information technology becomes widespread. Even colleges affiliated with larger universities cannot afford the instructor time-commitment.

Given that studies to date indicate that there is no clear pedagogical advantage to Web-based courses, why would anyone consider developing one? While their evidence was anecdotal and based on a small sample, the instructors I have talked to about their courses were very positive about the pedagogical value of such courses. They found it exciting to have students as far away as Africa and Australia, and felt that their courses engaged students in a way that was not possible in the classroom. As studies in this area are still few and fairly recent, perhaps subsequent studies will support these instructors' enthusiasm. While not downplaying the problem with time, the professors I spoke with seemed to feel that they could develop ways of managing better—setting office hours, lowering student expectations somewhat concerning reply times, and so on. They did not seem to regret the loss of the classroom per se, and, while it might be because none are exclusively engaged with online courses, identity was not a problem. Indeed, the more active participation of students returns the professor to an even more traditional role, that of guide.

There are also good social reasons for continuing to develop online courses. The number one reason given for taking an online course was convenience. This convenience factor is important in approaching the problem of accessibility. While the cost of courses is always a factor, the flexibility of Web-based courses allows more people to get an education than ever before. And, if that education encourages active participation, so much the better. An increasingly educated populace is an ideal worth working towards—economically, socially, and politically.

Technology in education is neither the panacea that a few still believe it to be, nor is it the devil at the door of civilization as we know it. It is a tool, a delivery system, that should be used, but used appropriately. Classrooms, audio-visual systems, text-alone systems may be more appropriate for some courses. This recognition alone forces us to review our teaching style, course design, and overall aims, a valuable exercise in its own right.

Appendix: Canadian Universities Searched

Newfoundland	New Brunswick	Nova Scotia
Memorial	Mount Allison	Acadia
	St. Thomas	Dalhousie
	U. of New Brunswick	Mt. St. Vincent
		St. Francis Xavier
		St. Mary's
		King's College

Prince Edward Island	Quebec	Ontario
U.P.E.I.	Bishop's	York
	Concordia	Wilfrid Laurier
	McGill	Windsor
		Western
		Waterloo

Manitoba	Saskatchewan	Alberta
Brandon	U. of Regina	Lethbridge
U. of Manitoba	U. of Saskatchewan	U. of Calgary
U. of Winnipeg		U. of Alberta

British Columbia	Other
Simon Fraser	U. of Phoenix
U. of Victoria	British Open University
U.B.C.	California Virtual University
	Penn State World Campus

Notes

[1] Thanks to Cathy Kelly and Tom Carey for assistance with electronic sources, Les Richards and Gillian Dabrowski for their technical assistance, Dr. Philippa Carter for reading and commenting on a draft of this paper, and Chris Baker for her copyediting expertise.

[2] This informal search was undertaken in September 1999. Information was gleaned from a random Web search. Web sites vary in ease of navigation, and, while the pattern was clear, specific information may have been overlooked. A thorough investigation of university calendars would be necessary to confirm the results of the search. A complete list of the universities searched may be found in the Appendix. For information on distance education in the United States see the National Center for Education Statistics Issue Brief (1998).

[3] The departments at the Universities of Windsor, Lethbridge, and Alberta come to mind.

[4] In a recent University of Alberta study, 30% of the students gave "desire to work" as the reason for their part-time attendance (Keast, Broadbent, and Carswell 1997). At the University of Waterloo, 92% of distance education students have a job (*Waterloo Online* 1999. CD-ROM). At the University of Manitoba, 66% of the students were enrolled in campus-based and distance education courses concurrently. Lisa Guernsey notes that this trend indicates a lower average age of distance education students, which may require pedagogical adjustments (Guernsey 1998).

[5] Guernsey 1998. In the Alberta survey, females outnumbered males two to one, 60% were married, and 20% of those listed "family obligations" as the reason for part-time study (Keast, Broadbent, and Carswell 1997). At the University of Waterloo, 70% are female, 67% married, and 48% have children. Also, the University of Waterloo is a co-op university, and co-op students often have scheduling difficulties (*Waterloo Online* 1999. CD-ROM).

[6] Pamela Mendels of the *New York Times* recently noted that (in the United States) more than half the colleges and universities offer some part of their undergraduate programs online ("Universities Embrace Technology, But Distance Learning Faces Controversy." *The New York Times*, 6 January 1999). Steven Gilbert notes, however, that while college presidents and board members believe they must move ahead aggressively in applying information technology to education, they also have concerns about the cost and its ability to provide measurable educational gains in the short term (Gilbert 1997). David Noble states that at York University untenured faculty have been "required to put their courses on video, CD-ROM or the Internet or lose their job" and that they then have been hired to teach their automated course "at a fraction of their former compensation." Noble also states that at UCLA instructors provided their course materials to the administration "dutifully or grudgingly (it doesn't matter which) to be used online" (Quoted in Agre 1997; the original of Noble's article can be accessed at http://www.firstmonday.dk/issues/

issue31/noble/index.html). For arguments against Noble's assertions of administration force see Noble et al. 1998.

[7] The most thorough bibliography on comparisons between distance education and classroom instruction, which includes materials on technological instruction versus other means is the *No Significant Difference* phenomenon compiled by Thomas Russell (1999). The title of the book is also the consistent conclusion of these studies. Vivian Rossner-Merrill discusses some of the reasons why distance learning has not yet been accepted as an academic area in its own right (Rossner-Merrill 1996) and Olcott discusses the changes necessary to make distance education sustainable in the changing environment of higher education (Olcott 1996).

[8] This is a significant factor in both the development and the evaluation of Web-based courses (Annand and Haughey 1997; Gilbert 1996; Jaffe 1998). Arvan et al. (1998) discuss the replicability problem.

[9] While David Noble (1997, 1998a, 1998b) is certainly the most ardent proponent of this sort of argument, many people share some of the same concerns (see, e.g., Rush and Oblinger 1997; Berube 1998).

[10] Some recent studies include: Wideman 1996; Arvan et al. 1998; Hoey et al. 1998; Russell 1999; Wideman and Owston 1999.

[11] Gilbert 1996. Erhmann provides a particularly useful discussion of past revolutions and their benefits and losses by which we can evaluate the current revolution (Ehrmann 1999).

[12] Olcott 1996; Hara and Kling 1999. The first virtual university in the world has just been launched in New Brunswick, Canada ("Virtual University Launched in N.B." *Globe and Mail*, 2 October 1999).

[13] Images cannot be translated into audio for the sight-impaired, and software for turning text into audio is not always enhanced enough for the hearing-impaired (Personal conversation, Dr. Philippa Carter).

[14] Wideman 1996.

[15] Olcott 1996. A 1997 (U.S.) survey found that only 12.2% of institutions recognize information technology as a career path. Houseman, among others, divides instructors into three groups: those that have been on the cutting edge, those who are early, middle, or late followers, and those who reject technology. Followers are the most important group for, with their adoption of information technology, it becomes "mainstream." He notes that it is important when working with followers to allow them to progress at their own rate (Houseman 1997). For a description of the process from an instructor's perspective see Olcott 1996 and Gilbert 1996.

[16] Agre 1997; Noble 1997.

[17] Jaffe 1998, 27. Also see Rush and Oblinger 1997; Olcott 1996.

[18] Berube 1998.

[19] Gilbert 1996, 12.

[20] Benefits include more student-to-instructor and student-to-student dialogue, and co-operative research and learning skills (Poole 1997; Annand and Haughey 1997; Wideman and Owston 1999). See also Arvan et al. (1998), who deal with "efficiency gains." One must be cautious here as efficiency gains, in some cases, are made by replacing faculty with less expensive and (perhaps) less skilled staff (Gilbert 1996).

[21] Annand and Haughey 1997; Hara and Kling 1999.

[22] Annand and Haughey 1997; Poole 1997; Olcott 1996.

[23] A report, and annotated bibliography of a wide variety of Web sites is found in Markel Chernenkoff (forthcoming).

[24] Also noted as important was the ability to take longer to think out an answer and respond than classroom situations allow (Guernsey 1998).

[25] Noble 1997; Agre 1997.

[26] Noble 1998.

[27] Noble 1997.

[28] Wideman (1996) and Olcott (1996), among many others, share this view. Olcott argues that the value considered must not be simply projected fiscal benefits.

[29] Noble (1998a, 1998b) notes the success of recent resistance initiatives. Jeffrey Young (1998) notes that UCLA administrators, in a recent series of interviews, stated that they had no intention of claiming rights to online course material development. Further, in Canada there has been recent discussion regarding the implications of the commercialization of university research, intellectual property rights and copyright (Berkowitz 1999; Gilbert 1996). Don Olcott argues, and student choice of Web-based courses for convenience appear to support this contention, that market driven (or consumer chosen) higher education is not a fad and the challenge, then, is to retain the best of the traditional system while adapting to the current situation (Olcott 1996, 1997).

[30] However, the University of Alberta survey showed that the highest level of interest in alternative delivery systems for traditional text-based distance education courses was in computer-assisted courses and that students would be prepared to pay an Internet fee (Keast, Broadbent, and Carswell 1997).

References

Agre, Phil. 1997. "For Your Interest." Internet communication, 12 December 1997.

Annand, David and Margaret Haughey. 1997. "Instructor's Orientations Towards Computer-Mediated Learning Environments." *Journal of Distance Education* 12 (1/2): 127–52.

Arvan, Lanny, John C. Ory, Cheryl D. Bullock, Kristine K. Burnaska, and Matthew Hanson. 1998. "The Scale Efficiency Projects." *Journal of Asynchronous Learning Network* 2 (2): 33–60.

Berkowitz, Peggy. 1999. "Panel Softens Stance on Commercializing IP." *University Affairs* (July): 19–28.

Berube, Michael. 1998. "Why Inefficiency Is Good for Universities." *Chronicle of Higher Education* 44 (29): B4–B5.

Chernenkoff, Markel. (forthcoming) "Electronic Buddhism: Technological Resources for the Buddhist Scholar." Unpublished paper presented at the annual meeting of the Canadian Society for the Study of Religion, 1999.

"Distance Education in Higher Education Institutions: Incidence, Audiences, and Plans to Expand." 1998. *National Center for Education Statistics*. 2 January 1998.

Ehrmann, Stephen. 1999. "Technology in Higher Learning: A Third Revolution." *The TLT Group*. Electronic citation, 2 January 1999.

Gilbert, Steven W. 1996. "Making the Most of a Slow Revolution." *Change* 28 (March/April): 10–23.

———. 1997. AAHESGIT #215 (Part 1 of 2): "3 Years of Changes." *American Association of Higher Learning*. Internet communication. Source: Cathy Kelly, cnkelly@corr1.uwaterloo.ca

———. 1999. AAHESGIT #227: "Thanksgiving: Fundamental Questions." *American Association of Higher Learning*. Internet communication. Source: Cathy Kelly, cnkelly@corr1.uwaterloo.ca

Guernsey, Lisa. 1998. "Distance Education for the Not-So-Distant-Future." *Chronicle of Higher Education* 44 (29): A29–A30.

Hara, Noriko and Rob Kling. 1999. "Student's Frustration with a Web-based Distance Education Course: A Taboo Subject in the Discourse." *Department of Instructional Systems*. Electronic citation, 24 August 1999.

Hoey, J. Joseph, John M. Pettit, Catherine E. Brawner, and Shelley P. Mull. 1998. "Project 25: First Semester Assessment." *University Planning and Analysis, North Carolina State University*. Electronic citation, 1 January 1998.

Houseman, Jon G. 1997. "Infusion, Not Diffusion, A Strategy for Incorporating Information Technology into Higher Education." *Journal of Distance Education* 12 (1/2): 15–28.

Jaffe, David. 1998. "Institutionalized Resistance to Asynchronous Learning Networks." *Journal of Asynchronous Learning Network* 2 (2). Electronic citation, 9 January 1998.

Keast, David, Rozanne Broadbent, and K. L. Carswell. 1997. "Summary Report: Access to Part-Time University Studies." *Special Sessions, University of Alberta*.

MacEachern, Alan. 1999. "The :-) and :-(of Teaching." *University Affairs* (Sept): 23–24.

Noble, David. 1997. "Digital Diploma Mills: The Automation of Higher Education." Electronic citation, 10 January 1997. Source: Cathy Kelly, cnkelly@corr1.uwaterloo.ca.

———. 1998a. "Digital Diploma Mills, Part II: The Coming Battle Over Online Instruction." Electronic citation, 3 January 1998.

———. 1998b. "Digital Diploma Mills, Part III: The Bloom is Off the Rose." Electronic citation, 11 January 1998. Source: Cathy Kelly, cnkelly@corr1.uwaterloo.ca

Noble, David, Richard Shneiderman, Phil Agre, and Peter J. Denning. 1998. "Technology in Education: The Fight for the Future." *Educom Review* 33 (3). Electronic citation, 6 January 1998.

Olcott, Don. 1996. "Destination 2000: Strategies for Managing Distance Education Programs." *Journal of Distance Education* 11 (2): 103–15.

———. 1997. "Constructive Enlightenment and the Academic Heritage: A Response to Vivian Rossner-Merrill." *Journal of Distance Education* 12 (1/2): 271–76.

Poole, Gary. 1997. "Back to the Future: What Can We Learn from Current Debates on Educational Technology." *Journal of Distance Education* 12 (1/2): 9–14.

Rossner-Merrill, Vivian. 1996. "Transforming Vision Into Practice: A Reply to Don Olcott." *Journal of Distance Education* 11 (2): 121–25.

Rush, Sean and Diana Oblinger. 1997. *The Challenge of Information Technology in the Academy*. Bolton: Anker Publishing Inc.

Russell, Thomas L. 1999. *The No Significant Difference*. Raleigh, NC: North Carolina State University.

Wideman, Herbert. 1996. "Using Computer Conferencing as a Medium for Pedagogical Innovation: Two Case Studies." Centre for the Study of Computers in Education, York University. Electronic citation, 12 January 1996.

Wideman, Herbert, and Ronald D. Owston. 1999. "Internet-based Courses at Atkinson College: An Initial Assessment." Centre for the Study of Computers in Education, York University. Electronic citation, 6 January 1999.

Young, Jeffrey R. 1998. "Skeptical Academics See Perils in Information Technology." *Chronicle of Higher Education* 44 (35): A29–A30.

Academic Buddhology and the Cyber-Sangha: Researching and Teaching Buddhism on the Web

Brett Greider

Knowledge is power and permits the wise to conquer without bloodshed and to accomplish deeds surpassing all others.

— Sun Tzu, *The Art of War*

We know what we are, but know not what we may become.

— Shakespeare, *Hamlet*

The Bodhi tree of Buddhist teachings has many branches, many leaves, and baskets of leaves. Web pages like leaves on the tree may contribute myriad cyber-sūtras in the new millennium. The emergence of networked thinking and Web awareness, and spiritual revitalization beyond postmodernity to transmodernity (post-colonial and post-Eurocentric) may spell the intelligible textuality of a super-conscious interconnected global culture. The Internet is ongoing, evolving, impermanent, changing, yet it is our new "material culture" communications and learning tool, a photon-field of waving pages webbing round the planet. Can we contemplate, listen and observe with the Web? Can serious scholarship be done, and with what methods? Can stories, *sūtras* and *kōans* be told there? Can Buddhism students receive authentic Teachings on the Web? Might we anticipate religious activities such as rituals or ceremonies? Do virtual shrines signal a new phenomenon in Buddhism? Is the Digital Dharma potentially a new transmission, a "Novayāna"[1] of Buddhism? May it become a wildfire of flames passing to multitudes of minds, a branching and twigging of lineages? Is this co-arising fabric of inter-linking codification a field for emerging religious phenomena?

The Web (now a synonym for the Internet and the World Wide Web) is a new kind of fusion of symbolic languages, and therefore potentially a revolutionary symbol-system triggering and expressing religious transformation, "a sphere whose center is everywhere and whose circumference is nowhere." This interlinked co-arising phenomenon is approximately eight billion pages and growing at a rate of one million a day. It is estimated that eighty-eight million of the "Net-generation" in Canada and the United States alone will reshape our society and the future of education.[2] The Web includes alpha-betic-text based information fused with international, pluralistic, multi-lingual, and multi-sensory cultural representations. It involves the senses of sight and sound as well as text: its textuality is akin to a hyper-linked and synthesized collection of illuminated manuscripts interpenetrated by the sacred celluloid of "movies" and the digitized libraries of Babylon, Egypt, Tibet, Alexandria, Uspantan, London, Washington, D.C., and Beijing. It has more in common with today's most popular forms of culture-texts: moving images, digital-video and television, graphic design, animation and music. Yet it also broadcasts a sea of vital information on medical research, physics, scientific dis-coveries, economic data, political news, human rights documentation, and endless archives of significant texts from the round world of hu-manity. Libraries of sacred texts, some in parallel translations and numerous languages, are now accessible where before they were nearly impossible to find. One enthusiastic observer of this phenomenon, Jean Houston, says the Internet is "remaking human culture": "a new and very complex culture is growing up along the Internet's great river of information.... This dance of metamorphosis is reciprocal; the Internet is changing us, even as we refine the technology that extends its reach."[3]

The approach to teaching Buddhism with computer technology is complicated by the paradox of Buddhist teaching: is renunciation of technology a corollary of Buddhist teaching, or are all things appro-priate in a kind of *vajra*-vehicle for the Dharma? This question is ad-dressed in Peter D. Hershock's cautiously constructed study *Reinvent-*

ing the Wheel: A Buddhist Response to the Information Age. Hershock's contemplative and philosophical exploration of the issues, with the serious thoughtfulness of a monk-scholar, cautions against the peril of technologies colonizing human consciousness. However, he says the use of technology is ineluctable, and so appropriate intentionality and skillful means are required to address the potential of this revolution. Hershock recommends a very intentional approach to skillful use of technology: "[T]echnologies biased toward contributory appreciation will lead just as inevitably toward problems requiring ever more subtle and far-reaching cooperation and contribution. Through such technologies, we not only come to live in increasingly valuable worlds— the buddha-realms so lushly invoked in Mahayana sutras—but as increasingly valuable persons. As someone with unlimited skill in appreciative contribution, the bodhisattva is dramatically invaluable."[4]

Hershock rightly underscores that technology is merely the tool by which the awakening mind may develop further, based first on the preparation of the mind through contemplative disciplines and learning. The extraordinary potential of this planetary web of communication and symbol interactivity poses the most serious awakening of consciousness in our society, beginning with education:

> [W]e should first undertake a rigorous practice of opening ourselves to our present situation as an unlimited field of opportunities for developing more meaningful lives, for more dramatically realizing our interdependence and creative community. Meditative discipline allows us to initially establish such a heading for our conduct and we should be teaching our children to train their awareness through some meditative discipline before we teach them how to use a computer or watch television, before we subject them to the rigors of achieving literacy and numeracy. Given the massive amounts of time and money focused on inducing iconic awareness worldwide, the beginner's mind of our children is in danger of extinction. Unless it is actively conserved, the fresh and appreciative attentiveness we associate with children at their best will simply fade away into a past beyond recall, and in its place will be instituted very deep structures of resistance to movement in the direction of meaningful virtuosity.[5]

Neo-Luddites warn of the Web's demise. Ironically, a website for "Luddites On-Line" claims to be "the only place in cyberspace devoted exclusively to Luddites, technophobes and other refugees from the Information Revolution," and is devoted to undermining the Internet, and hailing a post-techno future.[6] Luddites (named after the early nineteenth-century European laborers who fought against the industrial revolution's impact on labor by "monkey-wrenching" its machinery) warn of the fragile nature of our slender electronic connections, the potential electro-magnetic pulse of a terrorist's bomb wiping out our computers, the toxic waste of obsolescent computer garbage, the mind-numbing effect on the brains of the young, the pace of reading superficial info-blurbs instead of great long books, and on and on (for a provocative treatment see The Unabomber Manifesto by Ted Kaczynski[7]). The Web also includes the many ills of humanity: exploitations and deceits, twisted immorality and hate, avaricious money mongering, and whatever else is common to our species. To be sure there are clear and present dangers.

But the Web is a technology like many of humanity's great inventions: alphabetic writing, wheels, the printing press, mailboxes, telephones, radio, televisions, jets, and so on. We have evolved because of them, although they have also been used for evil. The Web—at least as marvelous as these in its potential effects on humanity's future—is also changing international human rights reporting, allowing greater freedom of information and expression for the voiceless, exposing the politics of authoritarian regimes and their propaganda, and giving greater access to world news and cultural views. It has sparked unprecedented economic expansion. The impact of this first wave from the oceanic Web—a mere decade in its infancy—signals that this revolution is only a glimpse of what is to come. Internet2, wider bandwidths, wireless connectivity, and exponentially expanding new technology will increasingly transform our present experience of the Web. Surfers know that waves come in sets, and this is only the first wave of the coming tsunami.[8]

Conceptual Horizons of Buddhism on the Web:
The Web as Evolving Religious Field of Study

The Web as a communication network has literally connected people from all regions of the planet through an interwoven fiber-fabric of linking documents, graphics, audio and video. This Web has created for the first time in human history a means to share information and knowledge almost instantly on a global scale, crossing all national borders into nearly every culture. Since the introduction of HTML (Hyper-Text Markup Language) code in 1990, the exponential expansion of the Web and new code-languages has appeared like the sudden birth of Pierre Teilhard de Chardin's "noosphere": a neural network of human knowledge expanding like a global glowing mind surrounding the planet. Teilhard biographer Ursula King describes the concept:

> Just as the zone of life—the total mass of living organisms—was the biosphere, a living layer above the non-living world of the geosphere, so there was yet another, thinking layer, a sphere of mind and spirit surrounding the globe. It is like a thinking envelope of the earth of which all humans are part. All contribute to it through their thinking, feeling, connecting, and interacting with each other, and above all, through their powers of love. The emergence of the noosphere is an important step forward in becoming human, in the process of transformation he called "hominization."[9]

It is little wonder that Teilhard's 1925 vision of the noosphere has re-emerged in the cyber-culture as a prophecy that foretold the sudden emergence of the Web. "All around us, tangibly and materially, the thinking envelope of the Earth—the noosphere—is multiplying its internal fibers and tightening its network; and simultaneously its internal temperature is rising, and with this its psychic potential."[10] Although Teilhard's "noosphere" is adopted as a paradigm by various New Age religious movements,[11] its application as an analogical way of seeing the Web in a Buddhist context is provocative.

The World Wide Web has emerged simultaneously as the current networking "tech-knowledgy" of communication for both the transmission and evolution of this historical project of an interdependent civilization. Can the collaboration of students and teachers, acculturated to new forms of media and information design, create with Dharma teachers and scholars a new sense of Buddhism's message for the twenty-first century? "The Buddha, the Godhead, resides quite as comfortably in the circuits of a digital computer or the gears of a cycle transmission as he does at the top of a mountain or in the petals of a flower," Robert Pirsig wrote in 1974.[12] It has taken a decade for Web to arise, yet already it seems Teilhard's and Pirsig's comments have meaning in ways they could not even conceive. Although Buddhism in the West has yet to emerge as a pluralistic intercultural phenomenon, I think we are seeing its potential emergence within a new framework of communication in the Novayāna of the West. These concepts are not exactly new, and we have been expecting a communication revolution that better represents the collective mind of Buddhism.

Transmodern Teaching

Learning to listen and to observe the Buddha Mind through new media may transport students to a new paradigm: a transmodern, planetary and intercultural interconnectivity analogous to the Buddha's original orally-transmitted Dharma. I hasten to say "analogous" because what is emerging is unprecedented: a historical groundswell of awareness of our planet's ecology, the inter-connectivity of all of its species, and the intercultural dialogue of Homo sapiens, that is remarkable and revolutionary. It is beyond "postmodern" and fits what Latin American philosopher Enrique Dussel calls "transmodernity": the emergence of voices from the four quadrants of the Earth calling for mutual interdependence of resources and human rights, ecological justice, and a new collective consciousness. "The transmodern project achieves with modernity what it could not achieve by itself—a corealization of solidarity, which is analectic, analogic, hybrid, and mestizo, and which bonds center to periphery, woman to man, race to race, ethnic group to ethnic group, class to class, humanity to earth, and occidental to Third World cultures.... This new project of transmodernity implies political, economic, ecological, erotic, pedagogic, and religious liberation."[13] In the coming decade computers will evolve to thirty-five times faster than today's machines, accelerating the multimedia interactive dimension of the Web. The prospects for rapid communication and interactivity, for virtual dialogue and teachings, and even for religious experience may accelerate the hybridizing of Buddhist learning and experience with the scholarly studies and methods of the university. Will students sense in new ways the transmission of teachings through digital-video, streaming-audio, cyber-shrines, and hyper-illuminated texts? Will new technology give a new generation opportunity to observe a vast array of sacred art? Can we imagine creating the opportunity to explore a temple in virtual reality, like the Mind Palace of *kālacakra*? These experiential pedagogical sites are already deployed, some as shrines and meditation temples, others as interactive virtual mandalas or digital neo-kōans.[14] Keeping in mind these theoretical and methodological issues, I now turn to some of the considerable pedagogical implications of teaching with new technologies.

Paradigm Shifts Happen

The emergence of a "global digital-neural system" of information is revolutionary, the way the Renaissance was a corner turned in European history. It may not have the grandeur of Rome and Florence, the classic stature of the great artists, yet it brings Leonardo da Vinci's *uomo universalis* to the frontiers of every society. The Web is changing the way we learn, the way we buy, the way we vote, the way we think, the way we live—for many reasons, good and bad and neutral. While many see in it a challenge to time-honored traditions and values, never before has a pluralistic and global humanity been given the opportunity to arise and freely express a common sense of morality and ethical concerns. Exposing evil and confronting tyrants, spelling out the standards of human rights, elaborating environmental manifestos, and proclaiming the rights of indigenous peoples are only a few examples of the Web's potential for raising human dignity to new heights. Far more dangerous are those parts of the world where the Web may be banned, where gulags may forbid sending the world messages, where human rights violations may not be broadcast, where scholars may not access information freely.

Comparable to what Thomas Kuhn has described in *The Structure of Scientific Revolutions*, the Web offers new paradigms for communicating information and knowledge. This particular paradigm shift has huge implications: the new framework for exchanging knowledge is constructed by participants who ineluctably recognize and enter into the new paradigm. As Kuhn says, "for this we must go native," meaning that full immersion in the emerging cultures and symbol-systems is a form of exploration that intellectually develops new theoretical frameworks to account for the phenomena. The new framework of the Web incorporates symbol-systems past and present from cultures around the globe. It can never replace experience and personal sensory immersion in the natural world, nor does it propose to (although some, like Ray Kurzweil, believe that it will someday).[15] The new paradigm constructs a framework for addressing the actual socio-political and intellectual challenges of a globalized civilization, a technology that gives representation to the marginalized (yes, across the digital-divide), a paradoxical tool of unparalleled potential for freedom of expression, whether good or evil. The caveat is that scholars who avoid participating in the Web may avert the challenge of creating and affecting the freest flow of information ever, while others jump aboard (as if the Jedi knights of Star Wars dropped their light sabers instead of engaging with the Force when they saw the Death Star!).

Instead, what I envision on the horizon is one of the most challenging and potentially exhilarating periods of religious history for religionists to study. Already we can find contemporary scientists joining religionists in the observation of this overwhelming emerging new paradigm.[16] Religionists and philosophers see the opportunity as an unprecedented dialectical learning and teaching environment that is akin to surfing a global mind.[17] The challenge is well expressed by Erik Davis in *Techgnosis: Myth, Magic and Mysticism in the Age of Information*:

As the high-tech juggernaut careens into the third millennium, I suspect we may need to open to such possible transmutations: to fire up
the alembics of the imagination, to tune in to the pagan pulse of
planetary life, to wire up the diamond matrix within. For many
earthlings, there is simply not much choice in the matter: A turning is
in the air. Slowly, tentatively, a "network path" arises from the
midst of yearning and confusion, a multifaceted but integral mode of
spirit that might humanely and sensibly navigate the technological
house of mirrors without losing the resonance of ancient ways or the
ability to slice through the greed, hate, and delusion that human life
courts. Against the specter of new and renewed fundamentalism, people both inside and outside the world's religious traditions are trying
to cut and paste a flood of teachings, techniques, images, and rites
into a path grounded enough to walk upon. Who knows what virtu-
alities will arise along the way? This path is a matrix of paths, with
no map provided at the onset, and no obvious goal beyond the open
engagement with whatever arises.[18]

Contrary to the technophobic perspective, many see the ineluctable potential for the arising of an epic period in humanity: a
"planetary morality" emerging with the free exchange of information
and knowledge that may be our last best opportunity to transform
our fragmentary civilization through awareness of the dangers and
potentialities of our historical moment. In a recent special issue of
Time, David Gelernter says, "Dignity is a necessity to fight for. And
come 2025, life will be better: not because of the technology revolution but because of a moral rebirth that is equally inevitable and far
more important."[19] Many of the most perilous threats to world
peace, quality of life, and environmental sustainability might only be
surmounted by global efforts through massive collective information
exchange.

The Web's Meta-Genre of Collective Symbol Sharing

Storytelling, sacred arts, theater, poetry, ceremony and ritual, movement and music are the genres of expression used by teachers
throughout human history. Shamans, priests, magicians and mystics

often employ some form of technology: sacred tools and arts that communicate the spirit, and symbol-systems to convey languages and texts. The Web is a powerful "teaching tool" if put to the task; a potentially transformative experience for the "Awakening Mind." It can incorporate all of these elements, and its potential has only begun to bud, propagating like a bodhi tree, with networks of interlinked Web sites by visionaries, writers, and artists. "Techno-shamans" and scholars are blending their strands of knowledge in a braid that questions traditional categories and boundaries. Can any worldview provide an explanatory orientation to this new paradigm?

The "Buddhism" of our globalized culture—especially expressed in an emerging form of instant world-wide communication—is changing the way we approach teaching Buddhism in the academy. The democratization of access to knowledge on the Web is changing our way of thinking about Buddhism, as well as adding to our resources. It is an unprecedented opportunity to exchange and compare teachings and to access scriptures, *sūtras*, teachers, *sanghas*, sacred arts, and texts from diverse cultures, historical contexts, and geographical locations. While textual and historical studies are the primary approach to university learning, the Web takes students "beyond texts" into the phenomenology of digital-textuality. We are witnessing the emergence of libraries of "illuminated manuscripts" on a scale unimaginable in the monasteries of Europe or Tibet. Teachers who have always worked with small classes, groups of students who have always sought wisdom from venerable teachers and professors, even monastics secluded in convents and monasteries, are now connecting to the classrooms, temples and libraries of an entire planet.

The Web's hypertextuality lends itself exceptionally well to Buddhist teachings. Erik Davis describes a monk's digital design approach for the Asian Classics Input Project publication as,

> a simple hypertext mock-up on paper, which draws from widely scattered sources to demonstrate the intimate relationship between morality and the concept of emptiness, the tricky and pivotal notion that all things have no intrinsic 'self-nature.' By selecting different keywords from the various citations, the user gets a feel for the complex web of

Buddhist philosophy. The interactive, probing nature of hypertext surf-ing is ideally suited for the logical, dialectical approach to enlightened understanding that the Tibetan monastic tradition prizes. "Ultimately, this system will be in VR cyberspace. You'll put on a helmet and come out two hours later, and you'll be much more educated.... There will never be very many people interested in these things. But the peo-ple who are will be able to learn it much faster, and in a much more powerful way."[20]

New Horizons in Teaching Buddhism: Teaching Digital Dharma

The Digital Dharma—named for the teachings of Buddha on the na-ture of reality—is an expansive network presence of Web sites repre-senting venerable teachers, monks and nuns, scholars, students, and novices (plus of course New Age doctrines, sectarian syncretisms, and dilettante personal pages). A variety of Buddhist "Web Rings"—"hyper-linked circles" of sites—monitor and manage the emergence of new Web sites for content and quality. As always, in religious revolu-tions critical thinking and analysis is crucial in our approach to the contents and material posted on the Web. Teaching Buddhism through the Internet begins with teaching-guides, which generate navigational and methodological strategies for approaching the ocean of information available. The multiplicity of pathways requires intel-lectual orientation and path-finding. The Internet represents a pro-found challenge to scholars and teachers to shape the global informa-tion system with responsible and substantial resources, while designing new ways of information delivery to communicate net-worked knowledge. The scholar/teacher's responsibility is both to create avenues of trustworthy information and to guide students in the navigation of the ocean of cyber-resources. The vast contents of the Web will be substantiated by scholars who build trustworthy and authoritative citadels of learning.

The Teaching Scholars Become the Students

Teachers have always been gifted with the task of inspiring and transmitting knowledge. The teaching of Buddhism in the Western academy is a relatively young tradition with a history and identity still in formation. Whether the emphasis is on "essential" issues, history and sacred texts, or on cultural anthropology of Buddhism, academic teachers of Buddhism are now at the threshold of a new framework in teaching. Malcolm David Eckel says in the *Journal of the American Academy of Religion*, "I am convinced that the time has come for the study of Buddhism to come of age, to acknowledge that it is involved in a sophisticated process of interpreting, appropriating, and shaping the values of the Buddhist tradition, and to bring this process of interpretation, criticism, and creativity into the discourse of the academy itself."[21] We are part of the unfolding tradition of Buddhism. Eckel talks of the "complex interweaving of voices, some Buddhist, some Western, some descriptive, some performative, and all informed by the realization that no realization or rhetoric is definitive or complete."[22] This is descriptive not only of the study of Buddhism on the Web, but also of teaching our students through this new textuality. Teachers of Buddhism today are doing what teachers have always done: using every means ready at hand for transmitting, illustrating and demonstrating the contents of their subject, and making it meaningful to students in their own cultural contexts. In the coming years this will mean teaching and studying Buddhism through the Web, adumbrating our traditional methods.

Students today often know far more about Web design and pagemaking than their professors. Without a doubt, contemporary university students are better acculturated to new technologies and media than their elders. They are less technophobic, and more readily eager to learn with the Internet; they know the power of the interweaving of voices, and the potential of visual media and multisensory intelligence. It is estimated that more than eighty million up and coming students of the "T-generation" (for technological) in Canada and the United States are digitally wired, literate in the new medium. Their disadvantage is the cultural orientation toward fragmented knowledge and clipped-information attention spans. But teachers have always guided students toward integrating knowledge and making sense of information. Teachers are meant to facilitate student learning, and to increase intellectual curiosity and creativity. A professor's navigational guidance and training in complex discourse is crucial to dealing with the almost infinite sea of information students now face on the Web. Yet our students often are on a quest for something more when they study Buddhism. As Eckel says, "For me the biggest unsettled question in the study of Buddhism is not whether Buddhism is religious or even whether the study of Buddhism is religious; it is whether scholars in this field can find a voice that does justice to their own religious concerns and can demonstrate to the academy why their kind of knowledge is worth having."[23] For this reason teachers of Buddhism need to approach the Web not only as a teaching and research tool, but also as religious phenomenon, a field of human consciousness.

Students learn from collaboration, exploration, research, discovery, and epiphanies that connect concepts. Stories, teaching, poetry, *kōans*, contemplation and meditation instruction have been the historical mediums traditionally associated with Buddhism. The alphabetic transmission of Buddhism to the West has been relatively brief and "Protestant" in its essentialism.[24] The contemporary direction is beyond texts toward cultural "thick descriptions" and experiential contextuality. Here we can make the analogy in our pedagogical model to the arising of the Web. Through working with and participating in the creation of the Web, students may sense the intangible yet interwoven photon-fabric of the Buddha Mind. As a teaching tool it is a parable of Trojan proportions, a loaded horse on wheels. How it is handled and how it is built is the responsibility of teaching scholars. In *The Medium is the Message* (1968), Marshal McLuhan suggested that the technological age would bring a resurgence of image, orality, and simultaneous participation, conjuring up the collective psyche of earlier oral cultures. According to Erik Davis, McLuhan predicted a "rediscovery of tribal, integral awareness that manifests itself in a complete shift in our sensory lives." McLuhan described the emerging electronic society as "a resonating world akin to the old tribal echo chamber where magic will live again."[25] After centuries of alphabetic textuality, is it possible that students may actually begin to feel again some connection with an oral tradition behind our logocentric belief systems by studying Buddhism on the Web?

Teaching Resources

The presence of Buddhist teaching and academic resources on the Web is overwhelming; a massive amount of available material to be accessed globally and nearly instantaneously. As teachers, we may serve to navigate, observe, critically contemplate, and create the presence of Web-based learning. Students are guided in their learning through our presentation of Internet materials in the classroom. At the classroom level, the Web is a "live" global show of resources, an archive of texts and multimedia for use in lectures. Graphic content is available as never before, and access to "sonic texts" (audio) and "visual performative" texts (digital video) allow teaching to be more multicultural. Where film created the possibility of thinking about diverse social contexts and multiple temporal contexts, the Web now expands the intellectual awareness of global and multi-faceted dimensions of knowledge for comparative and critical thinking. Navigating the scholarly sources and putting Dharma teaching in the context of contemporary cultural realities makes Buddhism relevant and motivating for students who might otherwise see their academic work as a fragment of their education.[26]

The content we create as Web authors must offer a meaningful framework for the intellectual awakening of students of Buddhism and religious studies. Students collaborating on building Web sites are challenged to awaken the mind in multi-dimensional intellectual activity. The Web-learning medium is integral to their cultural matrix: it offers more creative ways of expression than traditional scholarly genres, it moves them "beyond texts" in their exploration of cultural contexts and concepts, it opens a global and planetary awareness, and it perforates their ideological boundaries to become permeable to alterity and "Otherness." The pedagogical process of collaborating with peers in constructing Web sites incorporates numerous interdisciplinary aspects of their education. In building a Web site they are learning various skills and "multiple intelligences" simultaneously. Because their peers will evaluate them for a contribution that may be viewed by anyone else, they are highly motivated to explore their scholarly subject with academic fascination. Given that they are not submitting a project to be read by one professor alone, and returned with scrawled notes and a secluded grade, the substance of the actual learning content seeks to "stick" to a "site of meaning," and this "place" is appropriately made of photons, diaphanous digital light, a palimpsest overlaying texts of old and new. This offers an opportunity to instruct students about the nature of various Buddhist concepts, such as the *pratītya-samutpāda* of subatomic physics and galaxies, the energy of mind and the *śūnyatā* of existence, illustrated by analogy to the World Wide Indra-Net of the Web.

Collaborating and Knowledge Networking

One of the most productive pedagogical methods I have found for stimulating student learning is requiring collaborative workshops and projects for creating Web sites as part of the curriculum. Intellectual self-expression and incorporation of scholarship to create personal "stūpas" of knowledge, sacred resource temples for enlightenment practices (e.g., meditation instruction), and maps of information pathways, make the student learning process personally gratifying. Teaching Buddhism through collaborative teacher/student Web design puts the teacher back in the role of apprenticing and mentoring through the building of frameworks that students may carry beyond the classroom. (Examples of how to guide students into the Web and prompt them into collaboration, including training and models of teaching through the Web, may be found at Webquest.)[27] Teachers may often find themselves in the learning mode when students know more technical skills, and exchange their knowledge with the professor's guidance to content. Students unfamiliar with "tech-knowledgy" display high stress and reluctance toward these projects, yet experience a breakthrough when the threshold is crossed and the mission accomplished. Learning computer-literacy is never easy, but increasingly students are growing up with the Web and Web-page design. It is now more common for K-12 students to practice Web design than in many colleges and universities. University professors rarely retrotrain in technical skills, while their students are growing up with those skills expecting to use them in their higher education.

Web Workshops

One of the best solutions to this dilemma is for teachers to collaborate and learn from students. In my course on Latin American Religions, for example, students collaborated in building a Web site on Maya culture called "Heart of Sky."[28] Students received workshops in Web-page design, gathered and maintained their own pages, and linked each other's selected topics into an integral presentation. Working together made the learning process a form of creative workshop that developed open intellectual dialogue and teamwork. Like an ongoing sequential film, with many collaborators involved, the student Web site project grows beyond the text-based educational experience with digital imagery and other forms of sensory perception. This is by all means an opportunity for developing "skillful means" in communicating ideas and organizing knowledge.

Student Dialogues

Web-based learning also incorporates potential online discussion groups and conferencing as a means of carrying the classroom beyond the traditional walls. In my "bi-coastal" collaboration with Professor David Batstone at the University of San Francisco, students from our two schools collaborated together, meeting in our cyber-space classroom, and talking with one another in our weekly sessions through video-conferencing.[29] In one instance, students who had never met each other, living on separate coasts of the country, were able to build a learning relationship that resulted in profound insight. Students may access a Web site and participate in dialogue with peers and professors (including guest participants) whenever they choose to, enhancing their intellectual activity outside of class. Conferencing software offers the possibility of collating student contributions into portfolios of active participation in discussion. Often students who may not speak up in class feel comfortable "talking" online.

There is general agreement that there is no substitute for practice, for written texts, for teachings, and for the reality of "just sitting." Yet for the global sources of imagery and access to "sonic" texts (chants, Dharma talks, interviews, lectures, music) and video sequences of imagery, ceremonial and ritual components, and master teachers, the Web is unprecedented. The impact of visual and sonic textuality changes how students think, and the time-honored notion of textual analysis is difficult for a generation growing up on visual information and sound power, unless that textuality reflects this miraculous and momentous day in the sun. We are beginning to ask new questions in taking seriously the challenge of this sudden surge of information. Is the Internet a way of embodying authentic representations of culture? Will future scholars study the Cyber-Sangha as material culture expressing a planetary, transmodern Buddhism? Will the access to an interdependent and mutually connected community transcend the cultural contexts in new forms of Dharma insight? Can one study and learn practices, such as meditation instruction, through the Net? Can isolated individuals join a *sangha* that feeds the Buddha Mind through the senses touched by Web sites? Can the technological vehicle of the miraculous computer be used as the new *vajra* (and *vinaya*?) to reconnect community and individual enlightenment practice where we are?

Novayāna Digital Dharma, Cyber-Sages and Sūtra-Sites

A multi-faceted lens for understanding the new paradigm of the Web is emerging from contemporary Buddhism. The terminology for examining the Buddhism phenomena on the Web is both a response to the huge presence of Buddhist Web sites, and the need for a new language to communicate between the diverse cultural communities and traditions that now converse with one another. The religious phenomena of the Web provides a wide open field of study, and Buddhist Web sites provide an extraordinary example of its significance.[30] As the historian of American Buddhism Charles Prebish says: "Perhaps the most consequential impact of the aggressive spread of Buddhism into cyberspace, along with the creation of a new kind of American Buddhist sangha never imagined by the Buddha, is the uniting of all the Buddhist communities or sanghas...into one universal sangha that can communicate effectively in an attempt to eliminate the suffering of individuals throughout the world."[31]

The Cyber-Sangha (community of the four quadrants, disciples of Buddha) has emerged as an unprecedented *Dharma-kāya* and forum for exchanging Dharma views. This online "community of communities" of Buddhists is significant in several aspects: it constitutes an immense and diverse range of resources, archives, and educational programs for buddhologists and teachers of Buddhism; it represents a new plurality of Buddhist communities to study and examine; and it may actually be a historically revolutionary form of Buddhism emerging into the third millennium. Some are calling it a new branching of Buddhism, following Theravāda (Hīnayāna), Mahāyāna, and Vajrayāna. I have been using the term "Novayāna" to indicate a contemporary Buddhism that recognizes the Web as an embodiment of Indra's Net, and analogous to "interdependent co-arising" (*pratītya-samutpāda*, Buddha's "theory of everything").

The Indra-Net and the Internet

American Buddhism is emerging as a significant presence in the midst of this revolution partly because of its paradigm of "Web Awareness," the "Indra-Net," and the hyper-linked consciousness of "interdependent co-arising" and a "planetary ecology of mind." Indra's Net of the *Avataṃsaka Sūtra*[32] is an interconnected network of sparkling jewels infinitely reflecting one another. The Web has enabled the analogy of the interconnected Buddha Mind to make sense in a contemporary context. Erik Davis expresses this point:

> As you might expect, Western Buddhists nursing the digital dharma can hardly avoid making the punning leap between Indra's net and the Internet, another cunning artifice whose dynamic mesh of mind and photons takes the form of a nonlinear, hyperlinked, many-to-many matrix. For some, the formal resemblance between the Hua-yen vision and our planetary trellis of fiber-optic cables, modems, microwaves, screens and servers suggests that, in a symbolic sense at least, we may now be hardwiring a network of connections that reflects the nondual interdependence of all reality. At the same time, of course, the digital Overmind also reflects the anger, delusion, and greed that Buddhists claim drive the miseries of human existence.... The net of Indra works

its real magic by dissolving our habitual tendencies to divide the world into separate and autonomous zones: inside and out, self and other, online and off-, machines and nature. So the next time you peer into the open window of a Web browser, you might ask yourself: Where does "the network" end? Does it cease with the virtual words, images, and minds of cyberspace, or with the silicon-electronic matrix of computing devices, or with the electrical grid that powers the show with energies extracted from waterflow and toxic atom? As you contemplate these widening networks, they may alter the granularity and elasticity of the self that senses them, as well as changing the resilience and tenderness of the threads binding that self to the mutant edge of matter and history. I suspect there is no end to such links, and that this immanent infinity, with its impossible ethical call, makes up the real world-wide web.[33]

Photon Particle Web Design

Perhaps cyber-monks and nuns, scholars and students, may take instruction from the *kālacakra maṇḍala*, and apply some of the sacred arts methodology to Dharma design for a new millennium; to building an accelerated *vajra*-vehicle for the enlightening of minds. The particle *maṇḍala* is celebrated in Tibetan Buddhism through an elaborate sacred and multisensory artistic tradition. An entire cast of performers are involved: from the Vajra Master who choreographs, to the Tantric monks who patiently guide the particles of colored sand to the intricate details of the design, to the participants who come for empowerment through sacramental ritual. Everyone involved is aware that they are participating together in a vehicle to enlightenment. Through the deliberate attention paid by the monks to their art, the viewer is entranced with the beauty of the spectacular work of art. Yet both its climax and dénouement is in the moment of dissolution, when it is swept away and poured into a river—only then is its meaning is ultimately gained: all things are impermanent, subject to the Wheel of Time. When movies are made there may sometimes arise the sense that one is creatively involved in something bigger than the sum of the parts. The resulting celluloid text (film or now DVD) may be wondrous and invoke a world of its own. I wonder if constructing Web sites that become digital-citadels of cyber-sages might have something in common, or may become deliberate acts of sacred art sometime in our future? Were the illuminated manuscripts of the Kells, Lindisfarne, and Gutenberg new ways of reading sacred texts similar to the visual scripture of the *kālacakra maṇḍala*? Perhaps constructing photon-particle cyber-sūtras of the Web will become a deliberately religious process in the future for some Buddhists and scholars. A hermeneutics of hyper-texts and multi-media art forms may call for a serious paradigm shift in the traditional religious communities whose historical contexts are now subsumed by a pluralizing medium. Scholars and teachers should take note.

The disciplined mind of the tool-user is a crucial element in turning the potential of the Web into an accelerated vehicle to enlightenment, as an awareness of wisdom traditions. Cyber-monks, teachers, scholars, and information-designers are shaping a new way of intelligibility, of interpreting and understanding this genre of communication to a new generation of students and intellectuals. We are witnessing its emergence and formation, yet we are cautiously skeptical, suspicious and hesitant to embrace it as the next historical paradigm shift. H. H. Tenzin Gyatso, The 14th Dalai Lama, says "We all have a responsibility to shape the future of humanity." There is an ineluctable need to recognize that scholars and teachers are called to be elders mantled with the responsibility to create positive forces to counter negative energies, to make wisdom and compassion accessible in this new form of "Buddha Mind, Rainbow Body."

Notes

[1] At a large gathering for a lecture in the San Francisco Zen Center's series "Buddhism at Millennium's Edge," I asked Lama Surya Das if he thought we are seeing the emergence of a "Neo-yāna." "Speak English, young man," he said, and later said we might call it that. Whether we call it "Novayāna" (see Prebish 1999), or "Neo-yāna," following the now cult hit film *The Matrix* ("wake up Neo"), or the Cyber-Sangha (that excludes all contemporary Buddhists not online?), we are seeing the interdependent emergence of a very diverse new branching of Buddhism in the West.

[2] See Tapscott 1999.

---

[3] Houston 1999, 28–30.

[4] Hershock 1999, 282.

[5] Hershock 1999, 282–83.

[6] http://www.luddites.com/index2.html

[7] http://www.soci.niu.edu/~critcrim/uni/uni.txt

[8] See Kurzweil 1999 for what to expect in future machines.

[9] Quoted in King 1996, 88.

[10] From *The Planetization of Mankind*; quoted in King 1996, 89.

[11] See, e.g., http://www.skywebs.com/earthportals/index2.html.

[12] Pirsig 1974, 165.

[13] Dussel 1995, 138.

[14] E.g., Quan-yin virtual altar: http://la.znet.com/~quan_yin/.

[15] http://www. kurzweiltech.com/

[16] See http://web.mit.edu/bpadams/www/gac/.

[17] See Dave Lane's Neural Surfer (http://www.mtsac.edu/~dlane/).

[18] Davis 1998, 334.

[19] http://www.time.com/time/reports/v21/live/privacy_mag.html

[20] Davis 1994.

[21] Eckel 1994, 1099.

[22] Eckel 1994, 1106.

[23] Eckel 1994, 1108.

[24] See Eckel 1994.

[25] Davis 1998, 175; see also Erik Davis, *Corpus Cybermeticum: Digital Mysticism and the Religion of Technology* (http://www.levity.com/figment/ corpus.html).

[26] See the excellent online *Journal of Buddhist Ethics* (http://jbe.gold.ac.uk/) and the vast resources of Buddhanet Buddhist Information Network (http://www.buddhanet.net/).

[27] http://edweb.sdsu.edu/webquest/webquest.html

[28] http://www.uwec.edu/academic/curric/ greidebe/HOS/index.htm

[29] http://www.sojourners.com/soj9707/970732f.html

[30] See http://www.buddhanet.com.

[31] Prebish 1999, 232.

[32] See http://www.kalavinka.org/bookstore/huayen01.htm

[33] Davis 1998, 322–23.

Bibliography

Resources and more extensive teaching materials and examples for this chapter are available on the author's teaching Web site at the University of Wisconsin, "Buddha Mind, Rainbow Body" (http://www.uwec.edu/academic/curric/greidebe/BMRB/index.htm). Because links and sites are dynamic and impermanent, this printed chapter has few hyperlink references; for a dynamic Web-based version please go to the Web site.

Abram, David. 1996. *The Spell of the Sensuous: Perception and Language in a More-Than-Human World*. New York: Pantheon Books.

Bryant, Barry. 1992. *The Wheel of Time Sand Mandala: Visual Scripture of Tibetan Buddhism*. New York: HarperCollins Publishers.

Daido Loori Roshi, John. 1999. "Straight Ahead." Interview with Jeff Zaleski. *Tricycle: The Buddhist Review* 9 (2): 48–54.

Das, Lama, Surya. 1997. *Awakening the Buddha Within*. New York: Broadway Books.

———. 1999. *Awakening to the Sacred: Creating a Spiritual Life From Scratch*. New York: Broadway Books.

Davis, Erik. 1994. "Digital Dharma." *Wired Magazine* (August) Archive 2.08 (http://www.wired.com/wired/archive/2.08/dharma_pr.html).

———. 1998. *Techgnosis: Myth, Magic, and Mysticism in the Age of Information*. New York: Three Rivers Press.

Dussel, Enrique. 1995. *The Invention of the Americas: Eclipse of the Other and the Myth of Modernity*. New York: Continuum.

Eckel, Malcolm David. 1994. "The Ghost at the Table: On the Study of Buddhism and the Study of Religion." *Journal of the American Academy of Religion* 62 (4).

Gyatso, Tenzin, His Holiness The Dalai Lama XIV. 1999. *Ethics for the New Millennium*. New York: Riverhead Books.

Hanh, Thich Nhat. 1998. *The Heart of the Buddha's Teaching: Transforming Suffering into Peace, Joy, and Liberation*. New York: Broadway Books.

Hershock, Peter D. 1999. *Reinventing the Wheel: A Buddhist Response to the Information Age*. Albany, NY: State University of New York Press.

Hoopes, John W. 1999. *The Mayfield Quick View Guide to the Internet: For Students of Anthropology*. Version 2.0. Mountain View, CA: Mayfield Publishing Company.

Houston, Jean. 2000. "Cyber Consciousness." *Yes! A Journal of Positive Futures* 13. (http://www.futurenet.org).

King, Ursula. 1996. *Spirit of Fire: The Life and Vision of Teilhard de Chardin*. Maryknoll, NY: Orbis.

Kuhn, Thomas S. 1996. *The Structure of Scientific Revolutions*. 3rd ed. Chicago: University of Chicago Press.

Kurzwell, Ray. 1999. *The Age of Spiritual Machines: When Computers Exceed Human Intelligence*. New York: Penguin Books.

Nisker, Wes. 1998. *Buddha's Nature: A Practical Guide to Discovering Your Place in the Cosmos*. New York: Bantam Books.

Pirsig, Robert. 1974. *Zen and the Art of Motorcycle Maintenance*. New York: Bantam.

Prebish, Charles S. 1999. *Luminous Passage: The Practice and Study of Buddhism in America*. Berkeley: University of California Press.

Prebish, Charles S., and Kenneth K. Tanaka, eds. 1998. *The Faces of Buddhism in America*. Berkeley: University of California Press.

Stull, Andrew T. 1999. *Religion on the Internet 1998–1999: A Prentice Hall Guide*. Upper Saddle River, NJ: Prentice Hall.

Tapscott, Don. 1999. *Growing Up Digital: The Rise of the Net Generation*. New York: McGraw-Hill.

Thurman, Robert. 1998. *Inner Revolution: Life, Liberty, and the Pursuit of Real Happiness*. New York: Riverhead Books. 1998.